MANAGING A·M·E·R·I·C·A·N WILDLIFE

MANAGING
A ⋆ M ⋆ E ⋆ R ⋆ I ⋆ C ⋆ A ⋆ N
WILDLIFE

A History of the International Association of Fish and Wildlife Agencies

DIAN OLSON BELANGER

The University of Massachusetts Press
Amherst
1988

Printed in the United States of America
LC 87–30065
ISBN 0–87023–608–3 (cloth); 609–1 (pbk.)
Set in Linotron Sabon at Keystone Typesetting

Library of Congress Cataloging-in-Publication Data

Belanger, Dian Olson, 1940–
Managing American wildlife : a history of the International Association of Fish and Wildlife Agencies / Dian Olson Belanger.
p. cm.
Bibliography: p.
Includes index.
ISBN 0–87023–608–3 (alk. paper). ISBN 0–87023–609–1 (pbk. : alk. paper)
1. International Association of Fish and Wildlife Agencies—History. 2. Wildlife conservation—United States—History. 3. Wildlife management—United States—History. I. Title.
QL84.2.B45 1988
333.95′16′0973—dc19 87–30065
CIP

British Library Cataloguing in Publication Data available

TO

MY FAMILY, ABOVE ALL

Contents

Foreword by Robert M. Brantly xi

Preface xiii

Introduction 3

Chapter One ★ "From This Little Meeting" 10

Assembled for the First Time 10
A Consciousness of Conservation 13
The National Association: Born Again 17
A Future for Migratory Birds 20
The World War and Wildlife 25
The International Association: Agenda Established 27

Chapter Two ★ Building Game Management, Building an Association 30

Propagating Game: Farms and Refuges 31
Preserving the Dwindling Waterfowl 32
Big Game: Too Few, Too Many 40
The Value of Vermin 43
The New Deal and Wildlife 44
The Cooperative Wildlife Research Units: Management Training 49
The Pittman-Robertson Act: Linchpin of Wildlife Conservation 49
State v. Federal Authority: G-20-A, the Pisgah, and the Courts 53
The "Upbuilding" Years 57

Chapter Three ★ "Wildlife Is Big Business" 61

Progress for Wildlife 61
Progress in Professionalism 62

War Clouds 64
Postwar Reassessment 65
Postwar Water Policies 68
The War's Effects on Wildlife 71
The Dingell-Johnson Act: Pittman-Robertson for Fish 76
Federal Aid: Internal Controversy 78
Duck Stamps: Increased Fees 80
Federal Lands and Hunting 81
Flyway Councils and International Fisheries 83
The Exotics 85
Midcentury Review 87

Chapter Four ⋆ The Environmental Decade 90
Pesticides and Other Pollution 90
Recreation and Wildlife 94
Hunters, Anglers, and Neither 96
State v. Federal Authority: The Solicitor's Opinion, Carlsbad, and the Courts 101
Public Land Laws Reviewed 106
International Efforts for the Birds 108
The Legal Sphere 110
The Wildlife Reference Service 111
The Turning Point 112

Chapter Five ⋆ The Washington Presence 117
The Washington Office 118
The Antihunting Menace 122
Management Vindicated, Nonhunters Accommodated 125
State v. Federal Authority: The Marine Mammals 127
Endangered Species: More on Authority 129
International Trade and Endangered Species 133
The Bonn Convention Rejected 139
Management in Court 141
The Association in Washington 144

Chapter Six ⋆ The Agenda Reviewed, A Future Agenda 147
New National Priorities and Wildlife 147
The Sagebrush Rebellion 149
Fifty Years of Pittman-Robertson 151
Dingell-Johnson: New Identity, More Money 152
Continuing Concerns 154
Media Ventures 155

Contents

The Native American Rights Controversy 157
Lead Poisoning and Steel Shot 159
Resource Policies: Consensus at Last 165
In Retrospect 166

Appendices

A: Chronology of Major Developments in the History of Fish and Wildlife Management 169
B: Presidents of the International Association of Fish and Wildlife Agencies 184
C: Dates and Places of Annual Meetings, International Association of Fish and Wildlife Agencies 186
D: Honorary Life Members of the International Association of Fish and Wildlife Agencies 188
E: Recipients of the Seth Gordon Award 192
F: Recipients of the Ernest Thompson Seton Award 193
G: Digest of the Resource Policies of the International Association of Fish and Wildlife Agencies 194

Notes 203

Sources 227

Index 237

Illustrations follow pages 48 and 116

Foreword

The International Association of Fish and Wildlife Agencies came into being in 1902 and has been a strong but quiet force throughout the entire history of the conservation movement. Its records have been included in the *Proceedings*, in testimony, in files, in the papers of its leaders, and in the memories of some of its more tenured members. The records of its meetings for a number of years were lost. These were located by a search in the Library of Congress and placed into the 1980 *Proceedings* to provide at least that minimal documentation.

There was, however, no running record of the evolution of the Association—no single document of its activities, influence, and contributions. And, with the passage of time, its early and influential leaders were slipping away.

In September 1983 the Executive Committee requested that President C. D. "Buzz" Besadny appoint a committee to explore the possibilities of developing an Association history. That committee consisted of chairman Glenn L. Bowers, former Executive Director of the Pennsylvania Game Commission and current General Counsel for the Association; Chester F. Phelps, former Executive Director of the Virginia Commission of Game and Inland Fisheries and current Secretary Treasurer; and Mr. John S. Gottschalk, a former Executive Vice-President, Legislative Counsel, and Counsel. Following the Committee's explorations and deliberations, it entered into preliminary negotiations with History Associates Incorporated of Rockville, Maryland. The Committee recommended that the Association contract with History Associates to produce an Association history and to do the necessary archival work on the Association's existing records. That recommendation was approved in March 1985.

This history is the product of that process and of the work of History Associates and, in particular, of historian Dian Belanger. It is far more than was anticipated. It is more than a history of the Association. It weaves Association history into the history of the conservation movement and places Association activities in the context of the times. The end result is informative and engrossing, even exciting. It will make current members proud of their organization and its role in the conservation movement. It will become must reading for the serious student of conservation history and for all those who pursue a career in fish and wildlife management.

The Association is proud to publish its history. We are pleased with the work that has been done by History Associates and its able historian Dian Olson Belanger.

ROBERT M. BRANTLY
President

Preface

Managing American Wildlife is a history of the International Association of Fish and Wildlife Agencies, written for the Association. It chronicles and interprets the IAFWA's eighty-plus years of biological and political activity within a context of American and conservation history, especially the history of wildlife conservation. From obscure beginnings and years of fitful growth and uneven effectiveness, the Association has emerged as a major voice for wildlife interests today.

While literature on conservation is plentiful and representative of the gamut of points of view, almost nothing has been written about conservation efforts, especially wildlife conservation, on the state level, where in fact most of the responsibility for wildlife resides and where most of the professional accomplishment has taken place. This history of an organization of state and provincial wildlife officials addresses that gap. It is not a compilation of individual state endeavors. Rather, it traces landmark developments in representative states that highlight issues significant to all states as well as to wildlife resource conservation in general.

Managing American Wildlife emphasizes state game managers' insistence upon the right and necessity of state authority in wildlife administration. Parochial local interests, an encroaching federal government, and, in recent years, international agreements too hastily concluded have challenged state jurisdiction. How the states met these challenges and set their own agenda, while cooperating with the federal government in major programs, forms a central theme of the book.

The IAFWA history underscores the International Association's primary focus on management, the positive, scientific manipulation of fish and wildlife populations for the benefit of both game and their human users. Historically, game managers had to promote the goals of their profession against exploiters who thoughtlessly and excessively depleted wildlife resources; later they had to cope with individuals and organizations opposed to any management scheme that encompassed the acceptability of hunting and fishing. In addition, within constraints of personnel and funding (often federal), wildlife conservationists pursued scientific studies to solve biological problems in order to enhance the renewable but vulnerable resources in their charge.

The International's irregular but accelerating growth in sophistication and influence over the years is an example of the political and social significance of special-interest associations in American history. The IAFWA's advocacy of wildlife management and state sovereignty has shaped the formation of national and international policy to a degree that makes the Association's history a contribution to an understanding of American culture beyond the specific subject of wildlife.

Many persons nurtured the creation of this book. At the risk of an unintentional omission, I wish to thank the following individuals for their assistance and to absolve them of responsibility for any errors of fact or interpretation that remain.

Colleagues and support staff at History Associates Incorporated have been generous with help and encouragement. Philip Cantelon directed the project with a welcome latitude for my professional judgment and with helpful editorial advice. Wide-ranging conversations with Rodney Carlisle on problems and potentialities of historical research and writing guided me through many a substantive and stylistic quagmire. Fred Dalzell, Margaret Rung, Bret Birdsong, Bruce Montgomery, John Shaw, and Mike Patterson contributed capable and willing research assistance in whatever mode was needed. Gail Mathews and Carol Spielman processed the final words with meticulous accuracy and aesthetic sensitivity. DyAnn Smith Gates also typed sections of the manuscript and provided every office service with cheerfulness and competence. And they got it done on time.

Numerous present and former IAFWA leaders contributed their time, knowledge, and professional perspectives willingly and enthusiastically throughout the project. Jack Berryman and John Gottschalk, current and former Executive Vice-President respectively, provided continuing guidance and critical review of the manuscript in progress. The suggestions, support, and comments of Chester Phelps and Glenn Bowers were also appreciated, as were interviews, correspondence, and contributions from several other state, regional, and national wildlife conservation leaders.

Association attorney Paul Lenzini did his best to steer me to phrases describing legal aspects of the study that were both true and readable.

I especially thank my family—Brian, Marcel, and Lia Belanger—who nourished me and this effort in ways they might not even guess. Friends and relatives from years past who hunted and fished gave unknown but valuable assistance to this nonparticipant toward the comprehension and articulation of the subject. Growing up in the country in northern Minnesota, where fish and wildlife were neighbors, also helped. Thanks to my parents, Esther Olson and, in loving memory, Raymond W. Olson.

MANAGING
A·M·E·R·I·C·A·N
WILDLIFE

Introduction

Like wind and sunsets wild things were taken for granted until progress began to do away with them.

ALDO LEOPOLD

THE International Association of Fish and Wildlife Agencies is not a secret, though few are familiar with its mission, the scope of its work, or even its name.[1] The fact is, however, in the mid-1980s the Association plays a central role in the conservation of natural resources at the state, regional, national, and international levels. From tentative beginnings during the peak of America's first surge of interest in conservation under Theodore Roosevelt's forceful leadership, the Association has felt its way—learning simultaneously the science of wildlife management and the art of influencing public policy for the enhancement of game and nongame resources. Today, wildlife research conducted or sponsored by Association members represents the state of the art. The Association's voice is powerful and respected in the development, passage, and implementation of legislation, legal precedent, and executive policy.

Since its founding at the turn of the century, the International Association has promoted rational, professional fish and wildlife management; fostered public understanding of the need for sound management; encouraged collaborative relationships with other agencies and organizations with similar goals; and cooperated with other nations to develop workable international agreements to benefit wildlife resources. While these goals have continued remarkably unchanged, methods of implementing them have evolved with changing conditions for wildlife and changing societal attitudes. Management has remained the fundamental concept; it means the professionally directed manipulation of wildlife populations for the mutual benefit of the wildlife and their human users.

The states have been the core and focus of the International Association of Fish and Wildlife Agencies from the beginning. Indeed, the IAFWA is a unique nongovernmental organization composed primarily of state-level government agencies accountable for resources management. The Association's Governmental Members include the fish and wildlife agencies of all fifty states plus Puerto Rico, the Virgin Islands, and the District of Columbia. Eight Canadian provinces, the Yukon Territory, and the Canadian Wildlife Service are also members, as is Mexico's Direccion General de Fauna Silvestre. Each of these brings its own sphere of influence and technical competence to bear with governors, legislators, and national policy makers. Five federal agencies—the U.S. Fish and Wildlife Service, U.S. Forest Service, Bureau of Land Management, National Marine Fisheries Service, and Tennessee Valley Authority—contribute their knowledge and support as Federal Governmental Members. Together they form the voting body of the Association.

Other members include thirteen Affiliate Members, which are related organizations such as the American Fur Resources Institute, the Association for Conservation Information, and several regional fisheries commissions. Contributing Members such as the American Fishing Tackle Manufacturing Association and the Woodstream Corporation give financial support and specialized advice. The Republic of China (Taiwan) occupies a special niche as a Cooperating Member, and the Federated States of Micronesia is showing interest in a similar arrangement. Finally, over 300 Associate Members are individual wildlife professionals and representatives of private organizations personally committed to the cause of wildlife conservation beyond their official responsibilities.

IAFWA's member agencies employ about 90 percent of the professional fish and wildlife biologists in the United States; in other words, the nation's wildlife management expertise overwhelmingly resides in the International. The developing professionalism of state game officials has been an important theme of their story.

Leadership is key. Officers and an Executive Committee, all elected from the ranks of the state, federal, and provincial members, establish policy, priorities, and direction for the Association. A careful multistep nomination and election process through several chairs has evolved to ensure both continuity and stability of leadership and the promotion of skilled, dedicated individual leaders. Geographic representation on the Executive Committee is provided by the ex officio presence of the four Regional Association presidents, since 1975; and representatives of Canada and Mexico, since 1981. Strong leadership has enabled the Association to function and even prosper under historical adversities.

The four Regional Associations of Fish and Wildlife Agencies—Western, Midwestern, Northeastern, and Southeastern—bring together conservationists from states with similar physical and climatic conditions to explore common resource management problems and spearhead action both independently and through the International. All are increasingly active and dependable for the timely support of national issues. Each has also developed particular expertise and its own deeper involvement in specialized regional concerns. The Northeastern, for example, has been strong on influencing water policy, while the Southeastern's cooperative projects, such as those on wildlife disease and dove hunting, have helped all states. Both regionals have been effective on marine fisheries issues. In the Midwest the game managers have taken the lead on questions of agricultural land use. And the Western logically concentrates on public land policies, such as grazing fees and the conservation of streamside habitat. Regional positions, developed through Regional Association committees, guide Association policies and actions, which in turn are advocated by the membership at all levels. Recent support from Kansas and Missouri for the extension of the Fur Seal Convention, which hardly affects these states or their region, illustrates both political responsiveness and the ability to perceive a threat to management anywhere as a threat everywhere. Learning the power of mass action was accomplished early by the International's members.

Committees form the backbone of the Association and do the bulk of its work. In 1985 there were thirty-six committees, focusing on a wide variety of technical, administrative, and political topics, such as acid rain and wetlands, Native Americans and migratory wildlife, international affairs and grants-in-aid, professional improvement and law enforcement. Committee membership encompasses individuals from seventy governmental agencies and almost sixty cooperating organizations for a total of some 700 persons. The committees develop policies and positions for the Association's review and approval. Three regularly scheduled meetings each year provide opportunities for building consensus and planning action on the basis of committee recommendations; these are the annual convention in September, the spring conference in conjunction with the North American Wildlife and Natural Resources Conference, and the December meeting in Washington of the Executive and Legislative Committees where program and legislative priorities for the coming year are formulated.

Orchestrating all this since 1972 are the Executive Vice-President and staff of the headquarters office in Washington. When the Legislative Counsel, chief liaison officer for affairs on Capitol Hill, reports the need for action on a vital bill, for example, the Executive Vice-President can quickly be in touch with state conservation department heads to request information or persuasion directed to members of Congress. Likewise, state agencies can solicit timely political or technical assistance through the national office. In short, the Washington office is where information is disseminated and action organized. The computerized communications network includes wide-area telephone service and individual correspondence as well as weekly memoranda to agency directors and the monthly *Newsletter* to all members. Establishing its Washington presence was, by common agreement, the Association's most significant organizational milestone.

The Association manages an annual budget of some $300,000 and influences the allocation of millions of federal dollars. In 1985 the IAFWA, in concert with others, was successful in restoring to the budget $78 million in federal grants-in-aid funds that had come under the scissors of administration spending cutters. The Association uses a separate fund, collected from federal agencies' membership dues that cannot be used for normal operating expenses or lobbying, to support special educational programs. It contributed $40,000 in 1985 to Project WILD (Wildlife in Learning Design), for example, for independent producers to develop objective educational materials on wildlife management for use in schools nationwide.

Since 1983 a State Associate selected from applicants from state conservation departments has served a year-long sabbatical internship in the Washington office. The Association gains in productivity through having an additional professional to concentrate on objectives otherwise unattainable for lack of staff time. The State Associate, a mid career, top-level state employee, gains specific knowledge of new issues and a national perspective to bring back to the state agency, thus widening the latter's perspective as well as his or her own.

The State Associate program has been successful in both practical and philosophical terms. For example, with habitat loss the most serious contemporary threat to wildlife and 80 percent of that loss caused by agricultural expansion, farm legislation has great relevance for game managers. So when a State Associate became available to follow this specialized issue, the Association could multiply its effectiveness. The Farm Bill's passage in 1985 was a triumph for wildlife interests, and it enjoyed the support of agriculturalists, too. The act affects virtually all privately held agricultural lands, where a significant portion of American wildlife resides. It provides for conservation reserves; its "swampbuster" feature stipulates that no federal subsidies will be available for swamp drainage; and its "sodbuster" provision prohibits the introduction of new lands into agricultural production without loss of federal funds. Thus, implementation of the act will help reduce soil erosion, maintain cover land, prevent overplowing, and save wetlands. More abundant, healthier wildlife habitat is expected.

When other remedies fail, the International Association participates in litigation, though rarely initiating a lawsuit. Its enviable record in the courts, where it has intervened more than forty times in the last decade and a half in the interests of wildlife conservation, reflects the care of its case selection, the background work of affected members, and the skill of its consultant legal counsel. The Association's current support of the state of Colorado's defense of its right to allocate licenses for limited-permit big game hunts on a nonequal basis for residents and nonresidents (Terk v. Ruch) reflects its ongoing insistence on the states' authority over resident wildlife. Responsible game managers feel they must be able to regulate the take of scarce species, finance the considerable costs of scientific game production, and maintain local popular support if any controls are to prove durable. Reserving the bulk of limited licenses to state residents is therefore a needed tool of wildlife management. The courts have already recognized the authority of states to discriminate in favor of residents on hunting license fees; this case, if successful, will strengthen overall state management authority.

State authority over resident wildlife has ever been the dominant theme of the organized state conservation officials. Their history is punctuated with confrontations, sometimes acrimonious, over perceived federal encroachment on their management prerogatives. Congress and the courts have resolved some jurisdictional issues but created others.

Today the state-federal relationship is mutually respectful, usually cooperative and cordial. Association leaders and staff maintain close ties with members of Congress and their aides, especially those on pertinent committees, and with their counterparts in the executive agencies, especially the Fish and Wildlife Service in the Interior Department. Legislators and policy makers seek the International's expert advice on drafting official documents as well as garnering support for their passage and direction for implementation. Government records are dotted with

IAFWA testimony. The Association works just as hard to block undesirable legislation or regulations. Efforts of antitrappers and antihunters offer continuing challenges that so far the proponents of balanced game management have been able to contain.

In addition to galvanizing its own members into effective political action, the Association also works in coalition with numerous other organizations, sometimes unlikely allies linked only temporarily for a specific goal. Wildlife protectionist organizations, for example, invariably opposing the International on any management-oriented measure, have helped lobby Congress for reauthorizations of the Endangered Species Act and on bills to clean up water, air, and acid rain.

The Association has performed an active role in international wildlife affairs for seventy years, since the first migratory bird treaty with Canada in 1916. The states it represents have embraced the primacy of national and international law when necessary to protect species whose seasonal nomadism is intercontinental, but they want assurance of benefit to the wildlife before relinquishing proven state management. Stung by the loss of control over certain valuable and nonendangered state resources such as the bobcat under the Convention on International Trade in Endangered Species (CITES), state wildlife managers have steered the United States clear of the "Bonn Convention." This intended international agreement for protection of migratory wildlife could trade away American authority to international jurisdictions with no insight into local conditions. Even a protocol to amend the 1916 treaty with Canada awaits Senate approval after six years until the International Association and other wildlife advocates are satisfied with its protective features. On the other hand, the Association supports an international convention that seeks to identify wetlands of worldwide significance. And the international flyway councils of the western hemisphere have cooperated successfully for years to protect and enhance the year-round habitat of their shared migratory birds.

The International Association of Fish and Wildlife Agencies prefers its low profile, letting other organizations better suited for public relations snare the headlines. The conservation community knows the Association's expertise, both technical and political, and counts upon it. The state members appreciate that none of them alone or even in small groups can accomplish what the Association does working for all of them together. The costs in dues and participation are a bargain when compared to the results for wildlife and the management cause. The International Association, combining the influence of the states with that of countless other sympathetic interests, realized the expansion of the fish restoration program embodied in the 1984 Wallop-Breaux Act, which will triple federal-aid funding for sport fishing and recreational boating activities.

Working for principles of wildlife management and state authority, the International Association of Fish and Wildlife Agencies wields broad political power, embodies the collective scientific knowledge on wildlife administration, and enjoys the respect of conservationists worldwide.

It was not always thus.

O ⋆ N ⋆ E

"From This Little Meeting"

A continent without wildlife is like a forest with no leaves on the trees.

WILLIAM T. HORNADAY

THE first efforts of the International Association of Fish and Wildlife Agencies were modest in scope, uneven in result, and obscure in the overall scheme of contemporary history. But the organization made a hopeful, purposeful beginning nonetheless, playing out its role in a widening current of American thought and action.

Assembled for the First Time

The small band of state conservation leaders that convened at Mammoth Hot Springs in Yellowstone Park on July 20, 1902, came in response to the call of W. F. Scott of Helena, Montana. Not much is known about Scott, though he must have been an ambitious, progressive organizer. He was Montana's first state game warden, the office just having been created in 1901. In one year's time he had organized the state into districts headed by deputy wardens, advocated hunting and fishing licenses so that the users would support the protection and enhancement of their sport, and sought possibilities for useful action beyond his own borders.[1] *Forest and Stream*, a New York-based "Weekly Journal of the Rod and Gun" which covered the Yellowstone event and provides its only surviving record, reported the meeting as the intended beginning of a system of mutually beneficial interstate cooperation in game and fish management. It credited Scott with having "long been convinced of the practical results of associated action by authorities of the contiguous states in the work of protection."[2]

Eight agents from six states appeared for this first wildlife managers' convention. The scattered but generally northwestern locations of the six—Montana, Minnesota, Wyoming, Colorado, Oregon, and Utah—suggest that Scott might have issued a larger number of invitations, but only thirty-one states had a game official to send in 1902. Three continental states were yet to be admitted to the union. Still, the pioneers formed a "permanent organization," which they called the National Association of Game and Fish Wardens and Commissioners, and they elected Scott President.[3]

Forest and Stream reported also the reading and discussion of "several well-considered papers" at this meeting. From these papers, which presented the attendees' most urgent concerns, came the first goals of the Association. Commissioner John Sharp of Utah urged the abolition of spring shooting. Despite a growing awareness that killing wild waterfowl during their propagating season had dire consequences for future populations, only a few states had effective prohibiting legislation and eight had no closed season at all. Sharp called the killing of breeding birds, or any breeding animals, a quick and "sure route to extermination" and a "barbarous waste of nature's bounteous gifts." Besides, he argued, ducks generally were not in prime condition for eating at that time of year.[4]

State Game Warden D. C. Nowlin of Wyoming strongly recommended a system of nonresident hunting licenses, such as the forty dollars charged in Wyoming or the similar fees generally levied in Canada, since such taxes would bring in revenue, keep out "that class of hunters who kill for speculative purposes," and allow some knowledge and control of "what is done in the woods." Forty dollars, a lot of money at the time, would have deterred many woodsmen, but not those gentlemen-adventurers from the East whose hunting and spending habits the frontier states had every reason to encourage.[5]

T. Gilbert Pearson said later that Minnesota's agent Sam Fullerton had "pounded the desk as he made the radical statement that a resident hunting license should be required everywhere," but Pearson had not been there to see it. Fullerton did say, according to the written record, that he did not favor a license law personally, but "in self-defense every State must adopt it; for if one State allows free shooting, it will be made the dumping ground of all the shooters from the East, and its game will soon disappear." In any case, hunting license laws, for residents or visitors, were even more scarce than game officials to enforce them in 1902.[6]

Fullerton stressed states' authority. His contention that game was the property of the state in which it resided had recently been affirmed in the 1896 Supreme Court decision Geer v. Connecticut, and it would become the rallying cry of state agents fearful of federal encroachment on their management rights. Fullerton also acknowledged that the states, to be effective in their own game administration, needed to work with each other. He further called for the establishment of bag limits, restrictions to limit the activities of head and hide hunters, and the prohibition of selling game at all times.[7]

Iowa had passed the first bag limit law in the United States in 1878, allowing a hunter to take no more than twenty-five prairie chickens in one day. Other states gradually added their own limits on various species, but James Trefethen noted that "as late as 1895 Michigan's five-deer season limit was considered revolutionary." Oregon enacted its first bag limit law for trout in 1901 at 125 per day, and for ducks at 50 per day or 100 in any one week. These were restrictions! Sensitive observers began to see that such profligacy could not go on indefinitely, but any limit was considered an infringement of individual rights in many circles. Prodigious educational efforts would be required to change ingrained attitudes. The tension between personal freedoms and the greater good of society would ever be a major theme in conservation history, as in all history.[8]

Commerce in wild game had constituted a big business between market hunters and restaurant keepers for years, but by the early twentieth century wildlife administrators were becoming alarmed over dwindling game populations. In an effort to stop such large-scale sales, Congress had passed the Lacey Act in 1900, to prohibit the interstate transportation of game killed in violation of local laws. Convicted offenders, whether shippers, carriers, or consignees, would be subject to fines of up to $200. The law also made the Secretary of Agriculture, through the Bureau of Biological Survey, responsible for administering the act and, more generally, for the "preservation, distribution, introduction and restoration" of game birds, thus considerably enlarging the Bureau's duties and powers.[9]

The Lacey Act, the first federal wildlife management law, would survive many reviews and emerge generally expanded over the years. The bill had breezed through an inattentive Senate after passing the House by a margin of more than five to one, but almost half the latter body had not bothered to vote. The game commissioners, while thankful for the Lacey Act even as they apprehended their first relinquishment of state power, could see that much more work would need to be done—in Congress, the state legislatures, and public forums—to inform and convince the nation that wildlife would remain a renewable resource only with careful planning and vigilance.[10]

By the early years of the twentieth century there was a noticeable shift in emphasis on game as a recreational, not a commercial, resource that was attributable in some measure to the concerns that had brought about the Lacey Act and agitation for other regulations. W. F. Scott's own contribution to the 1902 convention proceedings, for example, was a paper on the advertising potential of fish and game resources for stimulating growth and investment in the West. Scott noted that "protection of game plays its part in the upbuilding of our great Northwest. Millions of dollars of Eastern capital have been invested here whose owners were first attracted by the hunting and fishing, and nothing should be overlooked that will induce others to come and do likewise."[11]

Taken together, then, the state game agents' interests created an agenda for the new organization: to insist upon state authority over resident wildlife, to foster cooperation among states in matters of mutual concern, to seek federal assistance on broader problems, and, overall, to conserve wildlife for future use and enjoyment by legislative or regulatory means. Eighty years later these goals would still be guiding the Association's activities.

A Consciousness of Conservation

The broader context within which the eight men met at Yellowstone must be examined in order to understand fully their mission. Their jobs were to preserve fish and wildlife resources, and both the survival of wildlife and their jobs were at stake. The prospects did not look promising. Big game was disappearing in the West, either by systematic slaughter, as in the case of the buffalo, or by the push of encroaching settlement, as in that of the pronghorn antelope. Lesser animals everywhere were falling prey to greedy hunters killing off the breeders of next year's "crop." A "frontier mentality" that seemed to assume an infinitude of resources still prevailed. Later scholars sometimes called the latter half of the nineteenth century the Age of Extermination. It was, literally, for some, like the passenger pigeon. Once darkening the skies in profusion, the species' last survivor died in the Cincinnati Zoo in 1914.[12]

The problem, not a new one, was how to limit the wildlife harvest to the natural seasonal increase. The solution was later called conservation, but before the term was used generally in this context, individuals and groups were acting on the principle. Perhaps more than any other person, Theodore Roosevelt personified the growing awareness of wildlife as an invaluable but vulnerable resource. His extended hunting and ranching experiences in the West in the 1880s gratified his lifelong passion for animals and galvanized him into action to save imperiled species from extinction. So, in 1887, Roosevelt, wealthy and already politically influential, called together a select group of like-minded friends and proposed the formation of a gentlemen's hunting and game protection organization. The result was the exclusive and powerful Boone and Crockett Club, whose interest in the pursuit of big game led it to promote national forests, national parks, game refuges, and other means to encourage the restoration of depleted populations of America's most magnificent mammals. Such policies were not as paradoxical as they seemed; the club members recognized that accepting absolute prohibitions on hunting on reserved lands would ultimately ensure enhanced hunting in the surrounding areas.[13]

Gifford Pinchot, Chief of the Forestry Division (after 1905, the U.S. Forest Service) of the Department of Agriculture and a personal friend of Theodore Roosevelt, took credit for conceiving the idea of conservation. Modern scholars sometimes question whether Pinchot was quite as central to the birth of the movement as he claimed, but they salute his skill as a publicist and propagandist. In any case, Pinchot described in his autobiography, *Breaking New Ground*, the flash of insight that overtook him as he rode alone in Washington's Rock Creek Park on a "moody" February day in 1907. As he reflected on the problems of other resources (soil, water, fish and game, minerals) that overlapped with forestry, he suddenly saw "one single question with many parts." The self-educated, versatile geologist WJ McGee had articulated the concept in 1906 as "the use of the natural resources for the greatest good of the greatest number for the longest time," and Pinchot and his Forest Service associate Overton Price coined the term "conservation" to name it. President Roosevelt enthusiastically took up the cause, one he had lustily promoted as a private outdoorsman, and made conservation a cornerstone of his administration.[14]

Gifford Pinchot's moralistic platitudes justifying conservation in terms of Christianity and motherhood sometimes grate on modern ears, but his effect in his own time was considerable. In *The Fight for Conservation* of 1910, he defined conservation in terms of the development and *use* of resources. Proper use meant, in his view, the application of scientific methods for development, the elimination of waste, and the more equitable distribution of the natural bounty. He spoke of the interrelatedness of resources and wrote chapters about each as he named them, but he mentioned fish and wildlife only in passing and enlarged upon them not at all. He couched his arguments as much in terms of the prevailing Republican Progressivism as in terms of saving the resources, and, to the worry of fish and game wardens, he felt that conservation was the business of an activist federal government. He wrote in 1924, "I have very little interest in the abstract question whether the nation is encroaching upon the rights of the states or the states upon the nation. Power falls naturally to that person or agency which can and does use it, and . . . the nation acts . . . [while] the states do not." Pinchot's legacy would be appreciated selectively by state wildlife agents.[15]

Even earlier than Roosevelt and Pinchot, practical wildlife advocates had been busy urging conservation of the living natural resources. Henry William Herbert, under the pseudonym Frank Forester, wrote popular works on sportsmanship and game protection beginning in 1840. He was prominent in the New York Association for the Protection of Game, founded in 1844, the nation's oldest such organization. Charles Halleck established the journal *Forest and Stream* in 1873 that T. S. Palmer later credited as being "a potent force in moulding public opinion in favor of conservation" for half a century.[16]

Halleck's successor, Dr. George Bird Grinnell, published *Forest and Stream* for thirty-five years, frequently advocating policies considered radical or "utopian" but that eventually became hallmarks of conservation achievement. A prolific writer, he had consistently opposed spring shooting and supported protection for migratory birds. He adopted the slogan "Stop the Sale of Game" in 1894, long before the idea had popular credibility. Grinnell organized the first Audubon Society, in New York, in 1887 and was an officer in numerous other organizations promoting wise use of resources.[17]

G. O. (for George Oliver) Shields, a colorful and somewhat bizarre character, founded the Camp Fire Club in 1897 and the League of American Sportsmen in early 1898. Neither organization endured, but each had some influence working with others such as the Boone and Crockett Club. Shields also published the journal *Recreation*, which took upon itself the task of shaming "game hogs" into reforming their habits. For example, a newspaper account told of two Georgia hunters taking "first prize for killing blackbirds recently and sending to town a bunch of 900 of the songsters, the result of one day's hunt." Shields denounced the pair in *Recreation*, saying they were "unquestionably game hogs of the Southern razorback variety." When a Kentuckian caught sixty fish in one hour, Shields scolded, "Instead of boasting of your shameful work, you should have gone and hid yourself in the Ohio River swamps until the mosquitoes could have had time to suck the bad blood out of you." Whether Shields's methods of public humiliation worked or not, the culprits got a lot of publicity. Maybe they liked it; they continued bragging in print.[18]

These diverse conservation interests converged in the early years of the twentieth century, the wildlife officials of the six states in Yellowstone being a part of the much larger picture. The state agents, however, appeared less inclined to philosophize than to work for practical solutions to practical problems. Particularly mindful and appreciative of having their champion Theodore Roosevelt in the White House, they sought cooperative, legislative, and regulatory remedies for their most urgent issues.

Laws to regulate hunting in America existed as early as the colonial period and slowly evolved over the years. These required closed seasons on some species or prohibited certain methods or equipment. Massachusetts established a closed season for deer as early as 1694. Maryland, in 1730, prohibited the killing of deer by firelight, with fines to be paid in tobacco. Massachusetts and New Hampshire had the first game wardens around 1740. Rhode Island enacted the first law against spring shooting in 1846. The first hunting licenses were required for nonresidents in New Jersey in 1873 and for residents in Michigan and North Dakota in 1895. By 1880 all of the states had game laws of some sort. For example, nonresident market hunters had to pay a tax in Arkansas in 1875 and by 1903 were outlawed altogether. As already noted, Iowa limited the take of prairie chickens in 1878. An 1894 federal law forbade hunting in Yellowstone National Park. Still, the list was short.[19]

If game laws were few and weak, enforcement was weaker. Even in the states that had administrative machinery for managing game, budgets were inadequate and the officials more often than not had little training for the work and even less authority. Usually politically appointed and dependent for their income on the fines they levied, they soon learned which violators to avoid apprehending. T. Gilbert Pearson, later recalling his campaigns to have systems of game laws and wardens established in all states, told how Florida finally passed the necessary legislation in 1913. The governor thereupon appointed an officer to head the game department who was "earnest" but "not skilled in the game of politics as it was being played in Florida." Two years later, in order to eliminate this unfortunate official, the legislature abolished all the state's game laws.[20] Professional game management was still mostly in the future.

Given the widespread interest in conservation and organization-forming prevalent at the time, it is not surprising to find the wardens and commissioners together in Yellowstone in 1902. Given the current state of the profession and the legal and political apparatus with which they operated, the quality of their presentations and the purposefulness of their agenda are both surprising and impressive.

Commissioner Sharp tried to express the spirit of the 1902 convention "assembled for the first time—but to be hoped not the last—for the purpose of exchanging views and devising plans for the better protection and advancement of the fish and game interests of our several States." Warming to his theme, he went on, "Let us indulge in the hope that from this little meeting held up among the majestic peaks of these grand old Rocky Mountains, a stone may be started rolling down the mountainside and across the great plains to the sea, gathering as it rolls all the fish and game wardens and commissioners in the Union into one grand fish and game league."[21]

The National Association: Born Again

But that was that. Nothing more happened. There is no record of the first convention-goers making future plans. That there was a future seems almost a happenstance, as explained by T. Gilbert Pearson, National Association of Audubon Societies President and former Association President, in 1934: "Upon the occasion of the meeting of the League of American Sportsmen in Columbus [Ohio] on February 10, 1904, Dr. T. S. Palmer, who always takes great interest in such matters, told me of the meeting of the game wardens in the Yellowstone Park two years before. He said a number of wardens were present, and we should get them together and revive the Association, which seemed to have died with its first meeting. Mr. Scott was there, and he agreed to the idea; so several of us assembled for a short conference." Pearson recalled that the group attempted little in 1904 except to reelect Scott as "chairman" and plan to have regular meetings in the future. Only ten officials from nine state game departments were present (Minnesota had two; others were Ohio, Pennsylvania, Idaho, Michigan, Montana, Oregon, North Carolina, and Washington), but this time all sections of the country were represented, making the gathering more truly national.[22]

The only contemporary record of the 1904 convention appeared in the sportsmen's journal *The American Field* in a short paragraph entitled "Notes." The account centered on a "meeting of the sportsmen," the League of American Sportsmen, though it was not named, where laws against spring shooting and for hunting licenses were advocated. The report continued: "A National Association of Fish and Game Wardens and Commissioners was also organized," its purpose being "the prosecution of game law violators and the compiling of decisions in support of its work in protecting the fish and game." Pearson noted this confusion about the Association's date of origin in his 1934 recollections, but considering the lack of visible activity in the interim, perhaps *The American Field* may be forgiven for thinking it was witnessing a birth.[23]

The third meeting (*Forest and Stream* erroneously called it the "third annual") of the Association took place in St. Paul, Minnesota, in January 1906. W. F. Scott presided over twenty-three attendees from fourteen state game departments. Three others represented related interests, which heralded the beginning of what were to become affiliate memberships of various kinds. These were Major John G. Pitcher, acting superintendent of Yellowstone Park; G. O. Shields of the League of American Sportsmen; and Dr. T. S. (for Theodore Sherman) Palmer, assistant chief in charge of game preservation of the Bureau of Biological Survey in Washington.

Charles Joslyn of Michigan delivered the major address, which focused on the rights and powers of the federal and state governments over fishing on the Great Lakes. He thought that the national government should control these fisheries in the interests of all the people, but favored education and state cooperation with the federal government rather than federal legislation to achieve fair, uniform policies for resource enhancement. He noted an increase in whitefish in the Detroit River thanks to federal-state cooperation there. Joslyn put a rather heavy emphasis on federal power considering the Association's expressed views on state authority, but Great Lakes fishing was an interstate matter and no discordant reactions were recorded in the journal account.

The Association adopted a constitution in 1906, apparently after some discussion, since it was reported as an "amended" document. The group also presented the newly married W. F. Scott and his wife with a "set of silver knives and forks . . . in recognition of his services to the Association" and reelected him President another time.

T. S. Palmer was made an Honorary Life Member in 1906, the first of what is still a short list of leaders so recognized. It is clear that he had already made himself invaluable to the Association with his knowledge of wildlife and affairs in the national capital, but the honor may have also reflected an organizational structure that did not permit a regular membership for someone who was not a state fish or game warden or commissioner. The provisions of that first constitution are lost to history, and bylaws were not adopted until 1912.[24]

Palmer asked the Association's help in securing passage of a bill to authorize the President of the United States to set aside portions of the forest reserve as refuges for wild game. Refuges were destined to become a major concern for the Association throughout its history, and Palmer was the ideal person to raise the issue and gain the attention of the group. He was a remarkable man, an ornithologist by training but also a medical doctor and one-time banker. He was particularly interested in game protection, and he put together, among numerous other writings, compilations of hunting license regulations and several on game laws over the years. His *Chronology and Index of American Game Protection, 1776–1911* became a standard reference work. Besides his professional expertise, Palmer, as a relatively highly placed official in the Department of Agriculture, had intimate knowledge of the machinery of the federal government. He eventually headed the Bureau of Biological Survey, established in 1885, and had much to do with the enviable reputation the agency enjoyed. Palmer also commanded the respect and affection of the Association members. *The American Field*, which covered the convention of 1910, said he "impressed his auditors as a big, brainy man, broadgauge, and devoid of anything calculated to warp judgment or obscure vision."[25]

Palmer seems to have dominated the activities of the Association in its early years. In 1907 he gave the members an "instructive address" in which he suggested that artificial propagation and feeding of wild game augment the older protection method of simply curtailing hunting privileges. He enumerated "novel features" in recent game legislation from his recently completed digest of game laws and court decisions. He also summarized the effects of game protection efforts in various states, and especially in Yellowstone Park, where an absolute ban on hunting was leading to impressive increases in wildlife.[26]

At the 1910 convention (there were no meetings of the Association between 1907 and 1910) the membership rejected Palmer's advocacy of putting game wardens under Civil Service regulation, but later he apparently prevented a crisis by the force of his personality and stature. Amos Ponder, attorney for the Louisiana Fish and Game Commission, said in a speech that he would "prefer that the fish and game remain without any protection rather than have the states interfered with by the general government." *The American Field* wrote that "sharp differences of opinion" and "hot talk" ensued. The journal continued: "Here Dr. Palmer scored, and evinced skill of high order in recognizing differences. He assured the delegates that the national government had no desire or intention of invading the rights of states, but on the contrary realized that nothing could be done without [their mutual] cordial cooperation. . . . Whatever of distrust had arisen was entirely dissipated by Dr. Palmer's broad attitude." The federal-state debate would continue, of course, and there would not always be a Dr. Palmer to mitigate the animosities.[27]

Other matters of concern to the Association in its first decade are suggested in the resolutions it passed. The first of these statements of principle appeared in the *Proceedings* of the 1907 meeting. It was an expression of appreciation for the "valuable work being done by the Biological Survey" and a recommendation to Congress that its appropriation be substantially increased. The members unanimously passed the resolution; follow-up action, if any, is not recorded. In 1910 several resolutions were offered and adopted, among them one proposing national legislation for the protection of migratory birds and fish "if it can be constitutionally enacted." The members also supported uniform state game laws and a federal law "for cooperation between the various state governments and the national government." The 1910 convention made Canadian and Mexican game officials eligible for membership in the Association, an indication of growing awareness of the international aspects of wildlife resource management. The 1912 delegates resolved themselves in favor of laws further restricting the sale of all wild game and of effective quarantine regulations for the shipment of "living, useful birds." They also heard a lengthy justification of Pennsylvania's law, upheld in the state Supreme Court, that forbade aliens to hunt, shoot, or possess a gun.[28]

A Future for Migratory Birds

If a single issue dominated the thinking of fish and game officials in the early twentieth century, it was the problem of migratory wildfowl. Concerned sportsmen could see that game birds were noticeably dwindling in number. Wild ducks and geese, readily available in restaurants and commonplace on household tables, could no longer survive the ravages of indiscriminate, uncontrolled killing by increasing numbers of hunters using ever more sophisticated, deadly weapons. Some states had bag limit laws (unbelievably liberal ones by today's standards), and pressure was mounting for an end to hunting during the mating season, but restrictions were inadequate and impossible to enforce. The main difficulty was jurisdictional. Who would protect, or, more accurately, who would regulate the taking of vagabond birds that seasonally crisscrossed the continent?

The states had long insisted, with court approval, that authority over wildlife belonged to the state in which the game resided, but few had any laws regarding migratory birds. As James Trefethen succinctly put it, "The prevailing attitude of the respective state legislatures, even those that had taken decisive steps to protect resident species, was that their own hunting constituents should not be deprived of shooting privileges so long as neighboring states permitted unrestricted hunting of the same birds. The result was a grim competition to see which state could kill the greatest number before the migrating flocks passed from the range of its hunters' guns."[29] Unless all states cooperated to save the birds, no one state's actions could be effective. So the slaughter continued, and some species were threatened with extinction.

Serious conservationists came to realize that only federal intervention could protect wildlife migrating over state lines, but convincing the public to accept restrictions on shooting and states that they should surrender a portion of their sovereignty was no simple matter. The official effort began in December 1904, when the congressman and naturalist George Shiras III, Republican of Pennsylvania, introduced a bill to bring all migratory game birds under federal control. Grinnell immediately threw the weight of *Forest and Stream* behind the bill, noting that the individual states were "ineffectual" in protecting migratory wildlife and had proven themselves unable to bring about uniform protective laws. "All technical considerations dismissed, and fine-spun theories of State and Federal jurisdiction aside, the true consideration of public advantage supports this measure."[30]

Shiras's bill died in the Committee on Agriculture. It was too revolutionary a concept, as suggested by Trefethen. Unlike the Lacey Act, which simply extended to game an accepted federal regulatory power over interstate commerce, the Shiras bill made the unprecedented claim that migratory game birds were a federal rather than a state resource. Contemporaries called it an unconstitutional violation of states' rights. The shooting continued. Shiras tried again, unsuccessfully, in 1906. He retired in 1908. Republican Congressman John W. Weeks of Massachusetts took up the baton in that year, introducing an identical bill. It too failed, but public support and political interest were gradually growing.[31]

By 1912, when a fresh effort was mounted, new and rededicated advocates pressed the measure. Of great significance was the recently organized American Game Protective Association,[32] formed in 1911 by firearms company leaders who saw that conservation of game was in their interest. Without wildlife to hunt there would be diminished need for their products. The game association's purpose was solely to promote wildlife restoration programs to preserve and enhance recreational hunting. John B.

Burnham became its aggressive, effective President and the AGPA soon became a professionally staffed, citizen-sportsmen's advocacy group.[33] Its roster of members included many of the same people as the National Association of Game and Fish Wardens and Commissioners, its program remarkably similar.[34]

The American Game Protective Association, according to Pearson, "engineered" congressional hearings on new bills introduced by Congressman Weeks and his fellow Republican, Connecticut Senator George P. McLean. Federal and state game protective officials, state governors, and representatives of twenty-three associations and societies from forty-four states testified or wrote letters, an impressive endorsement and a first for the cause of national bird conservation.[35]

In an address before the state game and fish officials in 1935, T. Gilbert Pearson recalled that he had been the only speaker at the 1912 hearings who had not favored the enactment of the Weeks and McLean bills as they then stood. "My contention was that they should be amended to include protection for migratory insect-eating birds as well as migratory game birds." Pearson's views would have held great weight. By that time he was a respected insider at any high-level ornithological discussion as an Audubon Society spokesman and President of the National Association of Game and Fish Commissioners. Senator McLean gladly introduced a new bill that embraced Pearson's suggestion. This was a politically shrewd as well as conservationally wise move, since it garnered the support of farmers and nonhunters.[36]

Support may have been mounting, but opposition to the migratory bird bill was intense on constitutional and states' rights grounds. In Congress, Wyoming Republican Frank W. Mondell, the leading adversary, wanted no part of centralized "pestiferous interference" with what he insisted was a local matter. "Enact this legislation and there is no justification for a stand against the most extreme assertion of Federal police power in the States of the Union."[37] Later he warned that "regulations could be promulgated under which a barefooted boy . . . taking a shot with his airgun at the smallest and most insignificant of the feathered tribe, could be indicted, tried, condemned, and immured in a Federal penitentiary."[38] Senator Elihu Root, Republican of New York, also objected on constitutional principles but proposed a resolution that a convention among North American countries be negotiated to protect the birds and establish the constitutional authority for doing so.[39] The Weeks-McLean bill was passed, however, in a flurry of activity before Congress adjourned and before the treaty proposal could be acted upon.[40]

President Taft signed the Weeks-McLean Act on March 4, 1913. T. S.

Palmer prepared the Biological Survey's preliminary regulations for enforcement, and the federal government held regional public hearings to promote compliance and quell the considerable discontent. Agriculture Secretary David F. Houston of Missouri called together an unpaid fifteen-man advisory board of conservation leaders to assist in framing the regulations and encourage their acceptance. Among them were Grinnell, Burnham, Lacey, Shiras, Pearson, and Dr. William T. Hornaday, who would have much to say.[41]

Colonel J. H. Acklen, Association President in 1913, hailed the newly enacted Migratory Bird Law as a means of preserving the "fast-vanishing wildlife of our country." He noted, "The strong arm of the federal government whose little finger is more potent in effect than the entire body of any state, is embodied in the federal migratory bird law. We, therefore, have promise that the future will not be without the songs of birds to gladden the hearts of man . . . or to tempt him to the health-giving fields." He acknowledged that the law represented "a new moment, a great departure in game protection," and urged "careful footsteps" on the part of its enforcers. "If our first step is wisely taken; if we do not tread on the toes of the state authorities; if tact and judgment are used and the views and wishes of wardens considered, we will succeed." Acklen's tone suggested a diplomacy born of an awareness of tension and apprehensiveness within the Association. The migratory bird issue must indeed have been troublesome to the game commissioners. In effect, they were being forced to choose between preserving their power as state officials, or even their jobs, and preserving the living objects of their professional concern. Both were legitimate priorities. They went on record for saving the birds.[42]

The Migratory Bird Law severely curtailed market hunting and spring shooting. The Secretary of Agriculture now had the authority to declare closed seasons for selected species or even indefinitely prohibit their hunting. The law was almost immediately challenged, however, as unconstitutional and a test case involving a cooperative Arkansas coot hunter came before the U.S. Supreme Court in October 1915. Meanwhile, Congressman Mondell introduced a bill to repeal the law, and Senator McLean, even earlier, in April 1913, introduced a new version of Senator Root's treaty resolution.[43]

Congress passed McLean's treaty resolution. President Taft favored it and approached British authorities, who readily agreed to negotiate. Actually, Dr. C. Gordon Hewitt and James White of the Canadian Department of Conservation did most of the work for the British side. Dr. Palmer of the Biological Survey largely drafted the treaty, bringing to the task his expertise on game laws as well as the habits of wildfowl. There did not appear to be any serious disagreements to iron out, but it took more than three years for the international process to work. Considering, however, that England and Canada were engulfed in World War I during most of that time, it was remarkable that peripatetic birds got the attention they did. Finally, on August 16, 1916, the Treaty Between the United States and Great Britain for the Protection of Migratory Birds in the United States and Canada was formally signed by Secretary of State Robert Lansing and Sir Cecil Spring-Rice, British ambassador in Washington. The Senate quickly ratified it and President Wilson affixed his signature on August 22.[44]

The Migratory Bird Treaty required both countries to protect uniformly both useful and "harmless" birds that annually traversed parts of the United States and Canada. Its principal provisions were four: that all insectivorous birds important to agriculture or forestry be protected at all times; that no open season for any species be longer than three and one-half months; that both countries prohibit the taking of game birds during the breeding season; and that illegally killed birds not be shipped from one country to the other.[45]

The treaty was finally a fact, but on its own had no enforcement authority. Enabling bills of January 1917, fought by those, mostly in the West and Midwest, who still opposed the concept of federal control, at length passed, and President Wilson signed the Migratory Bird Treaty Act on July 3, 1918.[46] For its part, the Supreme Court never ruled on the Weeks-McLean Act, dismissing the case after the passage of the treaty act. Two years later, in 1920, the Court affirmed the constitutionality of federal regulation of migratory birds in the case of Missouri v. Holland, which challenged the treaty and enabling act as an infringement of the state ownership doctrine. The Court replied that state ownership of birds could not be established since wild birds "are in the possession of no one," and further that the federal government is not compelled to "sit by" while useful birds are destroyed for lack of sufficient state power or inclination to act. So, the task was accomplished. The treaty was now in effect and beyond question. It had taken some sixteen years, but the ducks and their cousins could have a future in North America, and so could the hunters.[47]

Dr. Edward W. Nelson, Chief of the Biological Survey, reported to the association of state game commissioners in 1918 on progress in enforcing the Migratory Bird Treaty regulations in the states. He noted that the "great antagonism" toward the treaty and his agency of the past few years had since changed to "almost universal harmony." Nelson acknowledged that regulations covering a large territory could not meet all local conditions and made the state game commissioners' work difficult, but he praised their "meeting the situation in the most friendly way" and promised flexibility where hardships resulted. Nelson's footsteps were very careful. He also seemed relieved that the problems had not been as bad as he had feared. These must have been delicate years for the Association, though the record says so only indirectly. No doubt game commissioners sufficiently interested in their profession to attend annual meetings recognized the importance of the new treaty law. The Association consistently voted resolutions favoring its passage. The malcontent commissioners suggested in Nelson's talk could have been from the ranks of the untrained political hacks that still held some state conservation positions.[48]

The World War and Wildlife

By this time the United States was also at war. Being "over there," World War I affected North America only indirectly, but as could be expected the intense spirit of patriotism that swept the country also affected the Association. At the 1918 convention Theodore Rouault, Jr., State Game Warden of New Mexico, got a standing ovation—not for his address on game farming, which was politely received—but for his plans to join the army.[49] The commissioners and wardens also reminded each other to preserve game for the hunting pleasure of the returning troops; suggested that some of them, especially the disabled, could be established in the important new field of game farming when the war was over; and credited the prevalence of hunting in America for the doughboys' preparedness and proficiency with guns.[50]

World War I also brought the wildlife community a real issue. That issue was food, specifically meat. The demand for food was sharply up, with everyone in apparent agreement that the fighting soldiers abroad should have first claim to the nation's beef. To augment the meat supply, however, various remedies were proposed that alarmed conservationists. Market game hunters, thought to have been "forcibly retired" by then, sought to resume their activity as a contribution to the war effort and asked state legislatures to relax all hunting restrictions for the duration of the hostilities. Theodore Roosevelt was furious with this and similar suggestions. "To the profiteering proposal of the Pseudo-patriots, the Patriots for revenue only, that protection of wildlife in wartime be relaxed, the united hosts of conservation reply: 'You shall not pass.'" The nation's natural resources must not be "destroyed for all time to gratify the greed of the moment." The state game managers said the same thing, with less color, in a 1917 resolution.[51]

Some fishing regulations *were* set aside, and fish commissioners cooperated in producing more food fishes and encouraging their consumption in order to conserve meat. Association President M. L. Alexander regretted the temporary breaking down of constructive law, but acquiesced "for the one great purpose." The shellfish commissioner of Florida went so far as to ask the Food Administration to approve the killing of a million brown pelicans that he alleged were eating $950,000 worth of food fish daily. T. Gilbert Pearson, sent to investigate, estimated there were no more than 65,000 pelicans on the Florida coast and found their diet to be mostly species unacceptable for human use. The pelicans were not sacrificed for the cause of liberty.[52]

The Association and other conservationists resisted attempts to loosen the game laws, recognizing that any short-term gains could easily mean extermination of some species in the long run. A specific apprehension arose when Alaska's congressional delegate Charles Sulzer introduced a bill in 1918 that would permit the sale of game killed legally north of the 62nd parallel until the war was over. Alaskans argued that scarcity (caused in part by the diversion of cargo ships to war service) had driven already outrageous beef prices even higher. All across the northern continent the native populations depended upon game for sustenance, and it was difficult to convince them and other frontiersmen that their abundant wildlife food supply should be controlled by forces thousands of miles away, or needed to be controlled at all. Game law enforcement in any case was a joke.

The Association grappled with the Alaska situation at its 1918 convention. Charles D. Garfield, convention delegate from Alaska, the territory's first, proposed a "home rule" resolution for Alaska. Bronx Zoo director, taxidermist, and one-time hunter turned absolute protectionist William T. Hornaday, who made his views known in every possible forum, objected on the grounds that only the federal government had the money and power to administer properly Alaska's game. More to the point, he called on the Association to resist any relaxation of hunting limits. The members, feeling torn and ill-prepared to comment on the issue, finally adopted a compromise resolution that called for congressional appropriations for Alaska's game and fish protection and the appointment of a resident Commissioner of Fish and Game. They further pledged their "hearty co-operation in all worthy measures looking for the betterment of fish and game conditions in Alaska."[53]

Dr. Hornaday then led the fight against the Sulzer bill. Speaking about it before the annual Conference of the American Game Protective Association in April 1918, he declared, "That the sportsmen of the United States would consent to a return of the old slaughter system embodied in the sale of game, is unthinkable, although it *is* true that the famishing [*sic*] lobbyist can, in the District of Columbia, still allay the outlying pangs of his hunger with quail in the New Willard Hotel at $1.25 a portion." E. W. Nelson of the Biological Survey, in consultation with Alaska expert Charles Sheldon, supported the bill since it was "just" under the circumstances, and the present law was disregarded anyway.

Hornaday succeeded in killing the bill. He also succeeded in alienating not only Alaskans but others, including dedicated conservationists offended by his narrow-minded, vitriolic sarcasm. But even his enemies conceded his effectiveness in the public forum. Indeed, if Hornaday's use of italics and exclamation points in his writing is an indication of his speaking habits, he must have been a potent, impassioned orator. He had intimate contact with virtually every conservation organization then in existence, including the Association, and sooner or later antagonized most of them.

As for Alaska, in 1925 it adopted a reasonable game code that all sides could agree upon. Trefethen called it a "thoroughly remarkable document," comparing it to the "theoretical ideal established several years later as the Model Game Law of the International Association of Game, Fish and Conservation Commissioners."[54]

In the end Herbert Hoover, head of the United States Food Administration, responding perhaps to strong letters from state game commissioners solicited by Nelson, issued a memorandum acknowledging the necessity of providing a maximum supply of game as food and the reality that some species were dangerously decreasing. The solution, he said, was to increase the breeding reserve "under present and even more progressive laws." Hoover concluded, "Since an attempted relaxation of laws would tend toward a rapid destruction of game, no emergency has as yet arisen sufficiently acute to warrant the Food Administration advocating the destruction of game, which forms a valuable national asset." The crisis passed.[55]

The International Association: Agenda Established

By the closing years of its second decade, the Association could be seen achieving direction and a greater sense of its potential for influence. At the 1916 convention in New Orleans the members asked the Secretary of

Agriculture to notify the state commissioners of pending legislation so that they could lobby or testify. They insisted upon sportsmen's representation on the advisory board to the Biological Survey that dealt with implementing the Migratory Bird Treaty and the Association's right to nominate individuals for the post. They supported specific game sanctuaries legislation. And they managed all this at a meeting that included a day-long Mississippi River cruise, in session, on President Alexander's yacht and a tour of the city by automobile.[56]

The association of state agents reached several organizational milestones in 1917. In that year the Association changed its name to the *International* Association of Game, Fish and Conservation Commissioners in recognition of its close relationship with Canada and the recent sealing of the Migratory Bird Treaty. Soon several Canadian provinces and federal agencies were members. The next year the Association proposed a migratory bird treaty with Mexico similar to the one with Canada, but that and Mexican membership would not occur until the mid-1930s.[57]

Also in 1917 the Association adopted, apparently with reservations about its ability to collect, a "state membership plan," which provided for four types of membership and stipulated the respective dues for each. State or provincial members would pay twenty-five dollars per year; individual, or "associate," members, two dollars; and life members, fifty dollars. Honorary life members, of course, owed no fee. This fiscal structure would hold until after World War II. The 1912 bylaws had made state and provincial game and fish wardens and commissioners, delegates of protective associations, and federal wildlife officials eligible for membership, but dues were payable by the individual, three dollars annually, "which amount shall be at no time increased." Earlier financial arrangements have been lost. In any case, the Association was not dealing in high finance. The audit committee for 1917–18 reported a balance of $123.58 after expenses from an income of $786.23. President Alexander commented that this report was "the best we have had for a long time."[58]

In 1919 Association Secretary Carlos Avery, Game Commissioner of Minnesota, announced that there were seventeen states or provinces enrolled, only about half of whose memberships were currently paid up. That was disappointing, of course, even though there were 130 associate members and two life members. Wresting twenty-five dollars from pinched state budgets was often difficult; worse, there were still several states with no official departments of game and fish. Aware of this deficiency, the members in 1916 had unanimously passed a resolution directing their secretary to communicate to the laggard state legislatures their "urgent request that enactments be passed creating such state organizations in order to properly assist in maintaining and protecting the wild life involved." Work toward the removal of game departments from political patronage occupied much attention.[59]

Meanwhile, the new "International" also was becoming more sophisticated internally. In 1918 a Committee on the Improvement of the Association recommended the establishment of committees on membership, to solicit state members and help them procure funding from their respective legislatures; publicity, since "there is nothing like educating people to the proper frame of mind to accomplish the results which the true sportsman desires"; uniformity of laws, to assist the states in mutual cooperation; endowments, for financial security; and program, so that conventions might focus on matters of "timely interest." It would take a while for these committees to become functional and effective, but the members seemed keenly aware that their organization could make—indeed was making—a difference.[60]

In just under twenty years, then, the International Association of Game, Fish and Conservation Commissioners had asserted state sovereignty over resident wildlife while recognizing federal authority over migratory birds. It had begun to work through the most promising avenues of law and regulation to conserve wildlife for future use. While still grappling with problems of growth and independence, the Association had established itself as an organization prepared in knowledge, dedication, and vigor to take on the challenging issues of the coming decades. There would be many.

TWO

Building Game Management, Building an Association

Ducks can't lay eggs on a picket fence.

JAY N. "DING" DARLING

SETH GORDON, pillar of the International Association of Fish and Wildlife Agencies for over sixty years, attended his first Association convention in 1921, an important year for witnessing both the continuity of conservation interests and the development of new approaches to game administration. As he later recalled, the major issues and recommendations of that session were the reduction of bag limits and improvement of law enforcement; the endorsement of the Public Shooting Grounds-Game Refuge Bill then before Congress; opposition to marsh drainage; and the removal of game and fish administration from politics. These priorities reflected, in fact, major issues of the conservation community for the next decade and more.[1]

Early conservation efforts had largely consisted of various restrictions on the taking of game. Moreover, a sizable bloc of learned as well as popular opinion had regarded wildlife as a finite resource that would eventually disappear. As McGee had put it, conservation would allow the greatest good for the greatest number *for the longest time.* Controlling hunting practices would postpone the final day—only that. But by the 1920s conservation leaders, while agreeing that hunting restraints by themselves could not preserve America's wildlife resources, would not accept the fatalistic view that game must inevitably be lost. Aldo Leopold, for example, perhaps borrowing from his first career as a forester, began applying the sustained yield concept of forest renewal to wildlife.

By mid-decade he was promoting the philosophy of "managing" game in a positive way. Increasing production by "artificial propagation or environmental controls," as opposed to negative protection alone, would produce a "crop" that could be harvested and still preserve the seed stock. In other words, by applying scientific principles, Americans could use their wildlife and keep it too.[2]

Propagating Game: Farms and Refuges

The idea of game farms, on which wild game could be scientifically and intensively raised for later release and their eggs sold for further breeding, gained popularity at this time. Illinois established the most extensive early state game farm in 1905. Private enterprisers dabbled in game farming as well. Richard Bache had set up a game farm of sorts around 1790 when he planted imported Hungarian partridges on his New Jersey estate. The International Association joined in the excitement in the postwar period, devoting several convention sessions to describing and promoting the concept. E. A. Quarles, Director of Game Breeding and Secretary of the American Game Protective Association, addressed the International in 1918, giving in detail his recommendations for establishing a successful game farm, down to the estimated cost of screens for rearing coops and the need for two cows, whose milk would nourish both the birds and the game keepers.[3]

In the end enthusiasm outdistanced positive results. Only a few wild animals, such as ringnecked pheasants, mallards, and grey and chukar partridge, proved amenable to introduction into the wild after close human manipulation. High initial costs which delayed return on investment discouraged participation in the experiment despite demand for the product. Meanwhile, fish hatcheries, game farms' aquatic analogy, were becoming common.[4]

More important, the concept of game refuges caught conservationists' imagination during the 1920s. Refuges would provide an inviolate sanctuary where animals could nest, rest, and feed in safety. As Leopold explained in 1933, such an area, closed to hunting, would stimulate population growth. The excess would eventually "flow out" and "enhance the productivity or abundance of game on the surrounding range." Here hunting could indeed be permitted without endangering the overall population, since only the overflow would be at risk.[5]

President Benjamin Harrison had created the first national wildlife refuge on Afognak Island, Alaska, in 1892. Theodore Roosevelt had used his executive powers in 1903 to establish a bird sanctuary on Pelican

Island, Florida, which became the first refuge of the National Wildlife Refuge System and the first made independently of a national forest. California had a state refuge as early as 1870 and possibly before that. Other states followed suit in the next few decades; between 1913 and 1925 twenty-four states organized wildlife refuges of some sort. One of the oldest and largest of these was the Grand Teton State Refuge, established in Wyoming in 1905 primarily for the protection of elk. Also in 1905, Pennsylvania set up a state refuge for upland game. Waterfowl received protection in Wisconsin's Horicon Marsh in 1891 and in Ontario and Iowa in 1907. The federal government showed its interest in preserving big game by creating refuges for Rocky Mountain mule deer in northern Arizona in 1906 and bison in Montana and elk in Washington in 1909. The International Association first urged the development of game refuges by convention resolution in 1916.[6]

Preserving the Dwindling Waterfowl

By 1920 conservationists were particularly anxious to provide refuges for waterfowl. Restrictive hunting laws and the implementation of the Migratory Bird Treaty had produced noticeable increases in the sizes of flocks seen, but the growth was both temporary and illusory. Americans, with more leisure than ever before, were increasingly seeking recreation in outdoor sports, and the nation's 6 million hunters now had improved firearms, the automobile, and even the airplane with which to expand their effective shooting range. They were beginning to represent more of a threat to wildfowl than the unbridled market hunters of an earlier era.[7]

Meanwhile, the habitats of ducks and geese were shrinking drastically. Supposedly useless swamp lands were being drained for agriculture and settlement in response to World War I food demands and postwar population growth. Too late came the realization that returning flocks of birds, finding their former nesting sites dried up, had to crowd onto smaller and smaller wetlands where sheer numbers meant death from polluted waters and competition for ever scarcer food. And where would they lay their eggs? In Oregon, for example, drainage of Malheur and Klamath lakes for irrigation projects steadily diminished waterfowl habitat there. Some of the world's finest breeding grounds eventually disappeared altogether and, in a particularly bitter irony, the lands thus exposed proved to be virtually useless alkali flats. One observer called it a "classical example of futile 'reclamation,' where every result was a loss." And the relentless droughts of the late 1920s and 30s were yet to come.[8]

Political problems compounded the waterfowl difficulties of the tumultuous 1920s. While the Migratory Bird Treaty empowered the Bureau of Biological Survey to regulate seasons and bag limits, the Bureau under Chief Edward W. Nelson was reluctant to take vigorous federal action for fear of antagonizing state game agents and the hunting public. At first Nelson seemed justified in assuming a relatively relaxed posture, since by official counts the waterfowl numbers were increasing. William T. Hornaday was quick to point out, however, that the only reason there appeared to be more ducks was that they were forcibly concentrated on shrinking wetlands. He demanded dramatically reduced bag limits. Nelson demurred, sincere in his belief that the waterfowl were coming back.[9]

Both historians and politicians have criticized Nelson's foot-dragging as well as that of the Bureau and its advisory committee of conservation experts. Frank E. Smith wrote that "despite the power of the 1918 law, the Biological Survey spent the entire decade of the 1920s refusing to utilize its powers to regulate bag limits or otherwise provide any meaningful protection for migratory birds. Without prodding from the Survey, Congress did nothing." Donald Swain also accused the Bureau scientists of cowardice in opposing organized hunters backed by the sporting arms industry; he accused Nelson of weakness and vacillation. Neither critic, however, showed any sympathy for the political realities with which Nelson dealt. His positions suggest a defensible preference for accepting lesser but attainable limits rather than insisting upon tougher measures certain to be opposed, ignored, or defied. Nor was Nelson receiving high-level executive encouragement for forceful action.[10]

Presidential leadership for conservation during the 1920s was undistinguished. Warren G. Harding (1921–23) owed his election in part to his sympathy for easing wartime restrictions of all kinds, and he showed no particular interest in conservation until shortly before his death. His administration unabashedly promoted unregulated private development of the nation's resources. Calvin Coolidge (1923–29) concentrated on decentralization and cutting federal spending. He paid little attention to conservation, although he did encourage the states to act on their own and cooperatively with each other to develop resource policy. Herbert Hoover, President at the end of the decade (1929–33) and Secretary of Commerce before that, cared deeply about conservation, but his individualist philosophy and voluntary approach to cooperative resources administration hampered positive accomplishment. The White House was not a beacon for conservationists during this decade.[11]

A final result of dwindling wetlands and proliferating hunters was a competition for shooting space, won by wealthy clubs that purchased or leased the choicest areas for the private use of individuals able to pay hefty membership fees. Hunters of lesser means were pushed into more crowded, less desirable spaces. More than one conservationist of the time revealed the worry that the "one-gallus man," feeling undemocratically deprived of his hunting rights, might look to other systems of rule and "add something to this Bolshevist business."[12]

Against this background and a great deal of urging in the conservation press, Indiana Senator Harry S. New and Kansas Congressman Daniel R. Anthony, both Republicans, introduced identical bills in 1921 that came to be known collectively as the Public Shooting Grounds-Game Refuge Bill. It provided for the creation of a system of federal wildlife refuges that would be combined with public shooting grounds. That is, the birds would be protected most of the year, but the public could hunt in these areas during a legally established open season. Funding for land purchase and law enforcement would come from a one-dollar federal hunting license.[13]

The International Association of Game, Fish and Conservation Commissioners immediately took up the New-Anthony bill at the 1921 convention. George Lawyer, Chief U.S. Game Warden in the Bureau of Biological Survey, spoke about all the swamp land that could be purchased and saved from drainage with the $2 million revenue expected from the federal license and of the expanded system of federal game wardens the bill would allow. Alabama Conservation Commissioner John H. Wallace, extolled for his knowledge and "preaching" skills, declared, "We must organize this country," and instructed the delegates how to educate sportsmen who in turn must pressure Congress. His was an early lesson in politicking that Association members would learn well. Guest speaker William Hornaday asked, "Will Our Vanishing Game Be Saved?" He spoke spiritedly on his own wider agenda, such as the necessity of cutting bag limits by half and quadrupling resident license fees, but his support of the game refuge bill was unequivocal. "The purpose of this bill is thoroughly admirable," he said, urging every "real sportsman" to support it actively. The members gave the game refuge bill their hearty endorsement and urged its early passage, calling it "vitally important to the conservation of migratory water fowl and necessary in order to furnish the masses of the people an adequate shooting area."[14]

The bill commanded widespread support within the Association, sportsmen's organizations, and even the national press. At congressional hearings the testimony was overwhelmingly in favor of swift passage. Association members, such as Carlos Avery, John M. Phillips of Pennsylvania, and T. Gilbert Pearson, contributed a good part of it. Those who counted votes found Congress solidly behind the measure. Or so they thought. The Public Shooting Grounds-Game Refuge Bill, in fact, failed to emerge from committee. It would be introduced again, and would fail again, more or less every year until nearly the end of the decade.

Ray Holland, longtime Secretary-Treasurer of the International Association and editor of *Field and Stream*, explained the failures of the game refuge bill at the next few Association conventions, revealing in the process that support for the measure was neither as enthusiastic nor unanimous as backers had thought, even though it would provide the machinery for implementing the much heralded Migratory Bird Treaty. Holland blamed the burdens of other business and "unsettled conditions" for preventing a full consideration of the game refuge bill in 1921. He also admitted that concern that the money collected would go into a general, not special, fund also contributed to its defeat. Forty states were solidly behind the bill, according to Holland, but he also noted that the Arizona state game commissioner, for one, not only opposed the bill, he refused to answer any mail on the matter. Dissension within the Association itself was beginning to surface.[15]

In 1923 Holland again had to report defeat, this time after the Senate had passed the measure by two to one and the House had widely supported it. But the game refuge bill was killed by ten votes when the House leaders of both parties, Republican Mondell of Wyoming and Democrat Finis James Garrett of Tennessee, opposed it, citing fears of federal encroachment in state affairs. Holland, in frustration, ticked off the provisions of the bill designed to allay such fears—state license requirements would not be jeopardized, refuges would generally remain under state jurisdiction, the poor could afford the minimal one-dollar fee—but it was already lost.[16]

And so it went. In early 1925, with a new bill (S. 2913, H.R. 745) before Congress, the *Bulletin of the American Game Protective Association* was both optimistic and anxious. It declared that states with excellent modern game conservation systems of their own welcomed more game refuges and that opposition was manifested "only where ignorance exists" and little was being done. It took the *Bulletin* more than half a column to list the conservation organizations, sportsmen's groups, national clubs, and varied publications that had endorsed the bill, including, of course, the International Association of Game, Fish and Conservation Commissioners.[17]

The *Bulletin* insisted that "this Bill does not encroach upon any of the rights of the states. It creates no new federal police power, and provides that the Federal Government can set aside no refuges or public shooting grounds except by permission of the legislature of the state concerned. The Bill does not require appropriation by Congress from the U.S. Treasury. The men who will directly benefit will pay $1 a year each towards the funds for its administration." The *Bulletin*'s arguments, couched in reassuring negatives, revealed disquiet not only about the bill but about larger societal problems as well. Fears of federal police power as exemplified by the proposed warden force, for example, were frequently raised, often directly or by implication in reference to ubiquitous, meddlesome federal agents trying to enforce Prohibition, in effect since the passage of the Eighteenth Amendment in 1919. It was not a good time to suggest additional regulation by "big government."[18]

When the International Association took up the game refuge question again at its 1925 convention in Denver, the issue of public shooting grounds was the focus of contention. As had become its custom, the Association invited experts to inform its members. This time they got an earful, not all of it polite. Will H. Dilg, National President of the Izaak Walton League and an aggressive ally of Dr. Hornaday, argued that public shooting grounds simply would not work. Too many hunters in a delineated space would kill off all the game in short order. He opposed the new tax and the increased federal warden force, quoting "a Senator" who called the whole bill "un-American and fundamentally and constitutionally wrong." John B. Burnham, President of the American Game Protective Association, countered just as strongly that public shooting grounds could work and indeed were working in several states. Without provision for public shooting grounds, he said, the legislation would amount to a "rich man's bill." When Dilg prepared to walk out on Burnham's remarks, the two exchanged bitter words over each other's tactics in Washington and elsewhere. Meanwhile, Hornaday himself, comprehending that the "so-called game-refuges" were "really convertible into shooting-grounds at the option of the Secretary of Agriculture," had reversed himself and was demanding the defeat of this "more-killing measure."[19]

The newly formed Western Association of State Game Commissioners also had difficulty reaching consensus. Western opposition to federal bureaucratic "tentacles," especially after World War I, was intense. The Western Association sent its president, David H. Madsen of Utah, to the International Association convention in 1925 to support the game refuge bill, but he admitted to having helped defeat earlier versions. The Western's records show much attention to the game refuge bill and no unanimity of opinion on it as revealed by worries over "the germ of paternalism" in "long-distance government" and the complaint that "this taxation by special license is getting to be a habit."[20]

In the end the 1925 convention of the International Association did a remarkable thing. Despairing, apparently, of reaching accord on the game refuge bill as it presently stood, the Association appointed a committee of five representatives, one each from the International Association, the Western Association, the National Audubon Society, the Izaak Walton League, and the American Game Protective Association, to study the legislation and try to draft a workable compromise.[21] This so-called Denver Committee was later enlarged and officially became the National Committee on Wild Life Legislation in 1928. In 1929 eight of its eleven members were affiliated in one way or another with the International. In its ten or so years of existence, the Committee exerted considerable influence in Congress. For his part, Hornaday heaped derision on the Committee, especially its chairman T. Gilbert Pearson, charging ineffectiveness, waffling, and egregious politicking. The Denver Committee drafted a new bill for the 1926 legislative session. It, too, enjoyed wide support but it, too, failed thanks to a filibuster by three western Senators who prevented its coming to a vote.[22]

Meanwhile, within the International Association support was cracking. For one of the few times during its history the Association called for a standing vote on its resolution favoring the Game Refuge Bill, and no one was very happy with the result. Fourteen states voted for the resolution, five against. Opposing were Oklahoma, Texas, Kansas, Missouri, and North Dakota, all in the midwestern plains. California voted affirmatively but was the only far western state present. The Western Association had already voted for a similar resolution, albeit with internal disagreement. Seth Gordon, showing his grasp of the central issue ("I am interested in doing something for the wild fowl of this country"), his political savvy, and his institutional orientation, worried about the effect of the Association's vote. "In view of the comparatively small number of states here represented, an action of this sort is going to be garbled by the enemies of this bill in a way that will be used to defeat the purposes of the sportsmen of the country." As an Associate, or individual, member, Gordon had no vote according to the bylaws. Finally, President E. Lee LeCompte of Maryland asked for a popular vote in hopes of recording a more accurate sense of the body even though it would not be binding. The delegates stood 29–2 in favor. More instructive than the numbers perhaps was the clear message that the members enthusiastically supported the game refuge concept. Their objections centered on other elements of the bill, such as the federal game warden force, the federal tax to fund it, and, especially, the public shooting grounds section, which was variously perceived as unnecessary, inimical to vested interests, or an outrageous license to kill.[23]

The next year, 1927, the members of the Association backed off from confrontation on the game refuge question. No particular bill was under consideration, and they bypassed the subject entirely except for approving a general resolution urging Congress to enact laws to honor the "solemn compact with Canada" that would "insure adequate refuges in which migratory birds may rest, nest and feed while in the United States."[24]

Meanwhile, waterfowl conditions were becoming precarious. In 1927 Gilbert Pearson went to see for himself the results of the drainage projects at Malheur Lake and was sickened to discover "only weeds" and "open flats over which whirlwinds chased each other like ghosts of the wildlife that had departed."[25] Several years of drought had lowered water levels and dried up shallow marshes, such as those at the mouth of the Bear River in northern Utah, a particularly important stopping off place for birds since it was a rather solitary oasis in arid country on the western flyways.[26] Congress at last appropriated $350,000 to reclaim the marshes by building earthen dikes, but by then less than 10 percent of the original marsh remained, as David Madsen, now Superintendent of the Bear River Marsh Migratory Bird Reserve for the Bureau of Biological Survey, reported to the Association in 1928. One positive accomplishment of the decade thus far had been a $1.5 million appropriation by Congress, its first, in 1924 for the purchase of bottom lands along the upper Mississippi River to establish a refuge for birds, other wildlife, and fish. This single refuge, an extensive area geographically, from northern Illinois to southern Minnesota, was at least a start toward the system of national refuges envisioned by the game refuge bill promoters.[27]

Finally, in 1928 Senator Peter Norbeck, Republican of South Dakota, with the assistance and backing of the National Committee on Wild Life Legislation, introduced a game refuge bill that was stripped of all mention of public shooting grounds and federal licensing. Funding would come from direct congressional appropriation. (Hornaday claimed it was his personal appeal to Norbeck that got the "vicious public-shooting-ground feature" eliminated and that the compromise bill was an embarrassment for the National Committee and its sponsoring organizations, but neither assertion was supported by evidence.)[28] This bill passed, as did an identical bill of Minnesota's Republican Congressman August Andreson. The Migratory Bird Conservation Act, or Norbeck-Andreson Act, was signed into law on February 18, 1929, following a few brief weeks of legislative activity and a personal visit to President Coolidge by Norbeck, Andreson, and Pearson to urge his signature. After eight years of dissension and debate, conservationists had finally acted on the common ground they had all along shared. It was a landmark act even if its incompleteness frustrated many.[29]

The waterfowl populations continued to decline, however, under conditions of drought, drainage, liberal bag limit laws, inadequate law enforcement, and insufficient funding for game refuges. Biological Survey Chief Nelson appeared before the Senate Committee on Agriculture and Forestry in 1927 to talk (at last, according to Hornaday and others) about the need for stricter bag limits in order to "safeguard the breeding stock." The subject got broader than Chairman Charles McNary of Oregon had anticipated when he asked Nelson if the law permitted the sale of birds. "No," said Nelson. "They are bootlegged, however. Since the Volstead Act went into force the bootlegging in wild game has increased tremendously. The same men who are bootlegging liquor bootleg ducks." While the Migratory Bird Treaty had been "pretty well respected" at first, since the enactment of the prohibition amendment, bootlegging had become a "regular industry" that was "really outrageous in places." The Noble Experiment was having some unanticipated and ignoble results for wildlife.[30]

As drought conditions worsened, Paul G. Redington, new Chief of the Bureau of Biological Survey, acknowledged to the International Association that the annual kill would have to be curtailed if waterfowl were to survive. At the same convention, 1931, Seth Gordon succinctly summarized the problems and limitations of current legislation, made a plea for unity and cooperation, and itemized specific actions that should be taken immediately to stem impending disaster. His proposed remedies called for ample refuges along flyways; adequate law enforcement to eliminate poachers, bootleggers, and market hunters; predator control; wildfowl breeding by states and private interests; and a migratory bird treaty with Mexico. To pay for all this he suggested a federal migratory bird hunting license of one dollar that could be purchased at post offices and affixed to state licenses. The convention body lauded Gordon's program and unanimously adopted it.[31]

The federal license law idea, while dormant, was indeed alive, since from the beginning congressional appropriations were chancy and could not be counted upon even when the monies were authorized.[32] Judge Lee Miles, Game and Fish Commissioner of Arkansas, had reintroduced the funding matter to the members of the International Association in 1930. Arguing that there would never be sufficient money from Congress to pay for inviolate sanctuaries for migratory birds, he declared that the gunners themselves would willingly support these costs if they had an equitable mechanism by which to do so. Miles proposed a federal migratory bird hunting license, pegged for reasons he did not explain at $1.10. Only a federal license would do, he said, since birds roamed not only nationally but internationally. Each year at convention this so-called duck stamp issue surfaced again, each time receiving the Association's endorsement while in Congress it gained support and momentum.[33]

The federal license finally became a reality in 1934 with the passage of the Migratory Bird Hunting Stamp Act, more popularly known as the Duck Stamp Act. The one-dollar fee was to be used to purchase and maintain migratory waterfowl refuges, with a small percentage reserved for administering the act. At last the federal migratory bird program begun in 1913 was not only alive in concept but was assured of the funding necessary to make it work. The hunters would thus support their own sport. This first application of a "user fee" represented the fruition of an idea that would eventually provide sustenance for much of wildlife conservation in this country.[34]

Big Game: Too Few, Too Many

Migratory birds, enormous problem though they were, were not conservationists' only concern during the 1920s and 30s. The lessons learned from trying to manage big game by the principles of restrictive hunting practices were different, but no less real or pressing.

T. S. Palmer's overview study, *Game as a National Resource*, in 1922 painted a discouraging picture of big game in America in the early postwar period. He noted, for example, that deer, the most important large animal killed for food, had become so scarce that in one-fourth of the states hunting had to be stopped altogether. Half of the states put does under statutory protection at all times. (Palmer never failed to make the point that doe laws not only conserved the breeding stock, they also protected human life, since the time it took to ascertain whether the deer had horns would also be sufficient to determine whether the object in the gunsight was an animal at all.) Elk, moose, and caribou were surviving under special protection.[35]

Guy Amsler, president of the International Association in the 1930s, remembered that in his state of Arkansas deer were so scarce that only about a dozen were killed during the 1922 season. He called his friend and fellow game commissioner Seth Gordon in Pennsylvania to inquire if Gordon had any deer to spare. Pennsylvania had plenty, so Gordon sent thirty to Arkansas. Moreover, he urged Amsler to establish state game refuges, the secret of Pennsylvania's success. Amsler thereupon set to the task, even plowing a farmer's field while a colleague talked the reluctant landowner into signing an approval for a local refuge. The imported animals prospered. In 1984 Arkansas's legal harvest was more than 50,000 deer.[36]

Big game refuges had been established early in the century, as noted. These sanctuaries made possible the replenishment of herds of bison and other truly endangered species, but sometimes the applied concept worked too well, with disastrous results. Protected elk in and around Yellowstone National Park, for example, became so numerous even before World War I that emergency winter feeding programs had to be initiated. Such good intentions yielded only overcrowding, dependency, and even larger populations. Not until World War II did conservationists face up to the need to reduce the herds to sizes the food supply could sustain.[37]

The Kaibab situation was demonstrably worse. In 1906 President Theodore Roosevelt had set aside the Kaibab Plateau in northern Arizona, most of which was already a national forest, as the Grand Canyon National Game Preserve in order to protect a herd of Rocky Mountain mule deer. The North Rim of the Grand Canyon and side canyons isolated the area like an island. Game conservationists applied the principles they thought they had learned and proudly observed the herd grow as they patrolled the plateau against poachers, reduced grazing rights there, and carried out a systematic extermination program against predators such as coyotes, cougars, wildcats, and even the few grey wolves that had frequented the area.[38]

The deer responded beyond anyone's expectations, the herd increasing sevenfold by the early 1920s to about 20,000 head. Since the presence of large numbers of visible deer attracted tourists to the North Rim, the program seemed at first to be a great success. But protection proved to be a cruelty. A 1925 census counted 30,000 deer, far beyond the carrying capacity of the forest. Seth Gordon, who had been on the Kaibab in 1925, reported back to the International Association of Game, Fish and Conservation Commissioners the next year. He minced no words. "Unless a reduction is made without delay that splendid herd is doomed, as Nature will in her own way bring about a drastic reduction on that plateau."[39]

The hungry animals were indeed stripping their browse higher and higher, eating tree seedlings, and finally destroying altogether the forests they depended upon. Naturally, self-destruction had to follow the loss of present and future food supply, and, sure enough, mass starvation quickly followed. When the Forest Service, which administered the area, and the Bureau of Biological Survey proposed a hunt of rather drastic proportions, they were attacked from two fronts—the "uninformed and uninformable sentimentalists and the professional humanitarians," who opposed what they called "wanton butchery," and the state of Arizona, which insisted upon the right to regulate its own resident wildlife.[40]

Arizona's position enjoyed precedent going back to Geer v. Connecticut in 1896, which had affirmed the right of state ownership. So when the Secretary of Agriculture directed the removal of deer from the Kaibab Plateau without regard to Arizona law, the state arrested the federal officials carrying out the program. In 1928 the Supreme Court, however, ruled that the United States had the power to protect federal lands and property, state game laws or any other state laws notwithstanding. Arizona did not fail to recognize the need for controlling the deer herd. Rather, it resented the federal government's high-handed disregard for state prerogatives and its unilateral action. Yet both sides desired better relations. When Paul Redington announced to the IAGFCC in 1931 that federal agents and the State Game Commission of Arizona were now acting in cooperation, the delegates applauded. In any case this clear illustration of the continuing conflict between federal and state authority over resident wildlife would be repeated in another decade on the other side of the continent, in North Carolina, and would have similar repercussions.[41]

Meanwhile, on the Kaibab the situation grew more deplorable before it got better. In 1931 Redington reported to the Association that the U.S. Forest Service had appointed a Kaibab Investigative Committee, chaired by Gilbert Pearson, to evaluate this "cynosure of all eyes," and recommend proper action. The committee concluded that the range was then maintaining less than 10 percent of the forage it had once produced and that much of this was unfavored varieties. The deer were still too numerous to allow recovery of the forest. The committee recommended heavy but supervised hunting of deer and the cessation of predator animal killing. In the end nature worked in its own way. Before effective action could be taken, the herd reached 150,000, and then in one appalling winter began a precipitous drop by starvation to 17,000.[42]

The Value of Vermin

The Kaibab crisis provided a compelling object lesson to conservationists on the perils of upsetting the balance of nature. A centerpiece of wildlife administration for years had been the control, that is to say the eradication, of "vermin." The term was an omnibus word used to indicate any animal considered pestiferous or destructive to desirable wildlife or their habitat, and conservationists had unhesitatingly called for their extermination in order to encourage the proliferation of favored species. English sparrows, for example, considered nuisances, were specifically exempted from the provisions of the Lacey Act. Hornaday, ubiquitous foe of those who would "slaughter" and "massacre" game, unblinkingly waged verbal war on his short but self-determined list of vermin. Predator control, a nicer name for the same idea, was an important part of the work of the Bureau of Biological Survey in the 1920s. Jenks Cameron, historian of the Bureau, proudly recorded the "commanding place that predatory animal control has come to occupy" in the Bureau's program. He described the appropriations for employing hunters and trappers and for purchasing rifles, ammunition, traps, and poison. "Poison is rapidly coming to supersede all other methods of suppression." Cameron noted that "by 1926 the cooperative predatory work had come to be well established in sixteen states, the cooperating agencies ranging all the way from the state governments to individuals."[43]

It would take a long while for conservationists to appreciate the essential role played by all organisms in the environment, including undesirable ones. "Wily stock-killing wolves, coyotes, cougars, or bears" on the Kaibab, for instance, could have by their natural predations prevented the deer from eating themselves, literally, into starvation. One young conservationist who was there to witness the Kaibab tragedy and learn from it was Aldo Leopold, a New Mexico forester who later became not only a game authority but also a land and wildlife philosopher. He was one of the first to call for an ecological ethic that respected the place of all things. By 1933 he had thought out and written his classic *Game Management* which outlined the possibilities, limitations, and responsibilities of manipulating game for the mutual benefit of the animals and human users. In other words, Leopold saw and comprehended the whole as well as the individual parts of game management. His call for flexible wildlife administrative authority in the hands of trained professionals to purposefully maintain animal populations in balance with the carrying capacity of the habitat recognized the need for new methods. He saw population imbalances threatening not only the deer of the Kaibab and the elk of Yellowstone but eventually other protected animals in other places such as deer in Pennsylvania, long hailed as the birthplace of successful game refuges.[44]

The New Deal and Wildlife

The same year that Aldo Leopold published his landmark study, the United States inaugurated a lifelong conservationist as President. Franklin D. Roosevelt's fascination for wildlife went back to his childhood days of bird hunting and collecting. He had worked on forestry and fish and game conservation as a private citizen, state senator, and New York governor. Like Herbert Hoover, he genuinely cared about the orderly development and long-range conservation of natural resources, but unlike his predecessor he had no philosophical impediments to taking decisive action. Besides, the times were as bleak as the nation had ever known. As unemployment and economic stagnation worsened, Roosevelt saw the waste of human resources, in terms of lost morale as well as productivity, as the nation's most paralyzing problem. So his administration took these two interests, conservation and employment, and developed far-reaching programs in public works to address both.

Conservation activities were an obvious approach for Roosevelt and his New Deal. The public domain was "by definition government's proper sphere." Private enterprise would be stimulated, not threatened, by public works in conservation. Neglected natural resources needed attention and could be worked on by unskilled labor, beginning almost immediately. Outdoor work was physically and spiritually healthy. Expenditures would be recovered from future timber growth, flood prevention, pollution abatement, and agricultural productivity.[45]

One of the earliest and ultimately most successful of the New Deal's numerous programs affecting conservation was the Civilian Conservation Corps, established in March 1933. The CCC did not initially address wildlife concerns directly or excite wildlife conservationists as having "epochal" promise, but it achieved some stunning results. In May 1933 Roosevelt approved the establishment of a CCC camp in the Blackwater Migratory Bird Refuge in Maryland; before World War II closed all the camps, thirty-seven more were activated. There could have been many more had refuge land acquisition been further advanced. Nevertheless, negotiating purchase options, surveying, building dikes and dams, fencing, and other aspects of wildlife restoration proceeded at a dizzying pace.[46]

Wildlife conservation was accelerated when Roosevelt appointed in January 1934 a presidential committee on wildlife restoration, naming to it Thomas Beck, soon to become the first president of the American Wildlife Institute, Jay N. "Ding" Darling, and Aldo Leopold.[47] They quickly recommended a $50 million allocation for wildlife restoration programs involving the rehabilitation of submarginal lands for game and other wildlife species. They further called attention to the appalling plight of migratory birds.

Roosevelt named Darling, an outspoken political adversary but ardent conservationist, gifted sloganeer and cartoonist, and dynamic mover of bureaucratic hurdles, as Chief of the Bureau of Biological Survey. In the year and a half of Darling's tenure, he intensified law enforcement against market hunters and spring shooters, acted on proposals for waterfowl restoration that the Wildlife Restoration Committee had solicited from state conservation agencies, instituted college training programs in fish and game management, and insisted on strict season and bag limits for the badly endangered ducks. Proceeds from the Duck Stamp Act of 1934 provided additional monies specifically for migratory waterfowl refuges.[48]

The members of the International Association of Game, Fish and Conservation Commissioners lost no time in seeing the potential for their own concerns in the new federal attitudes. By the 1934 convention there was much to talk about, and the record is animated. Carl Shoemaker, Secretary of the Senate Special Committee on the Conservation of Wildlife Resources and former Oregon wildlife chief, addressed the delegates on "New Federal Legislation." Shoemaker was enthusiastic. "Interest in wildlife and the out-of-doors has gone forward by leaps and bounds during the past nine months. It is safe to say that the conservation and restoration program has been advanced fully a generation in less than a year." And later, "Conservation had a brilliant day in the last Congress." First, the Duck Stamp Act revenues would fund additional waterfowl refuges. Public Works Administration monies would allow immediate acquisition of submarginal lands for the same purpose. The Coordination Act encouraged remedial legislation for combatting water pollution and provided that before impounding waters, provision must be made for greatest biological use of the waters and adequate means for fish to migrate over dams. And the Taylor Grazing Act, by limiting grazing on the overused ranges on federal land in the western states, promised a rejuvenated environment for wildlife.[49]

The discussion that followed Shoemaker's remarks revealed the excitement, level of activity, and pitfalls of too much too soon. Various state conservation leaders rose to describe their projects or ask how to get one through the short-lived Civil Works Administration, the Federal Emergency Relief Administration, or the Civilian Conservation Corps. Confusion about which agency was which was apparent. Biological Survey Chief Darling and Seth Gordon, then in Washington as head of the new American Wildlife Institute, cautioned the game commissioners to submit sound proposals for funds, that is, proposals for well-planned projects with proper engineering. When Darling told the delegates, "You must have something that will hold water," he had in mind more than a figure of speech. South Dakota, for example, had built 320 lakes with CWA and relief labor, but inspectors found that not more than half a dozen of them were so made that they would retain water. Poor construction or sand pocket locations doomed the rest. Darling's concerns were broad. Besides the problem of wasting money and time, he said, people lost confidence in conservationists when their completed projects were "no good." But good things were happening, too. An Ohio convention delegate boasted about his state's three CCC and twenty-one CWA projects. "We had fine plans and specifications; our projects all hold water and are going to stay."[50]

At the next Association convention, in 1935, leading game commissioners gave follow-up reports on New Deal projects in their states. I. T. Quinn of Alabama described his department's participation in a program to acquire, through federal purchase, submarginal lands and reclaim them through tree planting, stream improvement, and game encouragement. Fish and game surveys, then 80 percent complete, would help the conservationists determine the actual and potential animal populations of an area. Quinn's elaborate plans included a breakdown of personnel hours required for game management and the cost of food supply, in seeds or plants, for various species of game. Quinn was determined and optimistic that Alabama's wildlife resources were going to prosper under this new program.[51]

Elliott Barker of New Mexico, recently reelected President of the Western Association of State Game and Fish Commissioners, showed his grasp of economic and political realities as well as his astuteness in achieving the greatest good when he described how the new Taylor

Grazing Act would benefit both the stock growers and wildlife according to the plan he had helped develop in his state. Federally controlled livestock grazing and range use would improve forage conditions, "which stockmen desire more than any one else," and, ipso facto, improve wildlife habitat over time, too. Barker argued that joint use of the public domain by livestock and wildlife would work far better for wildlife than "exclusive game ranges." Small animals were no competition to livestock and even large ones could reasonably share a restored range. Besides, public and private lands were already hopelessly intermingled geographically, and most of the water, for game or anything else, was located on private or state land. Barker, a practical man, went cooperatively after what would work. With justifiable satisfaction he told the delegates that "the President of our Wool Growers' Association worked as hard for our wildlife program as anyone."[52]

Barker's later recollections about that 1935 meeting put forth his own sense of the critical issue, obscured in the lengthy *Proceedings* account. Barker remembered that the conservation community welcomed the intent of the Taylor Grazing Act but objected that it said nothing about wildlife. "Stockmen said they had always taken care of wildlife and just leave it set." Barker would not. Finally, he won acceptance of a compromise statement that he remembered clearly almost fifty years later: "In making estimates of livestock on the public lands and in the allotment of grazing privileges, reasonable consideration shall be given to wildlife." The International Association was not satisfied with that, Barker recalled, the term "reasonable" having no meaning. So he reminded the delegates that if a man's being hanged depended on reasonable doubt, "reasonable consideration" certainly could be a guide in the management of wildlife. They accepted it. At that meeting he had also presented the cattlemen's views. Their spokesman could not attend and entrusted Barker to give all sides. There was no formal indication of his wearing two hats at this session, but it was a lengthy one and Barker, a relative newcomer, must have impressed the delegates. They elected him President of the International Association of Game, Fish and Conservation Commissioners for the next year.[53]

The 1935 convention resolutions supported public works projects affecting wildlife, the Taylor Grazing Act and the regulations adopted for its implementation in New Mexico, the Biological Survey's attempts to restrict the hunting of still dangerously depleted migratory birds, and federal efforts to alleviate stream pollution. In all cases the delegates called for consultation with state conservation departments before action was taken. The Association also urged the consolidation of all federal conservation agencies and pledged its "hearty cooperation" with the new American Wildlife Institute.[54]

President Roosevelt called a North American Wildlife Conference in Washington in February 1936, demonstrating his own continuing interest and responding to mounting concerns within the conservation community for game and fish resources. Elliott Barker, President of the International and the Western Association, was on the planning committee of twenty-five and enjoyed power and access along with the hard work. Everybody who was anybody in wildlife conservation was at the conference, including Hoyes Lloyd, former IAGFCC President from Ottawa, Canada, and Juan Zinser, Chief of the Department of Forestry, Fish and Game of Mexico, who would host the International Association convention in 1937. Members of Congress, national conservation organizations, and state game commissions abounded. Jay Darling and Ira Gabrielson, Darling's successor as Biological Survey Chief, played major roles as well. Later that year, when Darling had resigned and was campaigning for FDR's opponent Alf Landon with criticism of the New Deal conservation program, Roosevelt asked his staff to prepare a "short speech on Wild Life for me which would be, in effect, an answer to Ding." In the statement Roosevelt called the Wildlife Conference "the most important conference of its kind ever assembled. Its purpose, which it successfully accomplished, was to promote a conservation program of national and international character" that all interests could unite to support.[55]

In the same speech, Roosevelt proudly listed the wildlife accomplishments of the first two years of his administration: the promulgation of a national plan and policy for the protection, restoration, and maintenance of American wildlife resources, with appropriations for implementation of approximately $20,700,000; the acquisition or setting aside of two and one-half times more lands for wildlife than had been set aside for this purpose in all previous years; the achievement of the "highest point of efficiency" ever in coordinating the work among federal agencies and federal and state agencies; the ratification of a migratory bird treaty with Mexico; the establishment of college research and training programs on wildlife and ecology; and the imposition of "competent and drastic" regulations to reduce the waterfowl kill and preserve the breeding stock during the drought emergency. Darling, of course, had been responsible for much of this progress, and had urged a total hunting ban for a year. In any case, the nation's wildlife interests had never seen action of such magnitude.[56]

The clearly visible browse line and denuded shrubs of piñon and juniper on Arizona's Kaibab Plateau around 1930 dramatized the disastrous results of overpopulation caused by too many protected deer consuming and destroying their future food supply. Mass starvation followed.

(Courtesy, U.S. Forest Service, Kaibab National Forest)

Snow geese alight on preserved wetlands of the Sacramento National Wildlife Refuge in California. Preventing swamp drainage for agriculture or settlement and maintaining healthy marsh environments have been important Association concerns since waterfowl populations declined alarmingly in the 1920s.

(Courtesy, U.S. Department of Interior, Bureau of Sport Fisheries and Wildlife, photo by Peter J. VanHuizen)

William F. Scott, Montana's State Game and Fish Warden, convened the first meeting of state game officials at Yellowstone Park in August 1902. He became the first president of the new National Association of Game and Fish Wardens and Commissioners, the forerunner of the International Association of Fish and Wildlife Agencies.

(Courtesy, Montana Department of Fish, Wildlife and Parks)

Canadian Environment Minister Thomas McMillan (left) and U.S. Interior Secretary Don Hodel signed the North American Waterfowl Management Plan on May 14, 1986. This agreement was hailed as second in importance only to the Migratory Bird Treaty of 1916 between Canada and the United States.

(Courtesy, U.S. Department of Interior, photo by Steve Stewart)

In 1982 animal-rights advocates, objecting to hunting as inhumane, attempted to rescue thousands of deer threatened by flooding in the Florida Everglades by moving them to higher ground. Half of the frightened few that were actually captured died, while noisy crowds and milling news reporters added to the confusion. Hunters in a controlled management program ultimately saved more of the herd.

(Courtesy, Florida Game and Fresh Water Fish Commission)

This release of transplanted antelope in Kansas illustrates restocking, a successful wildlife management practice. Antelope, in danger of extinction from over-hunting and encroaching civilization early in the century enjoy abundance today.

(Courtesy, Kansas Fish and Game Commission)

Providing for the enjoyment of nongame wildlife, today a significant activity of state wildlife managers, was not an early Association issue. The worried but unharmed chick is a baby white tern.
(Courtesy, U.S. Fish and Wildlife Service, photo by Robert J. Shallenberger)

Idaho biologists in 1964 used fish shocking apparatus to collect fish samples for comparative DDT contamination analyses. The adverse effects of pesticide spraying had worried wildlife managers even before Rachel Carson's *Silent Spring* galvanized public opinion in 1962.
(Courtesy, U.S. Forest Service, photo by Lee Prater)

The Cooperative Wildlife Research Units: Management Training

FDR's reference to wildlife research and training in his 1936 summation acknowledged what was arguably Ding Darling's most notable achievement, the establishment of the Cooperative Wildlife Research Unit Program. The activist Darling, long frustrated by difficulties in recruiting qualified wildlife personnel, had persuaded his state conservation commission and Iowa State College to each match his personal contribution to support a training school in fish and game management at Iowa State in 1932. Indeed, Aldo Leopold, who helped survey Iowa's wildlife resources for Darling, had as early as 1925 urged technical education for game managers that they might enjoy the stature and practical results achieved by agriculture and forestry professionals, much of whose work paralleled their own. By late 1935 Biological Survey Chief Darling succeeded in launching a national cooperative training program, obtaining funding and other contributions from the Bureau, the affected state game departments and colleges, and the American Wildlife Institute, primarily a group of moneyed arms industrialists reinvigorated from the old American Game Association.

Housed at nine scattered land grant colleges, the Units offered graduate-level academic preparation for wildlife biologists. They also directed fundamental research, applied the results to local conditions, and disseminated the information to landowners through demonstration and extension services. The resulting certified game professionals and new techniques in wildlife management proved their fundamental worth almost immediately when implementation of the Pittman-Robertson Act required both. State wildlife management could only prosper under these complementary educational and legislative developments.[57]

The Pittman-Robertson Act: Linchpin of Wildlife Conservation

Conservationists hailed the Pittman-Robertson Act, or Federal Aid in Wildlife Restoration Act, as a landmark when it was enacted in 1937. It remains so. Carl Shoemaker of the Senate Wildlife Committee called it "the most dramatic and perhaps the most beneficial conservation legislation ever introduced in the National Congress since the enabling act for the Migratory Bird Treaty." Trefethen compared its far-reaching importance to the Lacey Act of 1900. The role of the International Association of Game, Fish and Conservation Commissioners was central at every step of its establishment; the law could be regarded as the Association's brainchild.[58]

The need for action in wildlife restoration was clear. The populations of several species were alarmingly low and decreasing, as repeatedly seen. The number of hunters was increasing annually. Habitat loss from drought and expanded farm production continued apace. The federal waterfowl refuge program was demonstrating what could be done, but the states also had an interest in preserving migratory birds, to say nothing of upland game, a responsibility solely theirs. The states, however, had no money.

Federal legislation was the answer, and a fortuitous congressional effort provided the clue. Congress was abolishing various excise taxes at the time, and conservationists saw their opportunity. Continue the excise tax on sporting arms and ammunition, they said, and apply the proceeds to wildlife restoration programs through the states. Carl Shoemaker presented this proposal, which he credited to Darling, to a receptive International Association at its 1936 convention. On June 17, 1937, Senator Key Pittman, Democrat of Nevada, introduced a Federal Aid to Wildlife Restoration bill. His colleague, A. Willis Robertson of Virginia, also a Democrat and former head of the Virginia Commission of Game and Inland Fisheries, put a companion bill into the House hopper seventeen days later.[59]

Senator Pittman's committee report laid out the scope and purpose of the bill. It would provide for a continent-wide, joint state and federal program for restoring all species of wildlife. The federal government would allocate restoration funds to states that complied with the provisions of the act by, for example, passing state legislation stipulating that license fees not be diverted to any other purpose than the administration of the state's fish and game department. Monies would come from the already levied excise tax on sportsmen's equipment, some 3 million dollars per year, and would be set aside for restoration purposes only. A state's allocation would be determined by a formula that would be equitable to all states: one half in the ratio of the area of a state to the total area of all states, one half in the ratio of the number of paid hunting license holders of a state to the total license holders of all states. At bottom, hunters would be supporting their own sport and enhancing wildlife for nonusers as well.[60]

The final bill further stipulated that no state could receive more than \$150,000 per year from the fund. The Secretary of Agriculture, who, through the Bureau of Biological Survey, would administer the act, could assure that no state received less than \$15,000 provided that the state put up at least \$5,000. In all cases the federal government would pay 75 percent of the total cost of a project, the state 25 percent and maintenance. Eight percent of the total proceeds would be reserved for administering the act. In 1946 the law was amended to permit up to 25 percent of a state's share of federal aid to be spent on maintenance costs.[61]

Shoemaker and others noted with pleasure that the Pittman-Robertson bill passed both houses unanimously and speedily, with little discussion or debate. The supporters of wildlife were organized and united, their cause compelling in both popular and official circles. It was not quite that simple, however. Some in Congress feared granting a foothold of control in state affairs to federal agents via the Secretary of Agriculture. Others did not approve designating tax funds for specific purposes. A few clarifying amendments and the comparison of the mechanics of the bill to the demonstrably successful Federal Highway Aid Act of 1916 put minds at ease.[62]

Shoemaker did observe, however, that Congress, though it was determining a new policy in wildlife administration, did not follow the usual practice of referring the bill to executive departments for advice. The lawmakers, apparently fearing opposition from the Budget Bureau and the Treasury over the special fund concept, simply assumed the total authority unto themselves.[63]

The Secretary of Agriculture, Henry A. Wallace, in fact gave his written approval to the act after its passage, noting that it would "undoubtedly stimulate" state wildlife conservation and that it was "sponsored and earnestly advocated by practically all of the conservation organizations, official and unofficial, in the United States." Wallace was responding to a request for information on the Pittman-Robertson Act from Daniel W. Bell, Acting Director of the Bureau of the Budget. Bell opposed the bill and recommended that President Roosevelt veto it on the grounds that it would set up an earmarked fund. Bell quoted Roosevelt's own budget message of 1937 that disapproved of funding except by direct appropriation because other methods denied the President and Congress the right to authorize and review expenditures.[64]

But Roosevelt signed the Pittman-Robertson Act without comment on September 2, 1937, and inaugurated a new era in wildlife programming.[65] Ironically, Pittman's own state of Nevada was the last to make itself eligible for Pittman-Robertson funds. Its county-operated wildlife agencies did not consolidate under a state umbrella until 1947. The other forty-seven states were in line by 1943, forty-three of these by 1940.[66]

Albert M. Day, as head of a newly created Division of Federal Aid in Wildlife Restoration in the Bureau of Biological Survey, had charge of administering Pittman-Robertson funds. He sent federal agents to confer with state conservation department officials to interpret the new program and answer questions. Final touches to the program were reviewed at the 1938 IAGFCC convention, which met early that year, in June in Asheville, North Carolina. The law was slated to go into effect on July 1. Day reported that seven legislatures and thirty governors had already formally assented to the provisions of the act. (Gubernatorial action would suffice until the legislature next met.) Interest centered on permissible projects. Day cautioned the game officials to choose projects "clearly within the purposes of the act" that would be "least subject to question" and suggested three types: land purchase for wildlife rehabilitation; development of land to improve wildlife management, such as cover planting or water stabilization; and practical research problems, such as game surveys or transplanting deer to areas where previous populations had disappeared. He emphasized, in response to "also heard" concerns, that the purpose was game management, not the eventual elimination of hunting through willy-nilly creation of refuges, and that the Bureau had no intention of "insidiously attempting" to take over control of resident game and dictate the conduct of state game departments. Day closed by calling the Pittman-Robertson Act the greatest opportunity ever presented for restoring the national economy as well as environmental resources, wildlife being "inescapably linked with the land." He asked for a "spirit of mutual understanding and helpfulness."[67]

Although Lee LeCompte criticized the red tape Pittman-Robertson's implementation entailed, administration was relatively straightforward. The state game departments would select their own projects and, upon winning approval from the Biological Survey or, after 1940, the U.S. Fish and Wildlife Service, do the work themselves with state-hired personnel. Lands purchased and improved by the states would become state property. The states were allowed two years to obligate their federal funds; after that they reverted to the national treasury to help finance the Migratory Bird Conservation Act. Projects to benefit fish were not allowed nor those for migratory waterfowl intended, but habitat restoration in general would naturally serve all species.[68]

After a year of the act's operation, Albert Day again reported to the International Association on federal aid for wildlife restoration. He was disappointed in the slow rate of progress, but reasons were evident. The newness of the concept meant that both the state and federal officials were learning as they went. States, the majority of which had never before had money for research programs, were moving slowly, "perhaps wisely," to better insure sound projects. Interpreting legal questions took time in the Treasury and Agriculture Departments. 1938 was an election year with all the uncertainties that implied. Day was particularly discouraged by the high turnover rate among game officials. In the one year since the Pittman-Robertson program had been inaugurated, twelve state fish and game administrators had changed. Continuity of commitment and purposeful action could not be hoped for with 25 percent of the personnel unfamiliar with what had gone before. Not all states were yet eligible for participation, and a few had flatly turned down federal aid. Some, like North Carolina, were hesitant to make plans that would require lengthy implementation, since the amount of anticipated revenue was uncertain and subject to the whim of the Bureau of the Budget. Despite all this, Day was able to describe a variety of restoration programs underway in several states.[69] The 1940 Pittman-Robertson report related stepped-up progress as everyone involved gained in experience and optimism for future growth and the Cooperative Research Units contributed more personnel and know-how. World events would soon overtake wildlife restoration as they did much else, but the foundation for wildlife restoration, having been carefully, even cautiously, laid, would prove solid for future building.[70]

State v. Federal Authority: G-20-A, the Pisgah, and the Courts

If state conservation officials' suspicions of federal encroachment on their prerogatives with respect to the Pittman-Robertson Act were ungrounded, their fears had a basis in the unhappy fact of Regulation G-20-A, promulgated in 1934 by the U.S. Forest Service. G-20-A gave the Secretary of Agriculture, through the recommendation of the Forester, the self-determined right to require the purchase of a federal permit to hunt or fish in a national forest, to set season and bag limits for such hunting, or to prohibit hunting in order to prevent undue damage to forest vegetation. The USFS insisted it intended only to protect the forests, in cooperation with the states involved, but as the states saw it, according to Elliott Barker, the regulation made it possible for the Forest Service to "take over complete control of wildlife . . . any time they felt it desirable to do so."[71]

Barker was President of the International Association in 1936 when Regulation G-20-A came up as a continuing sore point. He politely reminded Homer L. Shantz, Chief of the Forest Service's Game Management Division, that while federal and state authorities had worked amicably together in New Mexico, the western states found the regulation a hindrance to cooperation and suggested that the Forest Service instead help the states enact better regulatory legislation of their own. Further, they considered G-20-A to be without legal basis and threatened to carry a case to the Supreme Court if the regulation were applied. So far no harm had come, but the potential for federal mischief made state agents wary. As a California delegate put it, "We have no objection to sitting down around a table and shaking hands with a man, but we don't like to see him carry brass knuckles."[72]

E. V. Willard, Conservation Commissioner of Minnesota, made the case for state authority in terms of the historic right of state ownership of resident game. He warned of the potential loss of revenue and increased confusion that divided responsibility for wildlife would bring. Willard worried about executive department regulations more than the laws they were derived from, he said, and even more about states that voluntarily surrendered authority to the United States. He spoke specifically, ironically, about the Pisgah National Forest of North Carolina, which had been created from the Vanderbilt estate in 1916 by presidential proclamation. North Carolina, in order to encourage the establishment of this federal forest, had ceded control of the game within it to the federal government under the authority of the Forest Service. The price paid by the state seemed small at the time. The enormity of the consequences would soon be manifest.[73]

In 1939 Dr. Shantz spoke to the Association again. It was a fairly innocuous speech about the goals and policies of his department. The real agenda of the occasion emerged haltingly, almost painfully, in the discussion that followed. Mr. Shawhan of West Virginia emboldened himself to suggest that the Forest Service modify the attitude of some of its personnel and teach them to look "level-eyed," not down, at state officials, that cooperation did not mean "domination." The awkwardness of the moment was palpable, even in the blandness of the written record. "The Chair awaits further discussion. . . ." Delegate Stras at length got up in praise of federal-state cooperation over national forests in his state of Virginia. Finally Seth Gordon seized the moment. "Mr. President, these folks are very hesitant; I heard a dozen of them out in the hall ask some rather serious questions about a suit that is pending in North Carolina, and I think we may just as well have that out here and find out what it is all about." A nervous President Arthur Clark opened the "dangerous" subject asking that comments be confined "strictly to the policies involved and their meaning and probable effect in the future." He called upon John Chalk, North Carolina's Commissioner of Game and Inland Fisheries and, as it turned out, his own successor.[74]

Chalk laid out his state's difficulties. The trouble had started in 1932, when the Forest Service began to conduct public hunts on the Pisgah

Game Preserve, an area within the Pisgah National Forest, to control the deer population. Unfortunately, the Forest Service exempted hunters from the state's license requirements. That problem was patched up by legislative amendment, but in 1939 the Forest Service began trapping and shipping deer out of the state to relieve population pressures. North Carolina protested—first, that overgrazing was not a problem in the Pisgah and second, that if deer were to be moved, they should be transferred to another part of North Carolina, whose animals they were. North Carolina's overall deer population was small. When the Forest Service refused to discontinue the practice, the state arrested a few federal agents. Thereupon, the Forest Service sued Chalk and his assistants for interfering with operations on federal lands. The question was on the interpretation of the 1916 language of cession of authority, which the state claimed the federal government was interpreting too broadly.

The Pisgah problem was local. But its implications affected all states, as Seth Gordon pointed out. The 1939 convention delegates took action in the form of a resolution that called the Forest Service's interpretation of certain regulations in the Pisgah National Forest a violation of all the principles of the theory of state ownership of game and its lawsuit a threat to "long-established amicable relations" between the states and the Forest Service. The resolution pledged the Association to ask the federal courts to intervene if the lawsuit were not withdrawn. It passed unanimously.[75]

In 1940 Peyton Randolph Harris, counsel for North Carolina, reviewed the Pisgah case before the International Association. By then a U.S. court of appeals had ruled that the federal government had sole and complete jurisdiction over the game in question. Harris encouraged the Association to enter a friend-of-the-court brief in support of North Carolina's position if the case were to go before the Supreme Court. The state agents, mindful of the broader implications of the Pisgah case, unanimously passed a motion to intercede as amicus curiae.[76]

Shortly thereafter, the U.S. House of Representatives Select Committee on Conservation of Wildlife Resources took testimony on the Pisgah case in view of its state-federal jurisdictional "friction." Shantz and others for the Forest Service argued mainly for the need to protect the forest from overbrowsing. Seth Gordon, Vice-President of the International and Executive Director of the Pennsylvania Game Commission, was straightforward. "The several States need the friendly aid, guidance, advice, and cooperation of a coordinated capable Federal agency in their wildlife management programs, but the States will never improve their ability to handle their own problems if a paternalistic Government steps in and does their work for them or assumes their responsibilities. And if the Government usurps their revenue-raising functions by overriding their hunting- and fishing-license laws and setting up permit fees of its own it will sap their very life blood." John Chalk, President of the International Association as well as chief defendant in the case, reiterated his state's grievances and its attempts to act in cooperation with the federal authorities. In fact, the International dominated the proceedings, with oral or written testimony from the Association of Midwest Fish and Game Commissioners, the Western Association of State Game and Fish Commissioners, and the Southern Association of Conservation Officials in addition to several individual state agents. Harris cited chapter and verse of the statutory background of North Carolina's position, much as he had done before the Association's recent convention. For all that, the House Committee made a long but superficial list of recommendations about upgrading training and equipment for federal field officers and one calling for "closer cooperation between Federal and State wildlife agencies for the advancement of conservation in all its phases."[77]

The Supreme Court, in mid-January 1941, refused to review the circuit court of appeals' decision, which meant the legal fight was over and the states had lost. North Carolina had ceded exclusive jurisdiction over these lands to the United States. Therefore, regardless of state laws which might have otherwise applied, federal administrators could, upon evidence of injury to the lands from overpopulation, reduce the number of deer by hunt or transportation, even out of the state.[78]

But the states emerged victorious in another forum, the practical result being equivalent. During the early months of 1941 Seth Gordon, the new President of the International, and other state representatives met with Forest Service and Department of Agriculture officials at the request of Acting Forester Earle H. Clapp. After several sessions G-20-A was repealed and replaced with a new regulation, W-2, for state-federal establishment and maintenance of desirable wildlife populations. As Elliott Barker wrote in an editorial for the *New Mexico State Magazine*, "This new regulation has cooperation written into it and recognizes states' rights. If carried out in a spirit of cooperation, by all parties concerned, the results should be a great step forward in wildlife management." State game officials would remain vigilant in view of the past and the potential for mischief inherent in the legal record, but the change in federal policy seemed both real and basic. The future would prove it. The states had learned that together they held power and could use it, or, as Thomas Kimball of the National Wildlife Federation later put it, the G-20-A controversy "overnight" changed the International Association "from a bunny rabbit to a man-eating tiger."[79]

The "Upbuilding" Years

The impressive record of accomplishment of the IAGFCC before World War II belies the sometimes thin ranks with which the members fought their battles. Largely hidden from view also was the fact that there were still numerous states where official authority over game management was bandied about as a political plum. Heavy turnover, insufficient training, and lack of commitment to conservation goals were constant problems. Overall, however, game management was becoming professionalized and recognized within the respective states' political systems as worthy of independent judgment and action. Missouri's Senator Clark, during the Pittman-Robertson debates of 1937, boasted how his state had just constitutionally created the nation's first completely nonpolitical state conservation commission.[80]

In 1920 the Association had twenty-six state and provincial members paying dues, and 126 associate members. By the eve of the war, forty-seven states, provinces, and national agencies were members, but the numbers fluctuated greatly over the years, especially as the economic crises of the 1930s sapped state budgets. It was common for individual states to drop out for a year or more to save the $25 fee. Only ten states were paid up by the September 1921 convention, while three years later there were twenty-six states and provinces but only forty-five associates at two dollars each. In 1927, three years after that, seventeen states were counted. And so it went. In 1930 Secretary-Treasurer Ray P. Holland reported "with considerable enthusiasm" four new state memberships, including Montana, the founder, which somewhere along the line had dropped out. The total was thirty-two states and Canadian provinces or agencies. Income and state memberships were down in 1933, which Holland attributed to the "present financial situation of the country." In 1937 there were forty-one members, including Mexico. In 1934 I. T. Quinn introduced the first "lady commissioner," Mrs. Peck of Texas, to the delegates. This was accomplished with the "permission" of her husband and "amid applause."[81]

The four regional associations were in place by the mid-1920s. Association members and other conservation groups had for years attempted to develop uniform game laws for all states, but the widely differing needs and interests of the various sections of the country prevented the formulation of any workable system. The regional affiliates of the International Association were an obvious and instantly successful compromise that recognized the value of cooperation among contiguous states with similar geographical and wildlife conditions. The Western Association took the lead in the Taylor Grazing Act controversy, for example, because only in the arid western lands was domestic animal grazing a wildlife issue. All of the regionals, however, lent a hand to North Carolina in the Pisgah deer case because the states' rights issue affected all of them.[82]

Attendance at the annual meetings also fluctuated, although the quality of papers and discussions does not suggest this. In 1921 former president Lee LeCompte lamented that convention-goers enjoyed too much entertainment and not enough work. Barker remembered that in 1935, when the Regulation G-20-A controversy surfaced, only about twenty-five or thirty were in attendance, while the next year a much larger number convened, perhaps in response to fears about the regulation. Location undoubtedly had much to do with participation, with both distance and desirability of locale relevant factors. The 1937 meeting in Mexico City drew a smaller crowd but one that attendees remembered for its "red carpet" welcomes, including a uniformed motorcycle police escort that led them in a high-speed caravan over winding mountain roads from the border all the way to the convention site. Dr. Ira Gabrielson later joked that this was the conference where the audience consisted of "the man who was presiding and the man who was speaking and the man who had to speak next. The rest of them were out seeing the sights."[83] But if poor attendance frustrated leaders during the period, by the close of the 1930s members gravitated in earnest to the annual meetings in order to turn back perceived threats to their prerogatives lurking in the issues of the day.

The Association took the word "International" in their title seriously during the interwar decades. Canada was very active after the implementation of the Migratory Bird Treaty. Honore Mercier of Quebec was elected President of the International Association of Game, Fish and Conservation Commissioners in 1921, barely after Canada became eligible for membership, and J. B. Harkin of Ontario, Canada's Commissioner of National Parks, followed in that office in 1924. Ontario's Hoyes Lloyd, a conservation figure respected on both sides of the northern border, became Association President in 1929. He participated in Roosevelt's Wildlife Conference in 1936 in a leading role and regularly delivered papers at annual meetings. In addition, Canadians hosted conventions in 1920, 1924, 1930, 1934, and 1940, a remarkable contribution given their relative numbers. Their federal-provincial approaches to wildlife problems were always of general interest to the members, as Canada shared landlordship of migratory wildlife with the states and protected big game in numbers the United States could enjoy only in memory.[84]

Any number of conservationists had promoted a migratory bird treaty with Mexico similar to the 1916 agreement with Canada for almost that length of time, but action was slow in coming. Border states like Texas, not impressed by the political stability of their southern neighbor or the conduct of its border guards, recommended moving cautiously. However, by the mid-1930s, there was general agreement that cooperation was necessary and desirable. For some time Mexico had sent representatives to Association conventions, with Juan Zinser and others making occasional contributions to the proceedings. In February 1936 the sought after migratory bird treaty was signed, with provisions generally like those in the Canadian treaty.[85]

Perhaps in celebration of this achievement Mexico hosted the 1937 Association convention. Actually, Elliott Barker said that he had advocated a meeting in Mexico for some time, but "nobody wanted to go down there." Barker pushed the notion in the name of fairness, arguing that the Mexicans were "entitled to it" and had been discriminated against. Barker got to preside at that meeting, and proud he was as the hosts made celebrities of him and his Spanish-speaking family. As for Association membership, Mexico's was sporadic in terms of dues-paying participation, but the potential for mutual benefit was recognized on both sides of the Rio Grande.[86]

While certain dominant issues required special focus, other topics also engaged Association members throughout the period. Regulating the take of furbearing animals, for example, to conserve an important economic resource as well as particular wildlife species occupied much attention in Canada and the United States. Members saw the need for fish restoration projects in a period of increasing water pollution and water impoundment for irrigation or flood control. Several New Deal efforts affected fish populations indirectly, as did wildlife measures undertaken with Pittman-Robertson monies. Indeed, a restoration act for fish was proposed the same year as the passage of the Pittman-Robertson Act, but it would wait another dozen years before realization. Meanwhile, the Hawes Act of 1926 prohibited the interstate shipment for commercial sale of black bass, an effort to protect a favored and threatened species.[87] The Bureau of Fisheries carried on respected scientific research, maintained hatcheries, and regulated the catch of various species, especially salmon and bass, but still resources dwindled as overfishing, jurisdictional disputes, and thoughtless human intervention in the aquatic habitat took their toll. Support for an international treaty for migratory fish was beginning to grow. Perhaps because few people were sentimental about fish, specific restorative measures took longer than for furred or feathered fauna.[88]

Nonspecific issues included the relationship between landowners and hunters, a perennial one that required cooperation and sensitivity on both sides. The Association mounted ongoing educational efforts toward that end in various media. School children and scout troops also got carefully planned lessons in general wildlife conservation thanks to Association efforts. State-issued game and conservation periodicals began to appear. Guy Amsler apparently edited the first of these, a quarterly called *Arkansas Deer*, which appeared in 1924, with Amsler's slogan, "Education Means Conservation," on the masthead. It circulated among hunting license holders and had as its "avowed purpose" to "educate die-hard hunters away from their 'God-given' right to hunt where they pleased."[89] By 1940 twenty-five state magazines were circulating.[90]

One member called the progress of these years the "upbuilding of the Association." Indeed, the International was entering a new phase as a key organization in conservation. Seth Gordon had said in 1932 that there were more than 6,000 organized groups representing game and fish interests in the United States and Canada, so the prominence of the Association was a significant achievement.[91] Members were becoming increasingly sophisticated about their individual and collective power in effecting public policy and ever more active in the legislative arena. The seminal Game Refuge, Duck Stamp, and Pittman-Robertson Acts owed much to their commitment and determination. They learned lessons in the Kaibob and the Pisgah about both game management and jurisdiction that would be remembered for future application. Cooperative Wildlife Research Unit programs made wildlife workers and their work more professional. Members of the International Association were beginning to enjoy the fruits of their labors in enhanced wildlife environment, animal populations, and respect for themselves.

T ⋆ H ⋆ R ⋆ E ⋆ E

"Wildlife Is Big Business"

Fish grow on trees.
JOHN W. WALLACE

By 1940 three themes were becoming apparent in conservation literature and activities. One focused on progress in restoring wildlife and its habitat. Perhaps wildlife need not disappear after all, as had been long feared in the abstract and in frightening particular for two decades. The second was an awareness of the increasing professionalization of wildlife managers. More schools, especially the land grant colleges, offered improved education and training, and the field was slowly freeing itself from the bonds of political patronage. The last was a vague but hovering unease about world events. War had already erupted in Europe. How would it affect American conservationists, as game managers or citizens? Talbott Denmead of the U.S. Fish and Wildlife Service and General Counsel of the International Association of Game, Fish and Conservation Commissioners touched on all three when he reported to the 1940 convention. With an almost self-conscious lightheartedness, he opened by noting that "in spite of wars, rumors of wars, sun spots, elections and politics, the trend in fish and game legislation was upward."[1]

Progress for Wildlife

Denmead's report reflected the general priorities in wildlife conservation. At last Congress was tackling water pollution through various bills. Even though these accomplished relatively little at first, the lawmakers were beginning to recognize their responsibility and the need for clean water for all living things. Congressman Frank Buck's bill held promise as an analogy to the Pittman-Robertson Act for fish, proposing to apply a tax on fishing tackle to fish restoration projects. But it was opposed by the tackle industry and failed. The idea was planted, however. Senator Pittman sponsored a resolution that would make the Senate Special Committee on the Conservation of Wildlife Resources a standing committee, but it was stalled. Achievement was running far behind intent.[2]

The year 1940 also saw the states' court defeat in the Pisgah deer case, but optimism for wildlife management was not misplaced. Funds from duck stamps and Pittman-Robertson revenues were acquiring or restoring habitats, and game agents noticed increased populations of waterfowl and upland game. Ira Gabrielson, who admitted that "six years ago I myself reached the melancholy conclusion that nothing on earth could save the wildfowl," allowed himself a confident outlook at the dawn of the 1940s. The refuge program was already a success, he said. The application of new knowledge from academic training and scientific research was providing ways to influence birth and death rates of wildlife. Thinking like Pinchot and McGee, he saw the key to future accomplishment in the growing awareness that fish and wildlife conservation, forestry, agriculture, water and land use problems and plans all stemmed from the "same great root."[3]

Conservationists were learning how to cope with overpopulation, too. Wildlife forester Homer Shantz acknowledged that "we were slow in realizing that we could conserve too well and not too wisely," but now the country was enjoying good results with flexible, intelligent, collaborative programs. He noted that "the hunter, properly used, is the most valuable tool in perpetuating game animals. The control of land is also a vital necessity. It is a paradox that these tools, misuse of land and uncontrolled hunting, lead to the destruction of game, and that these same tools coordinated, planned and controlled offer the greatest possibilities of building back that which they once destroyed." He added that the beneficial use of such tools "points clearly to a need of cooperation if desired ends are to be reached." With the Pisgah confrontation still a fresh discontent, Shantz was both making a plea for cooperation and proclaiming its positive results.[4]

Progress in Professionalism

At the same time, educational requirements and opportunities for game managers were growing. The Cooperative Wildlife Research Unit Program was the key component, of course. The work at these few land grant institutions, in turn, stimulated improved wildlife curricula at other colleges and universities. The University of Wisconsin, which appointed Aldo Leopold to a newly created chair in wildlife management in the early 1930s, and Cornell University, for example, both developed extensive offerings. Pittman-Robertson projects, which demanded trained leaders, snapped up wildlife graduates.[5]

The International Association, at its 1938 convention, heard Herbert Davis, California Fish and Game Commissioner, note that despite low salaries for starting assistant wardens, 55 percent of the state's force held college degrees. In-service training and advancement potential for such "apprentices" enabled California to build a "superior" department. More and more states were placing their game departments under Civil Service requirements with overall higher salaries and job satisfaction.[6]

Aldo Leopold's evolving philosophy toward the natural world was winning a wider audience. He was describing the discipline of ecology, but that term would not be popularly adopted until years later. His presidential address to the members of The Wildlife Society in 1940 focused on "The State of the Profession." As usual, Leopold stressed what most of his listeners were only beginning to perceive. He called on conservationists to develop a land ethic, or a sense of balance, in approaching wildlife management. Pay attention to interrelationships, the history of wildlife, and the aesthetic value of noneconomic flora and fauna like wild flowers and songbirds, he said, in order to apply the scientific principles of land use more responsibly and effectively. Leopold asked game managers to share his "wonder" and "respect for workmanship in nature." Most of his colleagues were of a more straightforward, conventional bent, but with his professional credentials, compelling prose style, and commitment to the art of wildlife production, Leopold enjoyed uncommon esteem and growing emulation.[7]

Actually, one of Leopold's colleagues, Alabama Game Commissioner John Wallace, had much earlier suggested the need for ecological thinking. When Wallace told his fellows at the 1921 convention of the game and fish commissioners that "fish grow on trees," he was noting the effects on aquatic environment of careless soil management and forestry practices. Cut down the trees and there would be nothing to hold water in check, he said. Neither siltation nor uncontrolled water runoff was healthy for fish or other species. Game conservationists must pay attention to natural resources in balance. By the eve of World War II they were increasingly doing so.[8]

Meanwhile, the official federal structure for wildlife administration had also changed, which simplified state managers' communication with Washington. In 1940 Roosevelt transferred the Bureau of Biological Survey, then in the Department of Agriculture, and the Bureau of Fisheries, then in Commerce, to the Department of Interior. The next year the two bureaus were merged to form the U.S. Fish and Wildlife Service. Ira Gabrielson, Darling's hand-picked successor, became the Service's first Director.[9] Gabrielson's initial annual report boasted of achievements in wildlife restoration under Pittman-Robertson federal aid programs, wildfowl refuge successes from strict law enforcement and scientific research, and intelligent but cautious population control of various species.[10]

War Clouds

The opening and closing paragraphs of the Fish and Wildlife Service report were revealing. Both alluded, obliquely, to the war in Europe and how it might potentially involve the United States. Gabrielson took pains to warn against exploiting newly recovering wildlife resources "during any presently conceivable period of stress." He argued that "although intelligent wildlife administration can further the purposes of national defense, there is need, as with other resources, for extreme caution against a perversion of patriotic zeal that might endanger an important endowment that must be defended." And he made a larger point. "This national resource [wildlife], wisely managed, makes important, though in many respects intangible, contributions toward a national strength that is more essential than ever in times of emergency. That country is worth dying for which is worth living in." Enjoyment of wildlife was one recognized element of the good life of a nation.[11]

The International Association itself enjoyed the good life together one more time. The 1941 convention was held in St. Louis, with Conservation Director I. T. "Ping" Bode overseeing the local arrangements. President Seth Gordon remembered the banquet as "probably the zaniest" ever. "As we sat down, there in each large water goblet was at least one, mostly two fingerling bluegill cavorting around. And overhead, flying in all directions, were some of Missouri's most bewildered mallards."[12]

But then the fun was over. An FBI agent spoke to the members, many of whom had responsibilities in connection with law enforcement, on how they could be helpful to the Bureau in national defense. He gave the delegates tips on how to recognize espionage and sabotage and asked for their continued moral and active support. The fireballs of Pearl Harbor brought the United States into the world conflict, and everyone's attention turned. Many state game administrators, of course, would sooner or later be in uniform. For the others, higher priorities swallowed their specialized concerns. Early on, the government requested a curtailment of nonessential travel, and both transportation and hotel accommodations became difficult to arrange. So the International Association, made up mostly of workers in government at some level, postponed its 1942 convention, and then, as the war dragged on, the 1943, 1944, and 1945 meetings as well.[13]

Peter J. Hoffmaster, who had been elected president in 1941, presided at the first postwar convention in September 1946. That made him the longest-serving president since founder William F. Scott, but as he said in his opening words, while "dormancy did not completely overtake the Association during the recent five eventful years," its activities were "not numerous." Association records of the war years do not survive, but at the 1946 meeting I. T. Bode reported on the work of the Executive Committee which had tried to preserve continuity during the "trying interim." The officers of the Executive Committee and special committees had dealt with important issues and business matters and kept the membership informed "as best [they] could." Bode gratefully acknowledged the help of the Fish and Wildlife Service in assisting the flow of timely information. In 1942, for example, Gabrielson had called a meeting in New York City attended by conservationists from twenty-four states. Their discussions and report to all the states, circulated through the courtesy of the Fish and Wildlife Service, constituted what passed for a convention that year. In 1943 a special committee met to discuss the acute shortage of ammunition for hunting and to appeal to the War Production Board, but results were predictably unnoticeable.[14]

The Executive Committee continued to hold modest sessions. It met again in February 1945. The federal government had just requested that no large meetings be scheduled, so in lieu of a regular convention the Committee called for a "committee" meeting in June 1945 in Chicago to consist of as many state agents as could arrange to attend. Twenty-six states came as well as representatives of the Fish and Wildlife Service and the Army Engineers. The Executive Committee followed up on immediate concerns and met again just prior to the 1946 convention to draft resolutions from the recommendations of the 1945 "committee" plus several of their own for the consideration of the full International.[15]

Postwar Reassessment

Seth Gordon presented the Resolutions Committee's sixteen proposals in 1946, which by their number and content showed an Association anxious both to catch up and to move forward in wildlife conservation as well as to revamp its own structure and procedures to be more responsive and efficient. The Executive Committee had of necessity assumed the burdens of policy making and action, such as they were, during the war. Now Gordon's committee proposed to legitimize that role. Thus, Resolution No. 1 would empower the Executive Committee to meet at least twice between annual meetings, at the Association's expense, to consider interim issues and "advise with federal agencies in plans and programs involving cooperation with the states." This committee could also appoint subcommittees to study and report on special problems. The convention approved. Today, study committees working with the Executive Committee carry out the bulk of the Association's work.[16]

Alabama Game Commissioner Ben Morgan bemoaned the state agents' inadequate follow-up between conventions and lack of knowledge of "what is going on in Washington." He proposed that the Association increase its dues to $200 per year in order to "hire a man to live in Washington and represent this Association and keep us posted on what Congress is doing or trying to do." Cleland N. Feast of Colorado raised the ante to $500 but could not get a second. This was a rather radical change from the twenty-five dollars that had been assessed for forty years, as several members were quick to point out. Lee LeCompte warned that were such a dues increase to pass, the Association would likely be one of twenty state members, not forty-eight. C. R. Gutermuth of Washington, D.C., suggested that obtaining current information on congressional action from the newly established Legislative Service Bureau would be cheaper and just as effective. I. T. Bode worried that if a secretary were employed, after a few years the members would cease their own efforts and say, "Well, let the paid secretary do it." Finally, Ottawa's Dr. Harrison Lewis reminded the delegates that the Canadian members might take a dim view of paying extra fees to support a representative in the capital of only one of the member countries. Morgan's resolution lost. Both its components, a major dues increase and the employment of a "man in Washington," would be accepted eventually, but not without prolonged struggle.[17]

Another resolution proposed a special committee to review the Association's constitution and bylaws and recommend amendments to the 1947 assembly. Most agreed it was time to do so. Talbott Denmead, resigning after nine years as the IAGFCC's General Counsel, or chief legal adviser, confessed he had never seen a copy of the constitution, their basic legal document.[18] Seth Gordon, ever the institution builder, chaired the bylaws committee, too, and presented its report at the annual meeting the following year.

As Gordon read the proposed bylaws, he stopped periodically to explain member input and the committee's rationale. The first consideration was dues. An increase was clearly necessary; expenses had exceeded income that year by almost $300. Gordon noted that the committee had wrestled with increases ranging from fifty dollars, double the present amount, to $250. The original 1947 draft bylaws stipulated $100 for the states and twenty-five dollars for the provinces, but the Canadians had protested, wanting to be on "exactly the same level as anybody else" in the international organization. The final proposal read forty dollars for each governmental member, which would entitle it to four copies of the annual *Transactions*. No one ever explained why an amount lower than any previously proposed was settled upon.[19]

The committee also reviewed other membership categories. Associate memberships for individuals would remain at two dollars. The new bylaws eliminated life memberships, as there had been only two in the Association's history and no one knew what had become of those persons. Honorary life memberships could still be granted to individuals who had "rendered distinguished service in the cause of conservation administration." In the next order of business Seth Gordon nominated to that honor Ray P. Holland, who had retired as the Association's Secretary-Treasurer in 1946 after twenty-seven years of service. His colleagues unanimously ratified the motion.[20]

The new bylaws specified an Executive Committee of the President, two Vice-Presidents, a Secretary-Treasurer, a General Counsel, seven additional members, and the immediate past President. The Committee would choose its own chairman, someone other than the President. The bylaws empowered the chairman, with the approval of the President, or two-thirds of the Committee membership, to call a meeting of the Executive Committee at any time, but, curiously in light of the resolution of the previous year, they did not require any minimum number of meetings. The bylaws did give the Executive Committee broad interim powers, however. No one was to be salaried, but the Secretary-Treasurer was allowed $450 per year for expenses.[21]

The Association would meet annually, usually the second Monday in September, for a two-day conference followed (or preceded, if the Executive Committee so decided) by conferences or a concurrent meeting with the American Fisheries Society. This provision simply clarified a practice that the two organizations had begun in 1912. Twenty member governments would constitute a quorum. The President, with Executive Committee approval, could appoint standing and special committees and supervise their work, another recognition of a procedure already used.[22]

The members' brief bylaws discussion centered on relatively minor points. Various members debated over what to call the state commissioners. Officials? Executives? Administrators? The words had slightly different meanings to different people in different states or provinces. Finally, the members agreed to use the word "commissioners" and insert a clause to explain it. When C. R. "Pink" Gutermuth, former Indiana fish and game chief and now Vice-President of the newly created Wildlife Management Institute, wanted to change the cumbersome name of the Association, the members authorized him to head a committee to come up with something better by the next convention. But in 1948 this special committee recommended that the name remain the same, since no one could suggest a shorter one that would compensate for the loss of a name that represented an "old and well-established organization." So that was that. The Association had up-to-date written rules to go by for the first time in many years.[23]

Postwar Water Policies

Meanwhile, the International Association of Game, Fish and Conservation Commissioners had plenty of substantive work to do—on issues left in abeyance during the war, or created by it, as well as on new concerns. A top priority of the states was simply that of having conservation plans. The commissioners, well aware of the low national priority given fish and wildlife interests after World War I and wanting to avoid a similar situation now, urged each other to have state plans and programs complete as soon as possible, just as they observed the U.S. Fish and Wildlife Service doing nationally.[24]

A particularly crucial interest centered on federal water development policies and their effect on fish and wildlife. Dam building, dredging, and other water diversions or impoundments affected both aquatic and terrestrial environments. For example, during World War II the U.S. Army Corps of Engineers constructed a series of navigation pools along the upper Mississippi River which were then drawn down during the winters to maintain navigable depths downstream for essential military transportation. When the war was over, however, the War Department proposed to continue the drawdowns to benefit private navigation on the lower river. Naturally, dramatic fluctuations in water level were detrimental to fish and other animals, but wildlife interests had not been assigned a value in the planning or implementation of this or similar projects. Therefore, when the Corps of Engineers proposed a major flood control, navigation, and irrigation project for the Missouri River Basin, the newly reconstituted International Association of Game, Fish and Conservation Commissioners and their allies girded for action.

President Hoffmaster appointed a committee of three, Cleland Feast, I. T. Bode, and Albert Day, to study the Missouri Basin and other water impoundments as soon as the issue arose at the "mini-convention" of 1945. The attendees also took the immediate step of empowering their leaders to make specific recommendations to Congressman Willis Robertson on legislation he was proposing for wildlife interests in national water project planning.[25]

Robertson's bill became the Coordination Act of 1946 (Public Law No. 732). It required that all new federal water projects include provisions to prevent or minimize damage to fish and wildlife. No construction could begin without the plans being first reviewed by the Fish and Wildlife Service and the appropriate state fish and game commissions. The wildlife agencies had no veto power, but their recommendations had to be part of the overall proposal and reported as such to Congress. Moreover, the law gave the construction agency basic authority to fund wildlife programs within the project.[26]

The Coordination Act was actually an amended version of an earlier Fish and Wildlife Coordination Act of 1934 which requested but did not compel consideration for wildlife in water impoundments. Later, in 1958, the act was amended again to change the negative emphasis of 1946 to positive, from preventing damage to enhancing wildlife resources. The 1958 law required that wildlife conservation be given equal consideration with other aspects of water resource development, broadly defined, and that wildlife agencies' "justifiable means and measures for wildlife purposes" be adopted for "maximum overall project benefits."[27]

By the time the International Association met in 1946, the Coordination Act had passed, with considerable thanks to Executive Committee lobbying efforts. In highlighting water use issues, C. N. Feast reported at length for the special committee of 1945, making the same point from two directions. Wildlife must be established as a "primary purpose and a basic value" at the beginning, he said, for water projects to serve their needs. Here was an intangible, moral value, but he also made clear the economic value of wildlife. "Wildlife is Big Business," was his title statement. Millions of hunters and fishermen were purchasing licenses and spending billions in pursuit of their sport. Even though the Coordination Act was law, the Association must move immediately to establish contacts with the Army Engineers, the Bureau of Reclamation, or other federal work project agencies and insist upon a "general policy wherein lands acquired for all public projects should give first priority to public agencies for public use."[28]

The 1946 convention, in joint session with the American Fisheries Society, also heard a symposium on "The Missouri River Basin—Flood Control, Navigation and Irrigation and their Relation to Fish and Game." As P. J. Hoffmaster pointed out, the subject directly affected about one-sixth of the nation and was fraught with misunderstandings and conflicting views. It was a lively morning. All three speakers were federal officials: Brigadier General Lewis A. Pick of the Army Corps of Engineers, William G. Sloan of the Interior Department's Bureau of Reclamation, and Clarence Cottam of the Fish and Wildlife Service. The first two defended their agencies' work against some fairly hostile questioning. Pick ticked off numerous examples of clear water, full of fish, in lakes the Corps had constructed. Sloan talked about the importance of water in the West and the necessary compromise nature of the Missouri Basin project. Irrigation, flood control, navigation, power development, and recreational interests, including wildlife, all had to be served in some degree, and sometimes interests conflicted.[29]

Elliott Barker's question to the panel was one of the more politely phrased, but his complaint was typical. "I cannot imagine," he said, "any project that would involve the impoundment of water in [New Mexico] the benefits of which would not far exceed the destruction of wildlife values." But, would it not be possible to give "just a little more consideration to the fish life in some of our irrigation reservoirs?" When they were drawn down to the minimum, he said, sometimes completely drained, the fish were obviously lost. Sloan and Pick both insisted that their agencies built their dams to prevent such catastrophes and routinely consulted all interested parties for their specialized expertise, but Sloan also admitted that mistakes had been made through ignorance of fish and wildlife requirements and insufficient funding. The new Coordination Act would help remedy these problems, and the Bureau of Reclamation was glad to turn wildlife planning for its projects over to the Fish and Wildlife Service. Overall, Sloan was defensive and testy, "getting tired of these criticisms." Pick's answers were slick and aggressive, the comments of a man trying to present himself as a fisherman as well as an engineer.[30]

Clarence Cottam, the one wildlife careerist of the trio, concluded the program with tone and content more reassuring to the state conservation commissioners. The Fish and Wildlife Service, he promised, would insist that if impoundments destroyed wildlife habitat, these areas must be replaced. The Service would see to it that wildlife development measures would be taken, such as cover planting, pollution abatement or prevention, and fish screen and ladder building. Necessary water level fluctuations would be cushioned by more careful timing and an adequate flow over or around the dam maintained to allow fish below the reservoir. But Cottam also emphasized the positive possibilities for wildlife in the proposed impoundments—increased shoreline and water acreage, reduced silting, new wetlands, and irrigation-improved environments for upland game. The future looked promising, especially if the state conservation agents took their cooperative, integrative roles seriously, as they expected others to do. For their part, the state managers welcomed the potential for wildlife enhancement while remaining skeptical about the value of dams that seemed ill-considered and promoted for no other reason than that the rivers were there and engineers had the technical expertise to build them. The inimitable Ding Darling, disgustedly observing the overlapping efforts of multiple federal agencies racing to be first at dam sites regardless of "irreconcilable conflict" with natural conditions, opined that "three cooks trying to peel one potato couldn't get more in each other's way."[31]

The War's Effects on Wildlife

World War II created or focused several issues for wildlife conservationists. With the resumption of peace, hunting and fishing pressures were suddenly, sharply up. Ira Gabrielson produced figures that showed nearly 21 million hunting and fishing licenses sold in the United States in 1946.[32] International Association President Lester Bagley worried about the "inexplicable" magnitude of the increase and the likelihood that soon it might not be possible to "furnish hunting and fishing for all who desire to indulge in these means of relaxation." Returning soldiers, of course, accounted for much of the increase, and game populations, especially waterfowl, once again began a serious decline.[33]

Soldiers created an additional problem as well. A federal proposal to issue free hunting and fishing licenses to members of the Armed Services found no favor within the International. Its "committee" of 1945 and the 1946 convention opposed the granting of free permits to any special group including discharged veterans. Comments were few but forceful and met no opposition. Apparently the problem was one of loss of state revenue. "Up to that time at least no state had been successful in getting legislative appropriations to cover any deficiencies that were created in fish and game funds by virtue of the granting of these free permits." The International made it clear that its policy did not restrict the states from issuing such permits to convalescents or servicemen on furlough.[34]

World War II also created a wholly unanticipated issue for conservationists—how to deal with the unknown effects of atomic energy on wildlife. In 1948 the IAGFCC heard Dr. Elmer Higgins, Special Assistant to the Director of the Fish and Wildlife Service and liaison officer to the Atomic Energy Commission, on the new subject. He opened with a lengthy, semitechnical lecture on the nature of the atom and radioactivity, his message carrying the confident optimism characteristic of the period. Acknowledging that atomic energy offered "both a threat and a promise to conservation interests," Higgins dismissed the threat of drastic injury as "chiefly imaginary," short of atomic warfare. "The potential and distant dangers of genetic upset can be faced calmly in the realization that science is rapidly providing for their understanding, evaluation, and control." The promise, he asserted, was in expanding knowledge through research, especially the use of radioisotopes as tracers. Higgins proposed a long list of practical research questions of interest to wildlife conservationists, such as: "Can the mysteries of migration or the sizes of populations of waterfowl be investigated using radioisotopes?" and, "Is there a short-lived radioisotope with a radiation high enough to eradicate or reduce rodent populations without danger to crops or live stock (or people)?" Answering his own question, he guessed there was not, but he "would like to know."[35]

In later years the Association would have varied reactions to the threat and promise of atomic energy. It approved an atomic power plant at Hanford, Washington, as an attractive alternative to damming streams, but opposed ocean disposal of radioactive wastes in concern for the fishing industry and the safety of saltwater food products. Also confronting conservationists would be thermal pollution problems caused by water discharge from nuclear power plants into rivers as well as the direct threat to local wildlife from atomic testing.[36]

During World War II the War Department had acquired or appropriated vast acreages across the United States for defense purposes, such as bombing and target ranges and maneuver areas. At the conclusion of hostilities the War Assets Administration had the task of disposing of these lands, many of them classed as marginal or submarginal for agricultural or grazing use. In 1947 Senator Kenneth Wherry, Republican of Nebraska, introduced a bill to transfer some surplus lands to the states for wildlife conservation purposes. The International Association welcomed this legislation, which passed in 1948 as the Wherry-Burke Act, as a way to help relieve the pressures created by the great increase in the number of hunters and anglers and to enhance state conservation efforts.[37]

The game managers' elation was short-lived. F. R. Fielding of the War Assets Administration came to the 1948 Association convention to describe the policies and procedures of the surplus lands law. Basically, the law provided that lands could be transferred to the Department of Interior for migratory bird conservation or to the states for resident wildlife programs if the federal government, through the advice of the Fish and Wildlife Service, determined that the lands were "chiefly valuable" for the conservation of wildlife. That "if" became especially significant when Fielding noted that there would be competition for the surplus real estate. Recent legislation, Public Laws 616 and 829, gave priority to applicants for lands for park, recreational, and historic monument purposes and for use of civilian components of the armed services, respectively. Further, the states' proposals had to demonstrate need, show willingness to pay minor fees, and promote positive wildlife protection or propagation. Applications for programs involving unrestricted harvesting of game would not be considered. The net result was a convention of angry, frustrated state conservation commissioners who felt betrayed and foresaw hopeless entanglement in red tape. The delegates passed a blistering resolution "emphatically deploring" the War Assets Board's interpretation of the law and directing the Executive Committee to do whatever necessary to secure a revision of its current requirements.[38]

The surplus lands story ended with a whimper. To follow up on the resolution of discontent, Association President Lester Bagley appointed a Surplus Property Committee, which polled the states and got thirty-one responses. From those they learned that thirteen states were applying for land under the law; none had yet received any. But the questionnaires also showed that few states were properly applying under the regulations and that, indeed, the states were showing "but a slight interest" in available surplus lands. The Committee went to Washington but was "hard pressed for facts by which the case of the states could be properly made." The War Assets Board's interpretation was, in fact, correct; only lands that would serve no other useful purpose were available for wildlife use. With such lack of interest and lack of viable hope, the committee concluded that further work would be unwarranted.[39]

One of the state conservationists' greatest postwar vexations had to do with the administration of the Pittman-Robertson Act for wildlife restoration programs in the states. After nearly a decade the procedures understandably needed reexamination. In 1947 International Association President I. T. Bode appointed a committee headed by H. R. Ruhl of Michigan to consider revising the Pittman-Robertson manual, which they did in cooperation with the Fish and Wildlife Service. Overall, the new manual relaxed regulations and gave the states greater administrative responsibility. Another difficulty was simply the lack of qualified persons in the states to plan and supervise restoration projects. The state game officials could not devote the necessary time to this one aspect of their work. However, by 1948 thirty-one states had established "coordination projects" with designated coordinators to relieve game department heads of P-R responsibilities.[40]

A third problem was that if a state did not obligate its federal aid funds within a two-year period, the money reverted to the Migratory Bird Conservation fund. Nevada, for example, still had not passed the necessary enabling legislation for participation in the program, despite the conservation leadership of its federal legislators, so its minimum portion went back to the federal government. Unfortunately, when states did not use their money, it was difficult to impress Congress with their need for additional funds. In effect, those states not utilizing their allocations were penalizing those that did. Furthermore, when the federal funds were linked to state appropriations, and a state could not come up with its share, that entire restoration program was lost.[41]

But the P-R surplus caused the most unrest. Robert Rutherford, in his ten-year summary of the Pittman-Robertson program, noted that between July 1, 1938, and June 30, 1948, a total of more than $48 million had been collected from the excise tax on sporting arms and ammunition. Congress appropriated nearly $23.5 million to the states as its 75 percent contribution to restoration project costs. All of the $11 million income of 1947–48 was appropriated, but since collections had exceeded appropriations, especially during the war years, a reserve of almost $13.5 million had accumulated in the special fund. For example, in fiscal year 1943, the government appropriated $1.25 million for wildlife federal aid while the special fund contained $9.3 million.[42]

Rutherford noted that "this [surplus] is available for appropriation at a later date, when the Congress decides it is needed by the states." The members of the International Association were less patient about it. They wanted the money released. It would take a decade. At their first postwar convention in 1946 the delegates resolved to "go on record" in favor of congressional appropriations of not less than $5 million per year until the surplus was exhausted. The next year they directed the Association President to appoint a standing Pittman-Robertson Committee to advise the Executive Committee on administrative developments and measures regarding the impounded surplus. That Committee was made permanent in 1951 by a resolution that also urged the states and regional associations to clear policy questions and take action through it.[43]

The 1949 convention resolution proposed the distribution of 20 percent of the surplus annually until it was depleted. In subsequent years various formulas won favor; the point was to get the money moving. Finally, in 1954 Congress had three bills pending on the disposition of the P-R surplus fund. Carl Shoemaker, now General Counsel for the Association, summarized each, but his message to the delegates was that they simply agree upon one plan "to shake loose this money for wildlife purposes." The U.S. Comptroller General had recently issued a report suggesting that the unappropriated receipts be transferred to the general fund of the treasury. Shoemaker, speaking for the sportsmen whose taxes the fund represented, was blunt. "To put this money in the general fund would be an act of burglary comparable to taking our gasoline tax money to build state office buildings."[44]

Shoemaker had good news in 1955. The Bible-Price-Young bill, becoming Public Law 375 by frantic eleventh-hour efforts in the 84th Congress, authorized appropriation of the $13.5 million surplus to the states in five equal annual installments, over and above the regular annual federal aid allocations, beginning with the fiscal year starting July 1, 1955. And in August Congress further amended the Pittman-Robertson Act to allow expenditures for management of wildlife areas and resources under a broad definition that excluded little except law enforcement and public relations activities. The 1946 amendment to permit some federal funding for maintenance of completed projects still stood.[45]

Conservationists may have been frustrated by problems of implementing the Pittman-Robertson Act, but they sang its praises as a tool for improving relations between state agencies and the Fish and Wildlife Service and between landowners and sportsmen. They welcomed the variety of projects possible and the states' right to select their own based on specific needs. Western states, for example, concentrated on projects to benefit deer and elk, while in agricultural areas farmland game was emphasized. Waterfowl projects were popular in all regions of the country. The bulk of the money went for habitat improvement, trapping and transplanting for more favorable population distribution, and research to enhance reproduction and ensure scientific control of the harvest. In 1958 hundreds of projects were under way. The same year the Director of the Fish and Wildlife Service proudly noted the increasing cooperation between state game departments and other states, universities, federal agencies, and foreign countries for promoting wildlife enhancement.[46]

The Dingell-Johnson Act: Pittman-Robertson for Fish

Meanwhile, federal aid was also enhancing fish populations and their environments. Scientific efforts in fish management had been quietly succeeding for many years, but as with other wildlife endeavors, the need for funding was ever pressing. Furthermore, the number of anglers was increasing annually as transportation and leisure time improved, and sport fishing resources were straining to meet the demand. Immediately sensing the Pittman-Robertson potential for fishing interests, the Game, Fish and Conservation Commissioners in 1937 unanimously declared themselves in favor of legislation that would provide federal aid to the states for the development and maintenance of fishing resources. They proposed that the money come from an excise tax on fishing tackle and be administered through the Bureau of Fisheries. They were also careful to stipulate that the states have "legal recognition" in the establishment of standards and the selection of projects. They said all this again in 1941, couched, as were nearly all their resolutions that year, in terms of providing food, sport, and livelihood for millions in the interests of the "national defense and future welfare."[47]

When the war was over the International Association once again took up its annual and ongoing advocacy of federal aid for fisheries. By 1947 it had a new bill to endorse, that of Congressman John Dingell, Democrat of Michigan. Closely paralleling the Pittman-Robertson Act, it became the Dingell-Johnson bill with the support of Colorado's Democratic Senator Edwin C. Johnson. Various states quibbled with details of the legislation, but the Association favored it without hesitation. The Dingell-Johnson bill passed Congress in early October 1949, only to be vetoed by President Truman. The conservation community was stunned. Carl Shoemaker, in the National Wildlife Federation's *Conservation News*, wrote: "Thus comes to an end ten years of effort on the part of the sportsmen of America to provide themselves from their own contributions a sound program of fisheries management in cooperation with the Federal government and the states." Truman disapproved of designated funds, citing the same congressional policy of 1934 that Roosevelt had ignored in signing the Pittman-Robertson bill. The President called earmarking funds an "undesirable tax and fiscal policy" because it avoided "continuous budgetary and legislative appraisal." Moreover, he found its retroactive application objectionable.[48]

Dingell and Johnson tried again in 1950. Their House and Senate reports on the new bill, H.R. 6533, stressed the proven success of its model, the Pittman-Robertson program, now in its twelfth year of "outstanding" contribution to wildlife restoration. The House report continued, "To assure continuing smooth operations, members of the Fish and Wildlife Service meet periodically with the Pittman-Robertson Committee of the International Association of Game, Fish and Conservation Commissioners, to devise new policies and work out current administrative problems." All of the state game administrators had "heartily endorsed" the program, the cooperative nature of which encouraged progress without differences of opinion becoming acrimonious. Therefore, the feasibility of a similar program for fishery resources was ably demonstrated.[49]

Both congressional reports contained identical paragraphs that cleverly dispatched with two presidential objections as if they were one: "The President . . . questioned the propriety of earmarking funds collected by the tax on fishing equipment in prior years for use after the effective date of that bill, and also objected to its authorization of an appropriation of $2,000,000 to be used during the first year of its operation." These provisions were now deleted, the reports said, and no federal agency had problems with the present bill. If these arguments were slightly disingenuous, they worked. The bill passed. Truman signed it into law on August 9, 1950.[50]

The Dingell-Johnson Act provided that monies derived from the federal excise tax on fishing rods, creels, reels, and artificial lures, baits, and flies would be apportioned among the states annually for use in "projects designed for the restoration and management of all species of fish which have material value in connection with sport or recreation in the marine and/or fresh waters of the United States." Up to 8 percent of the income could be used to administer the act or help two or more states formulate cooperative compacts for migratory fish. The Secretary of the Interior would allocate the rest of the funds according to a formula of 40 percent in the ratio of the area of a state, including coastal and Great Lakes waters, to the total area of all states; and 60 percent in the ratio of the number of paid recreational fishing license holders of a state to the total license holders in all states. The states would have to put up at least 25 percent of the cost of their projects. They could spend up to 25 percent of the federal share on maintenance.[51]

During the first year nearly $3 million was collected under the Dingell-Johnson program and expended by the states. The desert state of Utah won the race to be first to get a D-J project approved; this was a study of the possible use of brine shrimp, Great Salt Lake's sole animal life, as fish food. Other projects were studies of the habits of marine and anadromous fish, ways to encourage use of less desired species, and techniques to improve habitat or technical equipment. States created and stocked new lakes and built access roads. They tried controlled poisoning of aquatic weeds and trash fishes and introduced new species. At the end of five years the Fish and Wildlife Service reported "major contributions" to the nation's sport fish resources from D-J funds.[52]

The International Association had urged that the Dingell-Johnson Act be administered by the same agency that handled the Pittman-Robertson program, and it was General Counsel Chester Wilson's happy assignment to report in 1950 that Albert Day, Director of the Fish and Wildlife Service, had promised to do just that. Harry Ruhl announced in 1951 that the Federal Aid Committee, which he chaired, had been asked to review the P-R Manual as revised to include the Dingell-Johnson program. He called it a "reasonably satisfactory working guide," though it could probably use some simplification. He also made the committee's recommendation, later passed as a resolution, that a "permanent committee continue to be a clearing house for federal aid matters even though questions of major policy must of necessity be referred to the association for action." The resolution acknowledged that neither the Federal Aid Committee nor the Association could legally bind a state or regional association but urged these entities to work through the Association before taking independent action.[53]

Federal Aid: Internal Controversy

In 1952 the International Association polled its members on whether they favored amending the Pittman-Robertson and Dingell-Johnson Acts, since many states were having problems with various federal aid details. Thomas Kimball's polling committee, however, recommended no modifications, for the simple reason that suggesting change could be dangerous. Mindful that they were operating with earmarked funds, a concept not favored by the Bureau of the Budget and Treasury Department and one they themselves might find discomfort with on the state level, the conservationists agreed that amending the acts would be "very unwise at this time." They had much to lose by intemperate action. In fiscal year 1953, P-R and D-J collections totalled $16.7 million. Pittman-Robertson monies had increased 11.4 percent; the Dingell-Johnson collections, starting from a lower base, were up 59.4 percent. These figures did not include other appropriations for wildlife through the Fish and Wildlife Service or the P-R surplus then still being withheld. Carl Shoemaker estimated that by 1960 revenues from the two federal aid bills, including both the federal and state contributions, would amount to a total of $300 million. Hunting and fishing license sales by 1957 were up to nearly 15 million and over 19 million, respectively. So along with the increasing revenue came that many more sportsmen to "keep satisfied."[54]

By the end of the decade, internal controversy long kept quiet disrupted the Association; it concerned the apportionment formula for federal aid funds, and specifically the interpretation of the term "paid license holder." Did this mean, as the Solicitor of the Interior Department had recently opined, one individual regardless of whether he held one or more licenses? Or did it mean the number of licenses sold, as federal officials had decided years ago in the interests of simplicity? Before long some states began requiring sportsmen to purchase separate permits to hunt different species of game in order to increase their federal aid allotments, to the competitive disadvantage of single-license states. Such states were gaining as much as $100,000 a year at the expense of their neighbors but at a cost of complicated fee systems wherein a hunter could be counted eight or ten times if he bought that many separate licenses. On the other hand, these states argued persuasively that multiple licenses were more fair to the hunter. Should a pheasant hunter who went out once or twice a year have to pay for a single license whose price bore the cost of supporting all of the state's big game conservation programs as well? The subject was becoming emotional as well as economic.[55]

The members of the International Association, increasingly distressed over their own lack of consensus and its probable unhealthy effect on congressional attitudes toward the whole federal aid program for wildlife, officially asked the Interior Secretary and the Department's Solicitor to delay making a final decision that would change past practice until the states' attorneys general could submit their legal views to Interior. This was in 1958. In 1959 Missouri's Conservation Commissioner William E. Towell, chair of the Federal Aid Committee, implored the Association to face the issue squarely and come up with a compromise agreement that all states would then support. He emphasized the "all," warning that "few lawmakers approve the principle of earmarked special excise taxes. Most manufacturers and distributors of guns, ammunition, and fishing tackle are not such ardent conservationists that they heartily favor a special tax on their products. It is not at all inconceivable that big business and congress could get together and repeal the P-R and D-J excise taxes if we continue to squabble among ourselves on how these funds shall be distributed."[56]

Meanwhile, the Executive Committee had polled the states on a distribution formula based on total license income and found not only no consensus but lack of response from several states. The Federal Aid

Committee also had difficulty coming to closure, but finally they agreed, by majority though not unanimous vote, to propose a resolution to request that the Fish and Wildlife Service direct that half of the apportionment be based on area as before and half upon "paid license holders" to be "defined and interpreted to count a maximum of one small game license and one big game license for any one individual." The Committee considered this the best compromise since it most nearly equaled the actual current distribution and would result in the least disruptive changes. The Committee also recommended that the law be changed if necessary to accommodate this formula. That recommendation and the delegates' knowledge that nearly a dozen bills to amend the 1937 federal aid act were before Congress at the time, suggested a potential for legislative mischief that calmed no one in the assembly.[57]

The Association finally embraced not the Federal Aid Committee's proposal but a simple statement that endorsed the "present apportionment policy" of the Fish and Wildlife Service, that is, the Solicitor's hunter-based interpretation for disbursement of federal aid funds, and urged states not satisfied with their own license structure to seek correction in their respective state legislatures. The route between the two resolutions was tortuous. Everyone agreed that the game commissioners must support whatever the majority decided, but arriving at compromise was tricky. The delegates finally defeated the committee's resolution, mostly on the grounds that it could open a Pandora's box in Congress and possibly the courts. Immediate past President John Biggs, who had favored the first resolution, offered the substitute "only in the interests of good will." Sensing the "sharp cleavage of opinion" and knowing the power of the federal government to change more than the states wished, he suggested they simply assume the burdens of reform themselves. His weary colleagues agreed.[58]

Duck Stamps: Increased Fees

Meanwhile, paying for and regulating migratory waterfowl programs remained an ongoing concern. The one-dollar duck stamp fee of 1934 was clearly inadequate by the forties. The International Association of Game, Fish and Conservation Commissioners in 1947 formally supported federal legislation to raise the tax in order to acquire and maintain additional refuge areas, part of which could be used as public hunting grounds. The public hunting provision gave some lawmakers and protectionists pause, but in August 1949, a new two-dollar Duck Stamp Act passed, which was estimated to bring in an additional $2 million annually. Clauses in the law that limited hunting to not more than 25 percent of any refuge area and prohibited it altogether during times of population decline reassured the cautious and gave state game managers room for flexible policy making.[59]

Unfortunately, as Harry Ruhl, chairman of the Committee on Changes in Allocation of Duck Stamp Funds, noted a few years later, in 1956, since the new law had doubled the duck stamp fee, the federal government began to reduce its regular appropriations for wetlands development and maintenance. At the same time land prices were rising as needs were increasing. Should the duck stamp fee be raised again? Ruhl could think of good reasons pro and con. The money was needed and three dollars was not much—less than the cost of a box of shells. But if marginal hunters refused to buy the stamp and either did not hunt or did so illegally, actual revenues would fall. Perhaps the states should increase their own fees and develop smaller refuge areas, which they could do more efficiently. The Association asked for more adequate federal appropriations without high expectations and considered numerous bills to amend the Duck Stamp Act to increase the fee or change the proportions of the proceeds that could be used for various purposes.[60]

The duck stamp debate continued through the mid-1950s. Carl Shoemaker had told the House Subcommittee on Fisheries and Wildlife Conservation in 1955 that nothing less than five dollars, which would bring in an annual income of $11 million, would do; but he despaired that sportsmen would accept such a tax even though they did not "say a single solitary word" to protest paying an excise tax for "something in the blind to warm them up." Shoemaker, representing the IAGFCC as its General Counsel for both duck stamp and P-R surplus legislation, testified that he cared only about the principles of both bills. "Whether you allocate 40 percent or 20 percent or 35 percent or 50 percent to the purchase of land, it does not make a particle of difference so long as something is done." Congress finally passed an increase in the duck stamp fee to three dollars in 1958. The Association's Duck Stamp Committee chairman Melvin Steen gave the committee's report in two words: "Mission accomplished." The new law allowed public hunting on up to 40 percent of a refuge, a liberalization appreciated by game managers, but some, like Shoemaker, thought the fee was still too low.[61]

Federal Lands and Hunting

Financial and political considerations aside, where would the hunters hunt? Land for public hunting had long been a precious commodity in short supply. The armed services controlled vast acreages, increased during the war, as seen. Most sportsmen willingly accepted wartime sacrifices of their shooting grounds, but with the resumption of peace wanted their recreation restored. They had already been disappointed in their allotment of surplus military lands under the Wherry-Burke Act. The International Association in 1949 resolved with some impatience that the military could no longer justify reserving the use of wildlife resources on military lands to themselves and their friends, that control of these resources should revert to the states for public benefit. When the Association further learned that certain hunting was occurring on military lands in violation of state law, it insisted such practices stop. But they did not.[62]

Association leaders planned a panel discussion on "Government Coordination in the Fish and Wildlife Field" in 1957, invited representatives of the military, and took them to task on just this issue. James Platt of the Department of Defense read an official policy that "restrictions on the use of areas under military jurisdiction by civilian sportsmen will be kept to the minimum deemed necessary by the local commander to insure safety, security, protection of government property, and efficient accomplishment of his mission."[63] The state agents, unsatisfied, promoted the enactment of Congressman Clair Engle's pending bill which would confirm that state game and fish laws, regulations, and maintenance responsibilities applied to federally owned or controlled military lands and ensure state game officials' access in order to enforce the laws and manage the game harvest. The California Democrat's bill would, according to the IAGFCC's determined resolution, "preclude further unnecessary encroachment by the armed forces on the wildlife resources of the nation."[64]

The Engle bill became law in 1958, but the state conservation commissioners found it was only a partial solution. The law applied only to military lands, while the wildlife problems existed on all federal lands. Worse, the states had to enact their own legislation accepting the return of jurisdiction over game and fish, and some of them were unaware that they must. So the issue stayed before the International. The Defense Department sent a Deputy Assistant Secretary of the Army to the 1959 Association convention to reassure the members of President Eisenhower's intent to conserve wisely these lands through multiple use, including the safeguarding of wildlife and recreational values. Jurisdictional misunderstandings continued, however, when the armed services charged hunting and fishing fees over and above state license fees for use on military lands, even though the money was slated for conservation on the reservations.[65]

Finally, in 1960, the Sikes Military Reservation Act provided an agreeable mechanism for securing funds for wildlife improvement on military lands, some 27 million acres worth, and protected states' jurisdiction over wildlife and licensing. The International Association of Game, Fish and Conservation Commissioners, especially President Clyde Patton, worked with congressional committees to draft amendments to the original bill that the Association could support. The Sikes Act authorized the Secretary of Defense to carry out "cooperative" programs with the Interior Secretary and the appropriate state fish and game agencies for the "planning, development, maintenance, and coordination of wildlife, fish and game conservation in military reservations." The law further allowed special, nominally priced hunting and fishing permits to be required, the revenues from which could be used only for implementing the cooperative plans. A 1968 amendment expanded the act to encompass public recreation resources. In 1974 the Sikes Act Expansion Act broadened the coverage of the original legislation to include virtually all federal lands (specifically Bureau of Land Management, National Forest, National Aeronautics and Space Administration, and Atomic Energy Commission holdings as well as military lands) and required federal habitat managers to cooperate with state wildlife agencies on programs for habitat rehabilitation and the protection of endangered and threatened wildlife. The Association provided leadership for all of these efforts and for a further Sikes Act Reauthorization in 1982.[66]

Various other land use issues were perennial with the International. In the West the competing interests of wildlife and livestock clashed over the question of whether federal grazing lands should be transferred to private or state ownership. The game conservationists, finding no credible assurances for the future of wildlife on lands controlled by cattle or sheep raisers, again and again opposed the release of public lands. The hunter-landowner conflict likewise never went away, although conservationists' ongoing educational and public relations efforts attempted to convince both sides of the mutual value of cooperation. The game commissioners also continued their educational programs on conservation aimed at school children. And they carefully monitored soil bank, forestry, and watershed development programs, all of which had a direct impact on wildlife.

Flyway Councils and International Fisheries

Specific resources won renewed attention, nationally and internationally, after World War II. Migratory birds, ever popular, ever threatened, were a high priority. The International Association of Game, Fish and Conservation Commissioners in 1946 introduced a proposal for migratory waterfowl management that was so sensible and timely that it was almost immediately adopted. The Association recommended that the U.S. Fish and Wildlife Service, before framing annual hunting regulations for waterfowl, meet in advisory conference with state game agencies and representatives of sportsmen's and other conservation organizations in each of the major flyway regions. FWS Director Albert Day had convened regional informational meetings that year, so the Association was commending that action and encouraging its expanded continuation.[67]

That migratory birds followed fairly well-defined routes in their seasonal travels had been established by official and private bird banding studies begun as early as 1803 by John James Audubon and carried out in earnest during the 1920s by the Bureau of Biological Survey. By 1930 the Survey, under the leadership of Frederic C. Lincoln, was able to map out four "great geographical regions, each with breeding and wintering grounds connected by a complicated series of migration routes." These were the Atlantic, Mississippi, Central, and Pacific Flyways, administratively created by the Fish and Wildlife Service in 1947. For many years hunting regulations for migratory birds had been managed nationally, but since sizes of populations, varieties of species, and numbers of hunters varied over the continent, such regulations were often unfair, unpopular, or ineffective. Indeed, overall curtailments of hunting seasons in 1946–47, just as postwar demands shot upward, may have spurred Association action. In any case, the IAGFCC quickly embraced the regional approach.[68]

Biologists and conservation administrators, meeting in the flyway committees called by the Fish and Wildlife Service, soon recognized the need for a more formal organization to promote and oversee waterfowl research and management programs. In 1951 the International Association proposed that a flyway council be established in each flyway to be composed of representatives of the official state wildlife agencies. Two members from each council would also serve on a National Waterfowl Council along with advisory, nonvoting members from Canada and Mexico, officials of the Fish and Wildlife Service, and representatives of prominent national conservation organizations. The Fish and Wildlife Service would further assign to each flyway a technical coordinator to serve as a state-federal liaison and an advisor in census taking, surveying, banding, and other research projects. The flyway councils and the National Waterfowl Council were operating by 1952 and continue to promote better communication, cooperation, and waterfowl management practices to benefit both the wildlife and their recreational users.[69]

From the beginning the flyway councils were ranked in importance with the Migratory Bird Treaty of 1916. They, as well as other international forums, gave the Canadians a platform from which to ask for consideration for Arctic dwellers who depended upon wildlife for subsistence. Their obvious need and the paucity of their numbers argued convincingly for an earlier migratory bird hunting season in the far North, since by the time the season legally opened, most of the ducks were gone.[70] The flyway councils also gave the state game directors an increased voice in migratory bird management, obviously to their liking, although the *Proceedings* noted more than occasional discontent over the extent to which flyway council recommendations seemed to go unheeded in Washington. By the close of the 1950s the flyway councils were working more smoothly, defining the concurrent missions of the states, federal government, and Canada, and addressing specific problems of too little habitat and too many hunters, pollution damage to ducks and crop damage by them.

Flyway councils were just one example of the increased international-mindedness of the conservation community during the late 1940s and 1950s, which reflected outward-looking attitudes in the United States generally as the country emerged as a global power following the world war. In 1955, after unsuccessful efforts going back to 1893, the United States and Canada established the Great Lakes Fishery Commission to combat the depredations of the parasitic sea lamprey on the great inland lakes bounded by eight states and the province of Ontario. It was none too soon. By 1955 the sea lamprey had caused such destruction to lake trout in Lakes Huron and Michigan that the commercial catch that year was 99 percent lower than the average catch of the 1930s. Recreational fisheries were as badly hurt. Through cooperative research and management programs the Great Lakes Fishery Commission has helped to control the sea lamprey and revive an enormous ecosystem in distress.[71]

The Exotics

A final topic with international overtones that continued to fascinate game commissioners was that of importing "exotic" species of animals. The subject itself was old. Oregon, for example, successfully introduced Chinese pheasants to North America in 1882. They became so well adapted and popular that Fish and Wildlife Service Director Albert Day later called them "almost naturalized citizens." Also in 1882, however, Oregon brought in carp, an action "regretted ever since."[72]

The game, fish and conservation commissioners asked Day to talk to them about exotics in 1948. He did so with misgivings. The success rate so far had been mixed, he said, and mostly a matter of chance. While Hungarian partridges and German brown trout, for example, had made themselves welcome, the best that could be said about English sparrows, introduced from Europe in the 1850s, was that an attempt in 1885 to study and control these aggressive, numerous pests had launched the Bureau of Biological Survey.[73]

Nevertheless, the IAGFCC appointed a standing Committee on the Introduction of Exotic Animals which polled the states and reported back in 1949. The states were definitely interested, especially in rebuilding wildlife populations where native species had dwindled or disappeared. The Committee carefully recommended that stocking of exotics proceed only on the basis of "research and factual knowledge" since "we have [already] made every mistake that it is possible to make." But since the legal and economic obstacles appeared to have been met through provisions of the Lacey Act, which permitted importation, and the Pittman-Robertson Act, which provided funding, the states were ready to move ahead. The Committee also recommended the Fish and Wildlife Service as the most logical central agency to research the desirability of particular species proposed for introduction. By 1951 the FWS, understaffed for the work, was making slow progress, mostly on attractive game birds. The Committee was just as anxious, if not more so, for additional knowledge on undesirable species in order to exclude them.[74]

In 1956 Clarence Cottam, Assistant Director of the Fish and Wildlife Service, was ready to make some serious conclusions and recommendations. It seemed to him that criteria for measuring success or failure had to consider "the ultimate good or harm" of the introduced species on society generally, not just its numerical strength. Introductions should be restricted to filling "ecological vacuums"; encouraging native game should take precedence over a "costly, illusive, uncertain and dangerous search for an exotic." Curiosity or sentiment should never govern decisions to release a new species, and greater care must be taken to ascertain that imported game was disease-free. Furbearers and big game animals should be studied as potential competition to livestock. Releases, if made, must consider timing, numbers, and sexual balance to give success a better chance and avoid wasting money. Cottam clearly did not expect much return on investment in exotic animal introductions.[75]

Despite Cottam's cold-water analysis, however, exotics would continue to engage the imagination and resources of many lovers and managers of wildlife. The Association pursued its interest in importations for several years, working closely with Dr. Gardiner Bump of New York under the nominal supervision of the Fish and Wildlife Service. No permanently successful introductions resulted, but for a time a few states in the West developed huntable populations of chukar partridge. The federal government terminated the project in the 1970s.[76]

Midcentury Review

A review of Association activity during the postwar decade and a half shows a body of state conservationists expanding their scope of activity, clout, and confidence. The Association reached its full membership potential of forty-eight states in 1950, and in 1959 the two new states, Alaska and Hawaii, also joined. Seven Canadian provinces and the Canadian government continued to participate throughout this period. Dues payment would continue to fluctuate somewhat over the years, but from this time on, the Association could count on at least limited support from every state and most provinces. It was becoming increasingly clear to Association members that they represented "big business." Many states now managed budgets of several million dollars annually along with enjoying increasing authority and less political interference. The International itself, however, was only then modestly moving toward more sophisticated financial practices, beginning in 1952 to place its cash balance in an interest-bearing savings account. The first year's income was $94.13.[77]

At the end of the 1950s International Association President A. D. Aldrich once again brought up the desirability, in his view the necessity, of employing a full-time salaried secretary or "field liaison officer" in order to expand the Association's interests and influence. Or perhaps such an office could be established jointly with the American Fisheries Society. Aldrich "hastened to add" that "we have at present no acceptable recipe for financing such an office." Actually, others had made Aldrich's arguments several times during the decade, but the thought was still premature. The Association amended its bylaws again in 1959, the major change being an increase in state dues to seventy-five dollars, Canadian and Mexican dues to fifty dollars.[78]

The International Association of Game, Fish and Conservation Commissioners, celebrating its midcentury anniversary just about the time the nation did, took time to review its progress and evolving direction as well as that of game conservation generally. Ding Darling, quoted at the 1951

Association convention by Clarence Cottam, was saying, "We have less of everything than we had 50 years ago but we have made progress in game management nevertheless." Making his case, Darling noted that "fifty years ago we were still shooting ducks and geese in the spring, without limit, killing prairie chickens by the lumber-wagon load; golden plover, sandhill cranes, and trumpeter swan were 'game birds'; our agricultural colleges were teaching farmers that they should drain their marshlands, cut away their mock-orange hedgerows, and plow closer to the fences in order to plant more corn." And so on, until conservationists awoke to the danger and took corrective action. Depredations to the nation's water resources by Army engineers, lumbermen, and German carp were at last being countered. And sportsmen themselves were being educated to conservation wisdom. Ever the cynic, Darling added that gains had almost always occurred against the "noisy opposition" of "knuckle-headed exploiters and politicians" and only when extermination threatened.[79]

Nevertheless, as Cottam continued, the list of accomplishments in game management over the Association's history was long and impressive. Some major requirements were not yet satisfied, however, such as the need for overall planning based on sound research, especially in land and water management. States needed more regulatory power and less political meddling. Everyone would benefit from more aggressive educational efforts aimed at sportsmen, landowners, and the public at large. Canada had made similar progress against analogous odds, but of course the much smaller human population decreased the human threat. Even so, Canadians also saw as their greatest need the development of a "sound and generally accepted ecological plan for all species concerned, including our own." Society's "concept of conservation," while becoming more sophisticated, was still inadequately formed, would remain dynamic.[80]

Whether conservation as a concept enjoyed widespread support during this period was debated, then and later. Postwar Association convention delegates were pleased to hear that their concerns were enjoying high favor in Congress. Indeed, General Counsel Livingston Osborne noted in 1947 that very often conservation measures were added to other kinds of bills in order to ensure their passage. And there was no shortage of conservation legislation. During the 80th Congress, in the first session, no fewer than 109 bills were introduced that directly related to fish and game. Twenty-two became law.[81] Indeed, there was soon too much legislation for the Association to consider and act upon effectively. Setting priorities and concentrating on a few key bills would have to become important functions of the Executive Committee, Legislative Committee, and General Counsel.

On the other hand, contemporary observers such as Stephen Raushenbush, one-time economic analyst for the Interior Department, thought that conservation in the 1950s was in danger of becoming "a lost cause," having lost its emotional appeal as a method to save the "national patrimony" for all citizens. Why? Raushenbush gave as "contrary forces" the great draining of resources occasioned by war or its anticipation, the ability of scientists to produce substitutes or find alternate sources, economical importation of resources from abroad, the current maintenance of a high standard of living despite the resources exploitation, and fear of too much governmental control. Besides, the conservation movement was becoming atomized, he said. Too many separate, single-interest groups competed for attention. Raushenbush was writing in 1952. He may have been right in a general way, but at least one interest group, the fish and game conservationists, were ahead of that kind of thinking. They saw that there would be no substitutes if wildlife were lost, and the only way to save the animals was to consider their environment as an interrelated whole. The 1960s would focus conservationists' attention even more on the ecological approach so long advocated by their most articulate leaders, and suddenly, dramatically, a popular cause.[82]

F ⋆ O ⋆ U ⋆ R

The Environmental Decade

We have met the enemy and they are us.

POGO

THE decade of the 1960s dawned with a palpable intensification of environmental awareness. John F. Kennedy, using his presidential initiative for a personal as well as a national interest, called a White House Conference on Conservation in May 1962 that focused on developing public policy for ensuring environmental quality. Stirred by Kennedy's ability to inspire the masses and Lyndon Johnson's legislative acumen, the "conservation Congresses" of the period turned out a record volume of conservation legislation. Stewart Udall, Interior Secretary to both Presidents, was a committed environmentalist and talented executive who nurtured the cause by directing federal action and shaping opinion with his popular writings. Official, professional, and lay literature on various aspects of ecology abounded.[1]

Pesticides and Other Pollution

Rachel Carson's *Silent Spring* created a sensation when it appeared in August 1962. In a chapter entitled "Needless Havoc," she wrote that "as man proceeds toward his announced goal of the conquest of nature, he has written a depressing record of destruction, directed not only against the earth he inhabits but against the life that shares it with him." "Black passages" of recent history included the slaughter of the western buffalo, market hunters' massacre of shorebirds, and the near extermination of egrets for their plumage. But now a new havoc loomed—"the direct killing of birds, mammals, fishes, and indeed practically every form of wildlife by chemical insecticides indiscriminately sprayed on the land." Carson, with impeccable research and a gift of language both forthrightly persuasive and starkly poetic, argued that indirect effects were equally insidious. Birds that survived pesticide spraying often lost their ability to reproduce or died from eating poisoned worms. DDT sprayed on forests leached into streams, killing young fish wholesale and destroying aquatic-insect fish food. The loss of western sagebrush sprayed to encourage increased grasslands for cattle left the sage grouse, antelope, and mule deer without food or shelter, and the unintended but coincidental killing of willows along stream beds wiped out the habitat for other wildlife and fish. The tragic litany seemed without end.[2]

The International Association of Game, Fish and Conservation Commissioners welcomed *Silent Spring* and its instant impact. Carson compellingly articulated for the masses concerns that state wildlife agents had expressed for some time. The Interior Secretary's annual report for 1950 had noted that "game specialists have become increasingly apprehensive of the use by agriculturalists of modern herbicides and insecticides because of the direct or secondary effect these chemicals may have on game." By 1953 Durward Allen, Assistant Chief of Research in the Fish and Wildlife Service, was warning the International about chemical destruction of wildlife cover and food even as he cautiously welcomed additional research in "managing plant successions" for potential creature benefit. "The rewards of knowledge or the penalties of ignorance will be great," he said. Unfortunately, as Allen readily admitted, no one knew very much about the secondary effects of pesticides in the early 1950s.[3]

The Association established a Pesticides Committee in 1958 and scheduled detailed reports in that and subsequent years. Ira Gabrielson, President of the Wildlife Management Institute, was alarmed by "the phenomenal growth in number, potency, and use of chemical pesticides." Three years before Rachel Carson, he used many of her examples to show how little was known and how little attention was being paid to pesticides' effects. But even a casual observer could see that the Department of Agriculture's program of controlling (eradicating) fire ants in the Southeast, for example, was leaving in its wake dead fish, birds, rabbits, frogs, and even worms in appalling proportion to their overall populations in the area. Were fire ants a sufficient menace to justify such overkill? Clarence Cottam, chairman of the Association's Research Committee, who called the reports on pesticides at the 1958 convention the most important papers of the meeting, pronounced the fire ant control effort "one of the most irresponsible and immature programs" he had ever seen proposed by a federal agency, its indirect effects "dangerous both to human beings and wildlife." Fortunately, Congress had recently directed the Secretary of the Interior to undertake continuing studies of the effects of pest control chemicals on fish and wildlife. By then some states were also beginning to use Pittman-Robertson or Dingell-Johnson funds for research on pesticide spraying or encouraging studies through the cooperative wildlife research units.[4]

Dr. Cottam had much more to say on pesticides at subsequent conventions. He acknowledged that wildlife, agriculture, and human life could benefit from wise use of chemical controls. Unfortunately, wisdom had been too often lacking. In 1962 Cottam hailed Carson's support of "the cause of the International" and agreed with her that the current approach of pest control by indiscriminate spraying would not only destroy unintended forms of life, it could also fail to eradicate the targeted victims, who were quickly becoming resistant to the milder forms of popular chemicals. Use of heavier concentrations, of course, would have all the predictable effects throughout the food chain.[5]

In 1966 the International Association adopted a statement of policy and guidance on the use of chemical pesticides that allowed room for wise use of pesticides based on "knowledge, skill, and restraint" but insisted that pest control problems be viewed ecologically, both in the long and short term. Only the least toxic chemical controls should be used, and only as a last resort and in the smallest effective amounts, concentrations, and areas. Rigid standards for use, careful record keeping, and continuing evaluation must be maintained. Each state or province should establish a pesticide control committee of representatives of conservation, health, and agricultural agencies to review every large-scale pesticide application. The Association reiterated its pledge to the pesticide policy two years later, but chemical pollution would remain a problem as persistent as the poisonous compounds themselves.[6]

Other forms of pollution disturbed conservationists during this decade of burgeoning environmental awareness. Seth Gordon, representing the Izaak Walton League, had first discussed water pollution at an Association convention in 1929. Industrial development and sewage dumping were fouling American rivers, with aesthetic defilement and losses to recreational and commercial fishing. By the late 1930s the International was backing antipollution legislation, mostly dealing with sewage disposal. The additional water pollution problem of siltation caused by poorly designed water impoundments or soil erosion came to popular attention in the 1940s. Pollution control was an indirect objective of the Coordination Act of 1946, while the limited Water Pollution Control Act (Taft-Barkley Act) of 1948 appropriated money for technical and financial cooperation among federal, state, and municipal governments for pollution abatement programs.[7]

Still, the quality of the continent's waters deteriorated. Parts of Lake Erie, oxygen-deprived from many sources but primarily the disposal of inadequately treated sewage, was showing signs of dying. Its fish were, for certain. Choice species such as sturgeon and cisco, whose populations had already been severely depleted by overfishing early in the century, could not recover in pollution-choked waters. For example, around 1900 the cisco yield had been 14 million pounds. It dropped by the 1930s to 746,000 pounds, and to 8,000 pounds by the early 1960s. Meanwhile, "rough" fish nobody wanted had replaced the desirable types and appeared to be thriving. While the lake and some species would eventually revive, the comeback of cisco and sturgeon remains slow.[8]

Pollutants unknown prior to World War II, such as radioactive materials, detergents, and pesticides, were also destroying natatorial life. Oil spills from offshore drilling rig accidents or the breakup of tankers was another new problem, and thermal pollution of rivers from power plants had already caused concern. The discharge from fossil fuel plants raised river temperatures enough to kill a variety of aquatic life in a wide area; nuclear plants, proliferating with the increasing demand for electrical energy, generated vastly more heat.[9]

The official federal position had been that water pollution was essentially a state and local responsibility while the federal role was one of support, coordination, and control of interstate contamination. The Association annually backed stronger measures to save fish and wildlife resources from the effects of aquatic filth, looking more and more to the federal government for money the states and municipalities could not raise.[10] Finally, in 1956, the Blatnik Federal Water Pollution Control Act improved the Taft-Barkley Act with tougher enforcement mechanisms and a $50 million appropriation for municipal sewage treatment plant construction grants-in-aid that would work something like Pittman-Robertson funding. The International lobbied hard for the bill and the next year helped in a "dramatic rescue" of its budget. Several Association members served on the nine-person Water Pollution Advisory Board mandated by the Act, among them John A. Biggs, I. T. Bode, Seth Gordon, and William Towell, all Association Presidents, General Counsel Carl Shoemaker, and Legislative Committee chairman Charles Callison.[11]

In 1965 a new Federal Water Quality Control Act, also sponsored by Minnesota's Congressman Blatnik, established a federal Water Pollution Control Administration to provide research and development grants and increased municipal sewage treatment plant construction grants. It also required the establishment of standards for water quality to aid pollution abatement in interstate waters by 1967. The International urged its members to influence the setting of these standards at scheduled federal hearings. The Clean Water Restoration Act of 1966 provided further grant aid for pollution abatement studies and programs in basin areas.[12] These measures helped to reverse the trend of human destruction of the natural environment, but at decade's end the International Association of Game, Fish and Conservation Commissioners was still reiterating the need for greater attention and more money to clean up America's waters.

Recreation and Wildlife

Providing varied recreational use of natural resources became a national priority during the 1960s. In response to increasing user demand and decreasing quantity and quality of the outdoor environment, Congress had established an Outdoor Recreation Resources Review Commission in 1958. The Commission and its advisory council, composed of members of Congress and leading conservationists, including several affiliated with the IAGFCC, were to inventory resources, determine trends and needs, and recommend policies and programs for 1976 and on to 2000. One outcome of its activity was the Land and Water Conservation Fund bill, intended to preserve, develop, and assure accessibility to all citizens of outdoor recreation resources. The International Association looked upon this bill as the most important legislation before Congress in 1963. The Legislative Committee sent telegrams to all states urging them to lobby for the bill and held two conferences on it with the Interior Department's Bureau of Outdoor Recreation, a new federal agency born of Commission suggestion to coordinate the overlapping work of more than twenty others. The Water Resources and Grants-in-Aid Committees approved the conservation fund bill as amended to give stronger consideration to fish and game values in the allocation of its funds.[13]

Congress enacted the bill in 1964. Like the Pittman-Robertson and Dingell-Johnson Acts, it created in the Treasury Department a special Land and Water Conservation Fund earmarked for certain uses, but its sources of revenue and spending policies were broader. Income would be generated from selected user fees, proceeds from the disposal of federal surplus lands, a federal motorboat fuels tax, and later, additional sources including unappropriated Treasury funds and continental shelf mineral revenue. Up to 60 percent of the annual appropriation from the fund would go to the states for land and water facilities development, according to a need-based formula determined by law and interpreted and administered by the Secretary of the Interior. The rest of the money could be spent by the federal government to acquire or develop federal lands. The law required each of the states to prepare a comprehensive statewide outdoor recreation plan and enact enabling legislation in order to receive from the fund up to 50 percent of the cost of an approved project.

The Land and Water Conservation Fund had many intended beneficiaries, but as A. D. Aldrich, past President and chairman of the Association's Grants-in-Aid Committee, put it, "We are confident that wildlife conservation will receive its just share of these funds if we stay on the ball." Measurement would be difficult, but by the early 1980s over $2 billion had been spent by states or the federal government through the fund with considerble direct or indirect benefit to wildlife. The International continued over the years to work for modifications in the application of the law to further enhance fish and game interests.[14]

State conservationists were also pleased in 1965 when the Federal Water Project Recreation Act recognized the legitimacy of recreational and fish and wildlife aspects of federal water projects, however they might feel about federal activities that might threaten their own jurisdiction. A problem, though, was the stipulation in the law that nonfederal interests pay half of the separable costs of a project, that is, the costs of those parts necessary only for fish and wildlife enhancement, and all of their operational, maintenance, and replacement costs. If a state could not afford the high price tag, that part of the project might be deleted altogether, which in turn could make future development of that resource more expensive and difficult. The International asked by resolution in both 1966 and 1967 that the Act be amended to delete the cost-sharing requirements for separable costs. The next two years it urged that Congress assure adequate funding for cooperative state-federal fish and wildlife studies during the earliest stages of water project planning. Congress took no specific action on these requests.[15]

Nevertheless, some verifiable wildlife progress accrued from the implementation of the Federal Water Project Recreation Act. For example, the Garrison Diversion Unit of the Missouri River Basin Project was intended to irrigate the drought-plagued farm areas of North and South Dakota, but the increased water also favored the more steady production of migratory birds in one of the most important waterfowl-producing regions south of Canada. Federal and state agricultural and wildlife interests combined their political and economic support for the project. The enlargement of the Bumping Lake Reservoir in the state of Washington was another example of state-federal cooperation for mutual benefit. The primary purpose of this project was to improve irrigation, flood control, and water quality, but it added importantly to recreational values and enhanced runs for anadromous and resident fish, various species of salmon and trout, respectively. Since anadromous fish migrate over interstate areas, the federal government picked up most of the tab. The Washington Department of Game was glad to support this project even though some purist wilderness proponents were not happy with it.

The International, however, emphatically opposed the Army Corps of Engineers' proposed construction of the Rampart Dam on Alaska's Yukon River that would have created a reservoir larger than Lake Erie. Here, 8,000 square miles of waterfowl-producing area would be inundated, big game habitat disrupted with an expected loss of 5,000 moose alone, and runs for tens of thousands of salmon destroyed. The project had no wildlife plan or funds to create one despite congressional dictates. The dam was not built.[16]

Even with a mixed record of achievement, national water legislation of the 1960s marked a new effort to involve state and local governments in decision making and give them a stake in federal water projects. It also considered broader ecological and social values in addition to strictly economic and short-term interests.

Hunters, Anglers, and Neither

The success of these environmental laws as applied to broad outdoor recreational purposes underlined a trend game conservationists had begun to observe. That was the increased use of fish and wildlife by nonanglers and nonhunters. Members of the International would have to modify their thinking and their programs to accommodate a new constituency even as they continued to serve their traditional interests. Formal studies indicated the diverging directions.

The International began the important practice of researching its market in 1955, when the first National Survey of Fishing and Hunting was conducted at its behest by the firm Crossley, S-D Surveys, Inc., of New York under contract to the Fish and Wildlife Service. Federal aid administrative funds bore the cost. Measuring only numbers of sportsmen (over twelve years of age) and their expenditures in pursuit of hunting and fishing, the survey confirmed the prevailing belief that these activities in America were big business. The survey team found that of the 48 million households in the United States in 1955, one out of three contained at least one person who hunted, fished, or did both, with more anglers overall than hunters. The total of 25 million sportsmen compared with 21 million in 1946. They spent 3 billion dollars for equipment, clothing, transportation, food and lodging, and licenses, with two-thirds of the total for fishing.[17]

Ohio State University economics professor R. D. Patton attempted to interpret the survey results for the delegates at the 1956 Association convention. He compared the 3 billion dollar hunting and fishing expenditure to roughly the same amount spent for electricity, telephone and telegraph, and physicians' services that year and nearly double that spent for all spectator amusements. But he noted that it was not as much as some earlier investigators had indicated. Patton reminded the game managers that much of the tangible value of hunting and fishing was too diffused to be distinguished as a wildlife expenditure. Could a gasoline station operator or motel owner know for certain that a customer was a hunter? The intangible value was even more difficult to assess. A product to show for the success of a fishing expedition could be assigned a dollar figure as food, but surely going fishing was valuable beyond the catch. Patton's message was that wildlife managers must educate legislators to judge the work of their profession on broad principles. Who could measure the worth of pleasure in the outdoors?

Patton drew other useful conclusions. Not surprisingly, there was less hunting and angling in or near urban areas, but sportsmen apparently willingly traveled great distances to shoot and fish. So he suggested developing recreational facilities where conditions were naturally favorable rather than providing less satisfactory accommodations closer to population centers. He promoted the multiple-use concept to maximize available lands for wildlife. Finally, he suggested family facilities at fishing and hunting sites and more attention to the manufacture of clothing and equipment suited to women to encourage that insufficiently tapped source of financial and moral support. In 1955 not quite 5 million women fished (one in eleven), and a half million (one in 128) hunted.[18]

The state conservationists found the 1955 survey so valuable that they asked for a new one every five years after that. The Census Bureau conducted the 1960 survey for the Fish and Wildlife Service in conjunction with its ongoing population inquiries. Daniel Janzen, Director of the Interior Department's Bureau of Sport Fisheries and Wildlife, reported to the International in 1961 that about 30 million hunters and anglers spent some $3.9 billion. Sportsmen were still increasing more rapidly than the overall population, particularly among women and teenagers. The number of female hunters had doubled during the five-year period, from 418,000 to 860,000. Hunters were more likely to pursue small game than either big game or waterfowl, while the bulk of fishers engaged in freshwater fishing. Waterfowl hunting was down, perhaps an effect of drought conditions. Research would be needed there. Disturbing news to the state game and fish commissioners was the evidence that almost 10 million people (or one in three) fished without a license, while one in five hunted illegally. The implications for state revenue for conservation activities, to say nothing of law enforcement, were serious.[19]

John Gottschalk, Janzen's successor, presented the 1965 survey results to the International Association the next year. They were, in a nutshell: "Fishermen numbers up—hunters down!" Increased fishing could be attributed to a growing interest in saltwater fishing and additional artificial ponds such as reservoirs. The game directors were disappointed but not altogether surprised at the hunting figures. Posted lands, lost habitat, and urban sprawl all curbed hunting opportunities. The most recent survey, concentrating on "substantial participants," revealed 33 million sportsmen spending $4 billion, but the higher numbers had to be viewed against a larger general population. Including more casual, or infrequent, participants might bring the number closer to 50 million. Americans spent 523 million recreation days fishing in 1965 and 186 million recreation days hunting, with about the same proportions as before not bothering to purchase licenses. The survey also found 3 million young sportsmen, ages nine to eleven, most of them boys. These newest statistics also included over 8 million money-spending, traveling, "serious" bird watchers and over 3 million wildlife photographers.[20]

Thomas Kimball, Executive Director of the National Wildlife Federation, for one, was frustrated and worried by emerging trends in wildlife use and attitudes about hunting and fishing. Protectionists opposed to scientific wildlife management particularly galled him. Contrary to what he saw as a growing popular connotation that sportsmen were wantonly cruel, vandalizing, "urban slobs," Kimball reminded the world that "with few exceptions, those who hunt and fish have made the greatest contributions toward preserving America's outdoor heritage—more than any other segment of our society." In particular, it was sportsmen who, through payment of license fees, had borne the costs of wildlife enhancement programs. Now, what was worse, other users were pushing out the real conservationists. "It is a fact that lands and waters acquired by hunters and fishermen now are being used by thousands of other outdoor recreationists. Water skiers and boaters, to be sure, are making it difficult—if not impossible—for fishermen to utilize lakes bought with fishing license money! Tourists, campers, picnickers, hikers and bird watchers want to use every square foot of lands purchased as public hunting grounds." Kimball urged regular congressional appropriations to fund recreation projects intended for the general public, with user fees and income from the Land and Water Conservation Fund providing maintenance only, which was about all they could handle. And he called for a broader outlook among conservation organizations so they could work together and not focus on narrow ideological lines.[21]

A few years later the editors of *National Wildlife*, responding to mounting tensions among hunters, nonhunters, and antihunters, asked seven leading conservation organizations for their official views on hunting. All seven—the National Audubon Society, Wilderness Society, Wildlife Society, Izaak Walton League, American Forestry Association, Sierra Club, and National Wildlife Federation—in varying degrees considered regulated sport hunting a legitimate use of wildlife resources and a proper tool of scientific wildlife management. The same magazine questioned Dr. A. Starker Leopold, son of the game management and ecology pioneer and himself an eminent wildlife biologist, on his "favorite form of recreation." He spoke of the physical and psychological pleasures of hunting and its salutary effects on game populations. These articles and many more vindicated the game managers' approach but also revealed an uncomfortable, unaccustomed defensiveness. Leopold, Kimball, and their colleagues continued to argue, however, that conservationists of all persuasions shared a joint responsibility toward insuring the future of wildlife.[22]

By the end of the 1960s, new patterns were clear. The numbers in the 1970 National Survey of Fishing and Hunting were impressive, but the categories were expanded. That year 128 million people participated in outdoor recreation of some sort, including hunting, fishing, bird watching, wildlife photographing, and nature walking. The significance was in the inclusion of groups that no one had thought to mention fifteen years earlier. Wildlife conservationists' mission was evolving to serve a growing but increasingly diverse clientele.[23]

As Kimball had alluded, competition for recreational land was becoming intense. The perennial concerns of hunters versus landowners and the availability of public hunting grounds continued to plague the state fish and game agents. The Association routinely returned to these subjects throughout its history, and it did again in the 1960s, this time as might be expected with added emphasis on the ecological consequences of land use choices. Jurisdictional disputes were also present, as always.

Private landowners had become increasingly reluctant to allow hunters on their property. Growing philosophical objections to killing and some hunters' reputations for obnoxious behavior were factors, but a serious concern was fear of liability in case of personal injury. Even trespassers had sometimes successfully sued for damages. The Legal Committee of the International, in an effort to induce landowners to open their property, especially those like mining and paper mill companies that held huge forested acreages, publicized a recent Tennessee statute that protected landowners by exempting them from having to assure users that their premises were safe or to make them safe except for "willful or malicious failure to guard or warn against a dangerous condition" or if they charged a fee. The committee hoped the Tennessee law would serve as a model for other states, and indeed, Michigan and Wisconsin had already passed similar legislation.[24]

In 1962 the International Association of Game, Fish and Conservation Commissioners convened a panel to discuss hunting in national park areas. The issue was timely in that new federal recreation areas established in connection with water development projects were often located on lands under National Park Service jurisdiction but outside park boundaries. The Forest Service routinely permitted hunting on analogous lands under its control, providing both recreation and animal population control, but the Park Service applied the stricter National Park criteria and prohibited hunting. The panelists represented various interests and proposed a wide range of solutions to problems of wildlife overpopulation, from cropping surplus animals by trained deputized hunters to turning game management on park-controlled lands over to the respective state game departments. Anthony Wayne Smith, Executive Secretary of the National Parks Association, took the International to task, or at least the "extremists" in it, for opposing nonhunting on national park and monument lands since it was allowed on national forest and even some wilderness lands. He appealed to the moderates of the Association to preserve what he considered a durable, workable dual policy. President Hayden Olds had just minutes earlier declared the International's "grudging" willingness to accept nonhunting in long-established national parks but not on newly formed land units where state game authorities were convinced that "you can have your wildlife and hunt it too."

The members blinked at the frankness of the discussion, but their resolution on surplus game problems on national park and monument lands was mild enough and passed without dissent. They simply reiterated their traditional insistence upon state responsibility for resident game, noting for the record that damages by overflow wildlife populations on surrounding state-controlled areas created a financial burden for the states. Commending the Interior Secretary's recognition of the problem, they promised the assistance of state big game technicians to his newly constituted national committee of respected conservationists, who were charged with solving the game control dilemma. The Association still leads efforts to keep lower-status national park lands open to the broadest public use.[25]

State v. Federal Authority: The Solicitor's Opinion, Carlsbad, and the Courts

Nevertheless, the ever simmering pot of contention between the states and federal government on jurisdiction over resident wildlife boiled over once again in the 1960s. Utah's fish and game director Harold Crane reported to the Association in 1963 the results of a questionnaire sent to all the states. Twenty-five, or half, of the state administrators felt that the states were relinquishing their responsibilities in fish and game to the federal government through increased federal activities and that present or proposed federal recreational programs usurped states' rights to manage wildlife resources on federal lands in their states. Forty-one states worried that loss of hunting rights on public lands would be detrimental to game management. Crane seemed to conclude, however, that strong state leadership combined with desirable federal guidance would reduce conflict and move their common program forward. He was too optimistic.[26]

Also in 1963 the Association's Legal Committee, long chaired by lawyer Nicholas Olds, rendered its interpretation of the law regarding jurisdiction over game in national parks, monuments, and forests. President Frank Groves had asked for this review, suggesting the presence of disturbing undercurrents that did not surface in the written record until later. Olds's Committee drew the distinction between ceded and unceded lands, the point which had caused confusion and controversy for years. If a state had ceded exclusive legislative jurisdiction over particular lands to the federal government, the land became a federal enclave over which the state had virtually no authority. While many national lands fit into this category, not all did, contrary to popular belief. In some national parks, monuments, and forests the United States controlled the land as an "ordinary landowner." Here, under proprietorial jurisdiction, the United States could prohibit or restrict public hunting and act to protect its property from damage by wildlife, but it could not increase hunting privileges beyond state law. The Legal Committee said it needed to study further the question of whether federal agents were required to obtain "concurrence" by state permit before undertaking a "protective reduction" of a game herd. Olds asserted that in any unceded national park or forest the state owned the resident wildlife and had sole right of management over it. And, he emphasized, the federal government recognized this right.[27]

In March 1964 Association President Nelson Cox, at the direction of the Executive Committee, appointed an ad hoc Federal Invasion of States Rights Committee, chaired by Frank Groves. The committee drafted a statement of "Aims, Objectives, and Responsibilities Concerning America's Natural Resources" and "Recommended Policies and Procedures Concerning the U.S. Fish and Wildlife Service and the State Fish and Game Agency," which its members then discussed with FWS officials in Washington. Both sides agreed their objectives were similar and their relations on the whole cooperative, but the International's Committee insisted upon a clear statement of mutual understanding. The statement read: "The federal government, through existing international treaties and agreements, bears direct responsibility and jurisdiction over specified migratory birds, endangered species, basic research, certain oceanic resources, and fauna of certain territorial lands beyond the continental United States. In similar manner, fish and resident species of wildlife are state resources under the direct responsibility and jurisdiction of the individual states."

The states rights committee, in "grave doubt," however, about the legality of recent federal intrusion into state functions and alarmed over proliferating federally controlled lands, went on to recommend specific policies and procedures in eight separate areas, most of which the Fish and Wildlife Service readily acceded to. For example, both sides agreed that the operating manual for administering federal aid programs under the Pittman-Robertson and Dingell-Johnson Acts should be made more simple and less restrictive. Court actions (ultimately unsuccessful) by some frustrated states on license counting for federal aid funding emphasized the need. The Fish and Wildlife Service hedged on the Association committee's request to honor states' "expressed wishes" that migratory waterfowl refuges be opened to hunting so long as the resource was not endangered. The Service promised to "conform whenever possible" but reminded the committee that it also had responsibilities to people who got their satisfaction from wildlife "just by having the opportunity to view it."[28]

The IAGFCC Committee's first recommendation was the one that set the federal-state controversy spinning again. The Committee asked that the Fish and Wildlife Service "refrain from assuming the authority to fix regulations controlling the taking of fish and resident game species on lands the service has acquired, as such function belongs solely to the states." As Chairman Groves calmly reported it, the Service, on his request, had said it would ask the Interior Department Solicitor's opinion and forward a "complete and detailed legal position paper" as soon as it was completed. Making that request proved to be a major tactical error.[29]

Deputy Solicitor Edward Weinberg's opinion came down on December 1, 1964. Gratuitously addressing a broader question than the one asked, he sweepingly declared that the United States had the constitutional power, specifically superior to state power, to control and protect its lands, specifically including the resident wildlife thereon. No qualifying conditions softened the blow. A fury ensued. The International Association of Game, Fish and Conservation Commissioners' Legal Committee, in intense, almost incredulous disagreement, drew up its own brief reviewing the legal precedents for its long-held position and suggested possible courses of corrective action. Proposed tactics ranged from requesting a conference with the Secretary of the Interior to induce a withdrawal or change of the offensive opinion to seeking court action or new clarifying legislation. Both of the latter two approaches could be dangerous; Chairman Olds recommended their adoption only as a last resort.[30]

Meanwhile, the Federal-State Rights Relations Committee (Groves's committee renamed, probably informally) reproduced for the Association members the Solicitor's document laced with case citations along with the Department's cover letter to the committee, both of which were based on the premise that ownership of game relied on ownership of the land. The Committee, calling this the European, not the American, system, felt it "imperative" that the jurisdictional question be settled "once and for all." Groves again acknowledged "the friendliest relationship and the best cooperation" of the Fish and Wildlife Service but insisted that did not obviate the pressing need for a workable memorandum of understanding to replace the Solicitor's 1964 opinion. Groves suggested the "Cooperative Memorandum" negotiated with the U.S. Forest Service to replace Regulation G-20-A with W-2 "more than a quarter century ago" be used as a model. If that approach did not work, the Committee agreed with the Legal Committee's proposed plan of action. Concluded Groves, "If this constant infringement of State Rights is allowed to go unchallenged, we might as well fold up and go home."[31]

It was Seth Gordon who calmed the exercised delegates. Reminding them of his involvement with the W-2 action, the then Secretary of Agriculture's eagerness to cooperate, and the virtual lack of trouble since then, Gordon begged his colleagues to not "spread blood all over the floor" if a "little bit of sensible approach" would work just as well. The present Interior Secretary Stewart Udall, he said, was "wise" and "foresighted" and had done more for the conservation program they all cared about than any in memory. By resolution the Association agreed to Gordon's approach, with the proviso that if the "historic states' rights are not satisfactorily recognized," the Association would take "whatever steps [were] necessary." More insistent resolutions followed. A 1965 meeting with states' attorneys general confirmed the states' unanimous agreement with the International's position.[32]

The next year was a busy one for the Federal-State Rights' Relations Committee. At a meeting with the Secretary of the Interior in December 1965, both sides agreed that the Department issue a mutually acceptable compromise policy without reference to the Solicitor's opinion or the Legal Committee's brief. Since legal issues contained in these papers could only be resolved through judicial proceedings, setting them aside was the simplest approach. The Department produced a document that Association President William Towell in January 1966 urged the members to accept even though it fell short of all their objectives. The Solicitor's opinion was "shelved," Secretary Udall being "no more anxious to revive it than we are," he said, and the limited scope of the statement, referring only to national refuge lands, could be expanded from this workable starting point. Further refinements went back and forth; in May, Udall forwarded the latest compromise policy, which was quite agreeable until Udall referred to the 1964 opinion again as the source of the Department's authority. The frustrated Towell just could not get the Solicitor's opinion "buried as deeply as [the Association] wished."[33]

Meanwhile, an Endangered Species bill, having passed the House, was before the Senate Commerce Committee. State conservationists, fearing the proposed federal protection for specified species might further threaten states' jurisdiction over resident wildlife, urged the inclusion of the Interior Department's policy statement in the legislation to emphasize their position. Udall suggested the policy be part of the bill's history but not the bill itself. In the end, both sides accepted a simple amendment to the Endangered Species bill, in lieu of the more cumbersome policy statement, that said that nothing in the bill would be construed as affecting the states' jurisdiction over fish and resident wildlife on federally owned lands or waters. In other words, the amendment simply reaffirmed the status quo, to allow for negotiated change at a later date. So far, so good. But when Udall sent the amendment to Senator Magnuson, chairman of the Senate Committee, he once again cited the Solicitor's opinion, unbeknownst to the Association and "much to the chagrin" of its officers and special committee. Nevertheless, this first, modest Endangered Species bill did become law in 1966.[34]

After all this, the International Association felt that the only permanent solution lay in federal legislation that clearly declared the intent of Congress to affirm the states' historically recognized authority to manage fish and resident wildlife within their borders on all lands except those specifically ceded to the federal government. The Legal Committee drafted such a bill to present to the 90th Congress. At its 1966 convention the Association approved the Committee's work and endorsed its plan of action. In 1968 Association President Walter Shannon testified at Senate hearings that "by law, history, and centuries of tradition," the ownership of wildlife was, and should be, separated from ownership of the land.[35]

While Congress worked its slow progress through several game ownership bills and state and federal conservation officials came tantalizingly close to agreement on their own, the National Park Service informed the state of New Mexico that it intended to remove about fifty deer from Carlsbad Caverns National Park to conduct research on deer-browsing depredation. The state would have issued permits for the killing but the federal agents did not ask, claiming the deer, on federal land, belonged to the federal government. New Mexico, having never ceded exclusive jurisdiction over the park area, sued the Secretary of the Interior. The International Association and several other states supported New Mexico as amici curiae. This was the moment. Nicholas Olds reminded the state conservationists at the 1968 IAGFCC convention that in this first attempted implementation of the 1964 Solicitor's opinion the lands in question were national park lands, not refuges, as purportedly limited the applicability of the opinion, but that did not seem to be the legal issue. The federal district judge ruled that the federal government could only undertake such a program if it could prove that depredations had occurred and had been caused by the deer; he issued a restraining order against further killing without a state permit. The federal government appealed. Olds called it a national test case that would "determine the very survival of state game and fish departments and programs."[36]

The U.S. Court of Appeals for the Tenth Circuit in Denver reversed the lower court in 1969, arguing that the Interior Secretary need not wait for actual damage to occur before taking "reasonable steps" to protect national park lands, that the property clause of the Constitution gave the Secretary statutory power to act through Congress without state interference.[37] The stunned members of the International Association of Game, Fish and Conservation Commissioners voted to appeal to the Supreme Court, but the high court never heard the case. Nor did specific legislation ever pass to clear up the federal-state controversy despite major efforts by the Association and other supporters. Instead, finally, in 1970, the new Interior Secretary Walter J. Hickel issued an official regulation that gave "force and relative permanency" to a departmental policy statement that "quieted the reasonable concern of the states for their right to manage fish and resident wildlife within their borders"—an action that won him commendation from the International.[38]

Harry Woodward, President of the International from 1969 to 1970, remembers how members of the Association found friends for states' rights in President Nixon's Interior Secretary Hickel and his Assistant Secretary, Dr. Leslie Glasgow. Woodward and Glasgow, in almost daily contact, worked out the regulatory details with the help of Chester Phelps, John "Bud" Phelps, and Ladd Gordon. Not everyone in the federal establishment approved, however, and Hickel delayed signing the new policy. The actual news that the regulation had been approved came to Glasgow from the White House as he sat at the 1970 IAGFCC convention's head banquet table. Woodward got to relay the whispered word to the cheering delegates.[39]

And so the state-federal jurisdictional matter was put to rest once again and the Association could get on with other affairs. The issue was not "solved"; Chester Phelps calls it "a sleeping dog—I hope." Generally speaking, however, prevailing thinking within the Association has evolved to the idea that state authority on federal lands could be better preserved or restored by piecemeal strokes than by broad jurisdictional measures.[40]

Public Land Laws Reviewed

Fortunately, relationships between the federal government and state conservation agents were normally cordial and productive. A good example of relative cooperation, though not without some differences, involved the public land law review activities of the late 1960s. In 1964 Congress established the Public Land Law Review Commission to examine and suggest improvements in policies, laws, and regulations affecting federal lands, their resources and uses. It was a large assignment; one-third of the nation's land was owned by the federal government, most of it in the West. The International Association of Game, Fish and Conservation Commissioners took an immediate interest in the work of the Commission, especially that on fish and wildlife resources but also the many other issues that indirectly affected game habitat and populations. Thomas Kimball told the state game conservationists that he thought they would be able to "speak their minds" to the eighteen-member Commission, which was composed of twelve members of Congress, mostly Westerners, and six citizens, with a twenty-five member advisory board. And he urged them to work closely together to insure that public fish, wildlife, and recreational values would not be subjugated to commercial interests in the Commission's final recommendations. In 1965 the Association established its own Public Land Law Review Committee to "assist and keep abreast of" the Commission's proceedings and named Harry Woodward as Special Liaison to the PLLRC. He and James B. White of Wyoming chaired the Association's Public Land Law Committee during its years of existence, 1965–71.[41]

The Commission's report to the President and Congress in 1970 drew general applause from the International Association. The Association's hard-working Committee, however, felt sufficiently disquieted about some effects of land policy on fish and wildlife to issue, in 1971, its own publication, *Public Land Policy Impact on Fish and Wildlife*, in response to the Commission's *One Third of the Nation's Land*. Urging adoption of the many "excellent" recommendations of the PLLRC, the Association also pointed out those "regressive" measures that could have adverse implications for faunal resources and forwarded its own proposals for a more enlightened approach. Foremost, the Association urged that the one-third public ownership of the nation's lands not be diminished in quantity, although favorable disposals and acquisitions could transfer control of particular acreages in order to ensure the "maximum net public benefit."[42]

The International Association's land law impact document, in outlining specific problems for wildlife management on public lands, also illustrated its general concerns during the period. It merits a closer look. For example, the Association implored federal agencies to coordinate their efforts and seek public input so the Agriculture Department, say, would not be draining swamps even as Interior was encouraging the development of wetlands. The IAGFCC opposed the PLLRC's recommended "dominant use classification" for public lands since wildlife could rarely compete in economic terms against such uses as forestry, agriculture, grazing, or water impoundment. A balanced, multiple-use concept would both encourage other uses and protect wildlife. The Association asked for legislative action to formalize the state and local governments' role in planning for projects varying from highway construction to range improvement and to provide additional federal financial assistance for comprehensive land use planning.[43]

The IAGFCC Committee's report praised the Commission's attention to environmental quality, noting that a good environment benefited people as well as fish and wildlife. It asked for environmental impact studies *before the fact* when planning for construction of roads, power lines, dams, or airports. It asked for rehabilitation of abused lands—which did not have to mean restoration to original condition, the state conservationists emphasized. Indeed, a mine turned into a lake, for example, could improve the aesthetics and usefulness of an area. Likewise, small, irregularly shaped clear-cut regions in forests could enhance both vegetation and cover for animals. The Association did not oppose mineral leasing on public lands but again cautioned against large-scale operations that would adversely affect the quality of the natural setting. Environmental protection must be an "overriding priority."[44]

The Association Public Land Law Review Committee's major departure from the Commission's report was once again over authority. "Unfortunately, the PLLRC Report avoids coming to grips with the federal-state jurisdictional problem, failing to state explicitly the premises which underlie basic PLLRC recommendations." While the Commission called for full "consultation" with the state wildlife agencies in order to avoid any action "inconsistent with state harvesting regulations," it presumed a superior federal authority over wildlife on public lands under the proposition that control over wildlife went with ownership of the land. The Committee, however, argued again that authority depended upon the sovereignty of the state, not land title, and allowed only a few specific instances where it believed federal power could outrank a state's, such as to make harvest restrictions even more stringent than those of the state or to remove fish and wildlife where necessary to protect other resources from serious injury. The overall tone of both documents suggested that each side was mindful of the new Interior Department jurisdictional regulation and anxious to make it work.[45]

International Efforts for the Birds

Another area of cooperation was in international waterfowl management, a renewed agenda item during the 1960s. The migratory bird treaties with Canada and Mexico and their enabling legislation established the cooperative concept, but these documents dealt only with regulating the harvest and shipment of waterfowl and the protection of certain species. They did not address the crucial problems of habitat management. Serious bird losses from drainage of prairie potholes as well as difficulties with crop depredations were particularly acute in the prairie provinces and states of Alberta, Saskatchewan, Manitoba, the Dakotas, and Minnesota. Canada and the United States, through the International Association of Game, Fish and Conservation Commissioners, had begun to discuss the possibility of an international waterfowl commission as early as the 1930s and seriously by the late 1950s. But difficult questions centered on jurisdiction and the financing of an international body dedicated to bird habitat management and research across national borders. Could the spending of United States dollars in Canada or Mexico be approved? Who would determine how they would be spent? A treaty to supplant the 1916 agreement with Canada seemed out of the question by then because each province would have to ratify individually—an unlikely prospect. Mexico, hampered by insufficient funding, had irregular involvement with its northern neighbors in conservation matters.[46]

Nevertheless, Association efforts to solve transnational bird problems continued. Its Waterfowl Study Committee drafted a proposed Convention on Waterfowl Management for the United States, Canada, and Mexico in 1960. Based on the successful Great Lakes Fishery Commission's organizational documents, it included detailed regulations on procedure and finance. Nothing came of that attempt, but in 1961 the United States and Canada established an International Migratory Birds Committee, representing both agricultural and wildlife interests, which developed a research program and made slow progress toward political accord. In 1962 the Association's Migratory Birds Committee suggested that an international executive agreement restricted to the prairie provinces and states, where the worst conditions existed, be implemented as a quicker, more expedient approach to specific habitat preservation. Meanwhile, John Gottschalk stirred lively discussion with his proposal that bird populations be deliberately decreased during dry periods by more liberal hunting regulations. "Why save birds when there is no place for them to breed? Save them for times of good water," he said. Gottschalk's recommendation found its way into the Association's Migratory Birds Committee's policy statements.[47]

During the next few years the Association, as per mandate of the 1966 convention, put its efforts into the creation of an international wildlife management policy intended for adoption by the respective national governments. The Migratory Birds Committee, most of the time chaired by Thomas Evans, drafted policies in 1967 and 1968, each a new approach in style and to some extent in substance, probably in response to internal disagreements and a disappointing lack of specific input by other members of the Association. Apparently, although everyone agreed that the problems were serious and a policy was of great importance, the Committee got more criticism than help. In 1969 the Committee meshed the two previous statements and asked for Association approval, but when the report was given, the convention proceeded with other business without taking any action. In 1970 a discouraged chairman Russell Stuart reported the Migratory Birds Committee's failure to submit a waterfowl management policy because of unfavorable responses by Canadian provinces as well as the Western Association. He recommended the appointment of a ten-member (five each from the two countries), two-year committee to report back with a policy in 1972. The Association agreed.[48]

But in 1972 this Committee admitted final failure and asked to be relieved of its responsibilities. Neither the Canadian nor U.S. Wildlife Service was willing to give up its own prerogative in formulating such a policy, so it did not appear that an Association policy would have significant value; differing provincial and state management philosophies got in the way of consensus; and the parties could not even agree on definitions of terms. So the committee recommended instead that the International Migratory Birds Commission of 1961 (at the time called a committee), which had laid effective groundwork for international cooperation under the guidance of the Canadian Ministers of Agriculture and Environment and the U.S. Secretaries of Agriculture and Interior, be reactivated to formulate policy and management guidelines based on input from all interested agencies and organizations. The International Association of Game, Fish and Conservation Agencies acknowledged that it could not do everything.[49]

The Legal Sphere

The International Association found itself engaged in new directions during the 1960s. Its mounting activity in the legal arena was one. The Association had first convened an interim Legal Committee in 1958 and resolved to make it a permanent standing committee that same year in order to ensure conservationists information and advice on legal interpretations that affected their increasingly complex work. That Committee demonstrated its value over and over during the trying times of the controversy over the Solicitor's 1964 opinion on federal-state jurisdiction, as seen. In 1966 the Legal Committee and the Public Land Law Review Committee recommended the hiring of professional legal counsel to assist in research, proposal review, and brief writing. Nicholas Olds consulted Ira Gabrielson, then President of the Wildlife Management Institute, who recommended the law firm of Oscar Chapman, Interior Secretary under President Truman. The firm, in turn, designated a young associate, Paul Lenzini, to "see if you can help these fellows." Lenzini remains the Association's legal counsel. Since the 1968 Carlsbad litigation, the International has participated in a number of lawsuits of national significance upon review and recommendation of the Legal and Executive Committees.[50]

It was the Legal Committee that first formally reminded the Association that violence of the times would have unforeseen implications for game managers and sportsmen. In November 1963 President John F. Kennedy was shot by an assassin. One response to this shocking tragedy was a spate of gun control bills introduced both in Congress and state legislatures. The Association vigorously opposed antifirearms legislation that would "restrict the purchase, possession, and use of firearms ordinarily used in the pursuit of outdoor recreation by hunting or shooting," in the name of proper game management and the constitutional right to bear arms. The wildlife officials were willing to accept reasonable controls over concealed handguns or "gangster-type weapons," they said, but time and again over the ensuing twenty years, as more political assassinations, rampages of crazed individuals, and the war in Vietnam brought about a popular revulsion from senseless violence, they would be obliged to reassert a right they had long taken for granted and considered basic. The conservationists also responded by devoting increasing time and resources to the positive issue of hunter safety and the recreational and management values of hunting.[51]

The Wildlife Reference Service

Finally, the 1960s were years of expanding activity for the International Association of Game, Fish and Conservation Commissioners as an institution. The creation of the Denver Conservation Library was a proud example. The Association had been seeking for several years some kind of central clearing house for information and data gathered by the states for projects under the Pittman-Robertson and Dingell-Johnson Acts. In 1965 the Bureau of Sport Fisheries and Wildlife, through the Department of Interior Library, contracted with the Denver Public Library for the latter facility to expend federal aid administrative funds to collect, index, store, and make available for reference use all existing and future P-R and D-J reports. As reported by the Association's Special Library Committee, it was a monumental task just to develop a cross-referenced Thesaurus of

Descriptors (some 4,000 headings in all) so that entries could be broadly cataloged for expeditious retrieval; another huge job was to collect all the reports that should be included, some of which were not labeled as federal aid studies. The lack of a standardized report format made computerized data entry difficult, but Bureau Director Gottschalk was reluctant to impose more federal regulations on the states during this time of jurisdictional sensitivity. So the Library Committee itself agreed to poll the state agents on their willingness to conform to a predetermined format in their project reporting. Only fourteen states responded, but most of them were agreeable in the name of future efficiency.

By the end of the decade approximately 11,000 fisheries reports from the inception of the Dingell-Johnson program in 1950 through March 1969 had been indexed and about 95 percent of them computerized on punch cards. About 60 percent of the available Pittman-Robertson materials, some 24,000, post-1955, were indexed; nearly 16,000 of these were processed. The Department of Interior Library continued to index the P-R and D-J published reports. By then conversion from punch cards to computerized magnetic tape storage was also under way. In addition, the Wildlife Reference Service at the Denver Conservation Library responded to hundreds of requests for information or materials annually. A newsletter informed potential users of what was available.

The program was a success. A major continuing task would be the annual renewal of the contract with sufficient funding so that the increasing demand for the library services could be met and the program expanded to encompass broader fish and wildlife literature, including theses from the Cooperative Research Unit programs. The Denver Library recommended that free priority reference service be continued for the research staffs of the state fish and game departments and the Bureau of Sport Fisheries and Wildlife, but the state conservationists themselves hoped that any employee of these agencies or graduate student could also be served. Others would be accommodated at cost, staff time permitting. By 1973 when Roberta Winn, the Library's first project leader, retired, the program enjoyed solid footing and support and found it necessary to employ quality-control criteria in the acceptance of additional reports. In a dozen years it collected and made available over 12,500 varied documents.[52]

The Turning Point

Strictly internal activities also showed the Association's growth in vitality, influence, and self-respect during the 1960s. The Professional Improvement Committee began a continuing effort in 1961 to recommend higher educational and performance standards as well as upgraded salaries and professional development for game managers in order to attract and retain the most able practitioners in the field.[53]

The Wildlife Conservation Planning Committee studied the Association's committee structure itself, seeking to consolidate and streamline the work of the several committees, finding more efficient and professionally sound methods of selecting committee members, and ensuring liaison with other organizations as appropriate. In 1960 this Committee recommended that three categories of committees be established and their terms of office and functions delineated. The first, Continuing Operational Committees, would include Legislative, Legal, Conservation Planning, Water Resources, Land Resources, Research, Migratory Birds, Grants-in-Aid, and Professional Improvement. The five Administrative Committees would concern themselves with Resolutions, Audit, Nominations, Time and Place, and Program. Special Committees, appointed by the President upon recommendation of the Executive Committee for as long as a specific need existed, might include ones on hunter safety, communications, or slogan development. The Association accepted these proposals as bylaws amendments, thus spelling out the President's responsibilities more clearly as well as those of the serving members. This structure held throughout the decade.[54]

The Wildlife Conservation Planning Committee became the Management Improvement Committee in 1965, charged with developing information administratively useful to the Association. In 1970 President Woodward proposed that the Committee draft permanent policies for the Association based on past actions that would eliminate the need to repeat resolutions on the same subject matter annually. The Committee, upon recommendations from members and review by the President and Executive Committee, dutifully drew up policy statements on seventeen subjects, from states' rights in fish and wildlife management to pesticide use to commercial shooting preserves. It recommended the adoption of these policies in 1971, but confusion over what to do with late-received suggestions led the body to defer a vote. In 1972 and 1973 the Management Improvement Committee reported that it was still revising various aspects of the policy statements. Would they ever be ready for formal consideration?[55]

Harry Woodward started issuing an informal newsletter to keep the members abreast of the latest developments and spur them to action when he became Association President in 1969. In conversational style he addressed issues of immediate concern, such as sensational, antihunting television programs that appeared with frustrating regularity at that time, current legislative efforts, committee work and progress, and upcoming meetings. Woodward called his newsletter *SUMAC-GAF*, deriving the name by reversing and abbreviating the names of the member countries—the United States, Mexico, and Canada—and adding the first letters of Game and Fish. (Woodward's first issue put Fish before Game in the title, but following member protest of the connotation, he cheerfully switched the order.) Chester Phelps continued the newsletter tradition when he became President, supplementing it with a regional "telephone tree" worked out, in those pre-WATS line days when the Association could not afford frequent long-distance calls, in the pattern of his daughter's school carpool arrangements. The President would call a few regionally distributed state directors, who in turn would call a few more in their general areas, and so on until everyone was informed.[56]

The International Association of Game, Fish and Conservation Commissioners had attained maturity in terms of internal structure and growth. State membership in the International remained fairly constant during the period, while provinces fluctuated somewhat more as dues-paying participants. Individual membership increased to 316 by 1970 despite an increase in Associate dues from two dollars to three in 1967. At that session the voting, that is, state, members approved without dissent an increase in state dues to $150 and Canadian and Mexican dues to $100. In 1968 John Gottschalk applied for a Fish and Wildlife Service membership in the International, which was accepted, thus broadening the governmental membership category to include, for the first time, federal agencies. The FWS had provided advice and assistance for years. Now, for the price of membership dues, it had a voting voice.[57]

Just three years later, in 1970, the Association again took a close look at its bylaws. The Bylaws Committee, chaired by W. Mason Lawrence of New York, recommended several clarifying changes in wording, to separate the office of Secretary-Treasurer into two positions with the proviso that one person could hold both, to allow more flexibility in the scheduling of annual meetings and those called by the Executive Committee, and to rewrite the confusing statement of duties of the General Counsel, especially as they related to the work of the Legal Committee. The Association quickly accepted all of these amendments.[58]

But two changes regarding membership were another matter. One extended eligibility for membership to any country in the western hemisphere, or "major political subdivision thereof." The second proposed to increase membership dues of the states and the United States government from $150 to $1,000. (Other member dues would remain at $100.) The debate which followed was spirited, the transcript liberally sprinkled with exclamation points. As the President called for the vote on dues, Bylaws Committee member Earle Frye of Florida interrupted to ask "if the reason for the thousand-dollar dues [had] been adequately pointed out." Answering the question himself, he instructed, "The idea, of course, is that this money will be used to put a permanent, full-time secretary in Washington. I wonder if everyone is aware of that. If they aren't, they are now!" At Woodward's request, those in favor said, "Aye." The record does not indicate that "No" votes were called for. The Association was about to embark on a new era.[59]

That the long-sought vote to establish a presence in the national capital should have carried so easily does not seem a given from the written record. While the Legal Committee, for one, had specifically recommended the establishment of a Washington office as early as 1960, a special committee chaired by Melvin Steen concluded against such a move in 1961. The projected need to quadruple dues could not be justified, it said. Perhaps the President could secure temporary assistance when needed. No less a figure than President William Towell had argued against it as late as 1966, arguing that the Association would lose its strength as a grass roots organization if it chose to become "just another lobbying group." Further, it would forfeit its international aspect with even greater dominance by United States politics. Nevertheless, the Association was finally ready to take that step first proposed in 1946.[60]

Harry Woodward's valedictory address at the 1970 convention showed a man well aware of the turning point the Association had just passed. He recalled the "orderly accomplishment" of the past while anticipating the new challenges and "much greater involvement" of the future. During his brief presidential term, he had witnessed and helped achieve several milestones. Interior Secretary Hickel had signed the states rights' regulation, and the Public Land Law Review Commission's report was in. The Internal Revenue Service had granted the Association tax-exempt status, which would encourage increased activity. The first Earth Day in 1970 focused everyone's attention once again on the environment and ecology, which was mixed good news to the game conservationists. "Almost instantly, however, we realized we had a so-called bear by the tail," said Woodward, because so many of these Earth Day "neophytes" were opposed to the orderly harvest of wildlife resources. The game management profession would have much work to do in leading such people to an understanding of resource management in the coming decade.[61]

As a closing note to the passing era and a call for the new, the International Association of Game, Fish and Conservation Commissioners presented to Seth Gordon its first Seth Gordon Award, an inscribed and mounted lucite owl, for his "half century of inspired leadership and distinguished service in natural resources management." Since his first Association convention in 1921, Gordon had never missed a meeting. Besides serving as Association President from 1940 to 1941, he had guided it and just about every other conservation effort known in his lifetime with "enthusiasm and expertise," helping create the environmental awareness then reaching popular heights. With the continuing issuance of the Seth Gordon Award, the Association hoped to foster leadership within its own ranks that would "direct the surge of public demand into channels leading to the eventual harmony between Man and Nature." The award is today the Association's most prestigious.[62]

A South Carolina wildlife official demonstrates the proper handling of firearms to a group of orphaned youths. Hunter education for safety and ethical conduct has been an Association concern for more than fifty years.
(Courtesy, *South Carolina Wildlife Magazine*)

Association President Harry Woodward presented the first Seth Gordon Award to Seth Gordon (left) in 1969 for his "half century of inspired leadership and distinguished service in natural resources management." The award, given annually for sustained leadership and service, is the Association's highest honor.
(IAFWA)

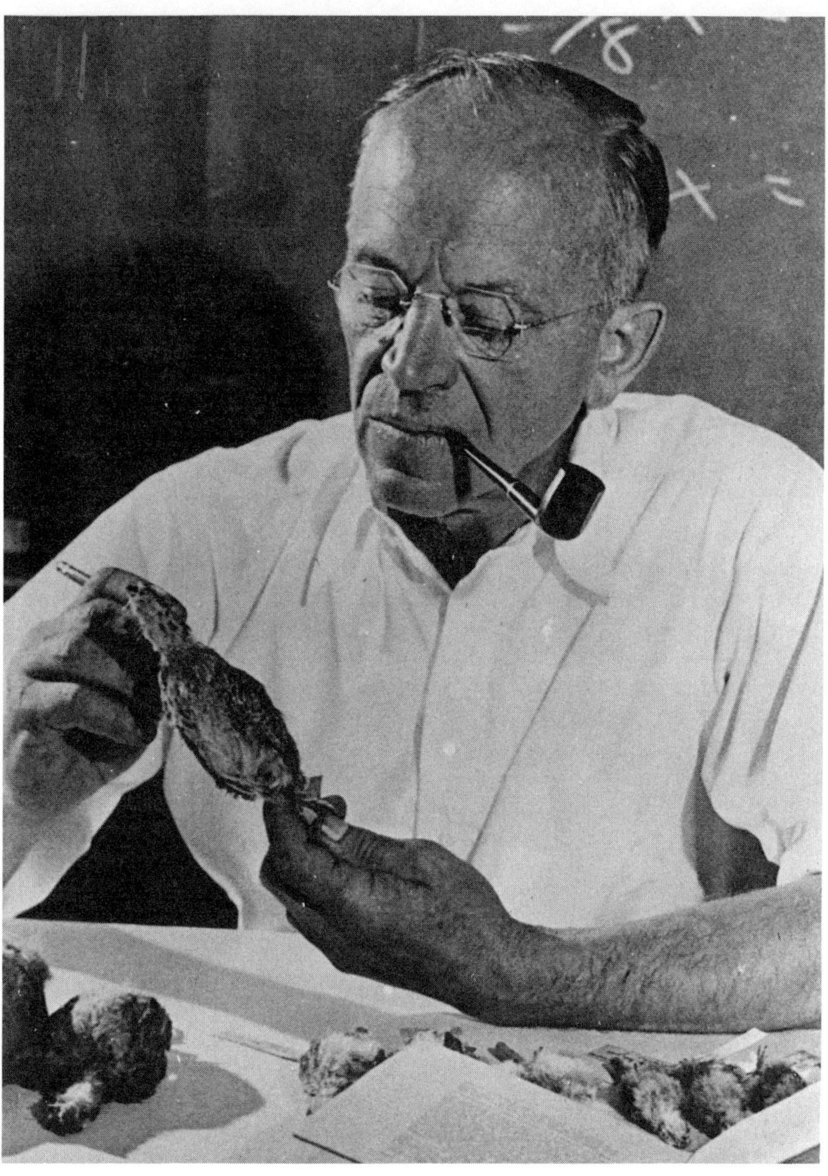

Aldo Leopold, acknowledged father of game management and softly eloquent champion of a land ethic that respected the interrelationships among all living things, is shown here in his scientific role examining study skins of bird specimens.

(Courtesy, Wisconsin Natural Resources Department)

WHY DRAIN OUR LAKES TO MAKE MORE FARMS WHEN WE ARE ALREADY SUFFERING FROM OVER PRODUCTION OF FARM PRODUCTS?

"Ding" Darling wielded uncommon influence for wildlife conservation during the 1930s and beyond, as much with his acerbic cartoons as with his gifts as an administrator, organizer, and spokesman.

(Courtesy, J. N. (Ding) Darling Foundation, Inc.; captions were supplied by the Darling Foundation)

The International Association of Fish and Wildlife Agencies has long advocated multiple land use, as shown in this Oregon scene of 1960 that juxtaposes recreation and grazing.
(Courtesy, U.S. Forest Service, photo by Paul R. Canntt)

Funding for this recreational boat launch in Pennsylvania was substantially assisted by proceeds from the federal excise tax on fishing equipment created by the 1950 Dingell-Johnson Act for fish restoration and management projects.

(Courtesy, Pennsylvania Fish Commission, photo by Russ Gettig)

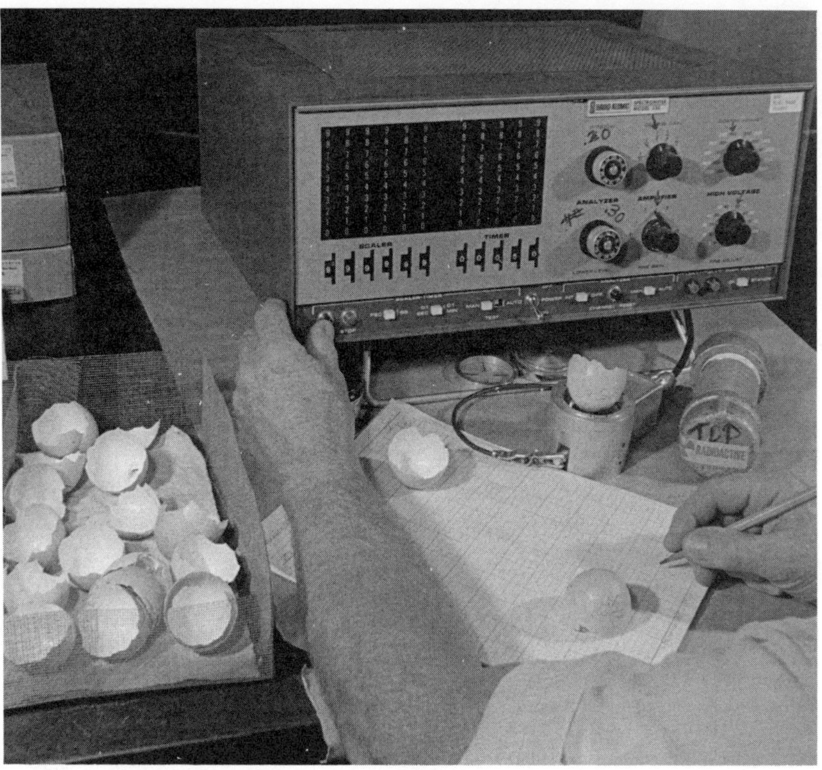

A biologist at the Patuxent Wildlife Research Center in Maryland studied the effects of pesticides on mallard eggshells in 1969. Small amounts of DDT in the ducks' feed produced eggs significantly thinner and more subject to cracking than the shells of ducks that ate untreated feed.
(Courtesy, U.S. Department of Interior, Bureau of Sport Fisheries and Wildlife, photo by Luther Goldman)

Wildlife managers have been particularly successful in replenishing wild turkey populations through transplant procedures. This release took place in South Carolina.

(Courtesy, *South Carolina Wildlife Magazine*)

F ⋆ I ⋆ V ⋆ E

The Washington Presence

When you are fed up with the troublesome present, with being "very twentieth century," you take your gun, whistle for your dog, go out to the mountain, and, without further ado, give yourself the pleasure during a few hours or a few days of being "Paleolithic."

JOSÉ ORTEGA Y GASSET

CONCERN for environmental quality continued to be a dominant theme in the 1970s, but emphasis shifted from faith in scientific and technological "progress" to a greater insistence upon social responsibility. The decade marked the heyday of congressional activity on environmental matters, beginning with the passage of the National Environmental Policy Act of 1970 and the creation of the Environmental Protection Agency. The lawmakers seemed at times to act with more heart than mind, however, with implementation problems a result for wildlife managers who preferred a rational approach to an emotional one. Emotions ran high as antihunting and "animal rights" advocates gathered support and the attention of the press.

Other societal issues affected wildlife. Public morality and accountability became central questions as the Watergate scandal enveloped an ever larger and higher placed circle of federal officials, finally including the President of the United States. Representatives of government at all levels consequently came under suspicion and closer scrutiny. The energy crisis, brought about by manipulated distribution and skyrocketing prices of Middle Eastern oil, led to double-digit inflation and a shaken sense of national well-being. Efforts to increase domestic fuel production affected wildlife habitat along with other aspects of the environment. Wildlife conservationists would have to confront all of these issues and more in the years to come. To face them more effectively, the International Association of Game, Fish and Conservation Commissioners attended to its internal agenda first.

The Washington Office

"Perhaps our most significant achievement this year has been to set the stage for the hiring of a full time executive vice president for the International," reported Chester Phelps in his President's message of 1971. Later, he unhesitatingly called that act the most significant achievement in the Association's history, but at the time his carefully phrased enthusiasm reflected perceptible trepidation among the membership. Going to Washington represented risk, costly risk. "Granted, our dues have increased drastically but of what significance is this sum in relation to the total budget of any state?" argued the hopeful Phelps. Federal wildlife legislation was proliferating, much of it concerning the regulation of resident species the states could better manage themselves. In Phelps's broad view, having a paid administrator and lobbyist was the only logical way for the Association to influence public policy with some assurance of success, and "the relatively insignificant cost [would] be repaid in many ways, many times." The sudden, almost sevenfold dues increment obviously created hardship and anxiety for the state directors who had not budgeted for it, but Secretary-Treasurer Walter Scott reported that all but six states had paid up in full and all of those six continued their participation with at least the old amount. By the next convention, membership stood once again at 100 percent. The members were ready for their new national role.[1]

As it happened, making the final decision to staff a Washington office proved easier than implementing it, which took three tries. President Phelps thought he had found the right leader in Forrest V. Durand, retired director of the Tennessee game department. Arrangements were sufficiently firm that Durand attended a national meeting and the Association had stationery printed with his name on the letterhead. The Association's bound response to the Public Land Law Review Commission's report of December 1971 also carried his name as Executive Vice-President. Then, precipitously, for "personal reasons," Durand declined the position.[2]

The first active Executive Vice-President of the International Association was Russell J. Neugebauer, who assumed the office on April 1, 1972. Although unfamiliar with the history and work of the International, he had long experience with the Wisconsin Conservation Department, the National Wildlife Federation, the Izaak Walton League, and as a private consultant. His background and continuing contacts with the media and Congress made him a natural for the job; both he and the Association looked forward to a productive relationship in enhancing the influence of the IAGFCC.[3]

Neugebauer's first folksy report to the 1972 convention showed him to be a fast learner and starter. While the Association as yet owned nothing more than a typewriter and filing cabinet, it had acquired an address and equipment in the law offices of Chapman, Duff and Lenzini, thanks to the intercession of Legal Counsel Paul Lenzini. The proximity of attorney and executive was, of course, mutually beneficial. The rent, a modest $250 per month, would soon go up when the Chapman firm moved, and the Association with it, to new headquarters on New York Avenue. Neugebauer, relying upon the assistance and institutional memories of leaders like Walter Scott, Harry Woodward, Les Voigt, and President Ralph MacMullan, set up a letter-based communication system with the state directors, outlined a "progressive, active program" that would keep the association on the offensive in Washington, began to draft an operational manual, and proposed that the International develop a *Reader's Digest*-type magazine to "get our message out to people all over the country" and possibly to help augment the Association's depleted treasury. He closed with an "I love being with you."[4]

MacMullan reported the "whopping long way" the Association had come during the year with the combined efforts of Lenzini "calling the shots" and Neugebauer doing the "leg work." With an efficient administrative system in place and better coordination at all levels, he was "extremely optimistic" that all the hard work was about to pay off. "I think we've taken our place on the shelf along with the other big organizations." Admitting to being "a full-scale worrier," however, MacMullan suspected that the International's financial situation was "not quite what it ought to be." In short, expenses were slightly over budget. He in no way suggested that the Association "even consider stepping back," but income would have to be raised somehow. He hoped it would not be by another dues increase.[5]

The International Association actually hired two people in April 1972. The other was Secretary JoAnna Matson, for whose willingness and efficiency Neugebauer had the highest praise. Matson wrote the thoughtful tribute for the next year's *Proceedings* when Russ Neugebauer died suddenly in December 1972 after just eight months of service. She called him "a sensitive man, dedicated to the cause of conservation, and to making the International a more effective organization." She continued to run the office for the next five months while the Executive Committee searched for its third director of Washington operations in little more than a year. That unfortunate interregnum did have the one positive effect of allowing the Association to accumulate a little advance cash to help pay for its bold venture.[6]

John Gottschalk, who became Executive Vice-President on May 1, 1973, was "perfect" for the job, according to Chester Phelps. The former Director of the Bureau of Sport Fisheries and Wildlife "knew the fish and wildlife business from A to Z" as well as everyone in it. He was a skilled administrator besides. If Gottschalk had a flaw, it was that he was suspect as a "fed." On the other hand, it was his federal service that gave him his vast fund of human and material knowledge. In any practical sense it was Gottschalk who established the Association's Washington presence.[7]

Gottschalk saw the Washington office as "a kind of listening post." He would try to find out what was happening on Capitol Hill and in the executive departments and report back to the states so they could take prompt, efficient action. Neugebauer had issued a series of reports, which Gottschalk would continue for the government members. But he also proposed a more formal, regular, and widely distributed newsletter for all members, including the associates, which the Executive Committee quickly approved. In order to make it a vehicle for disseminating information among the states as well as to and from headquarters, Gottschalk urged the state directors to forward their press releases, policy changes, or problem solutions so he could pass them on.[8]

Volume 1, Number 1, of the IAGFCC *Newsletter* appeared in November 1973, betraying no other evidence of being a "first." It sported the International's new logo, voted upon by the membership in 1972 from a choice of six selected by the International Symbol Committee. Professionally printed, brisk and businesslike in tone, the *Newsletter* featured an overview of the status of current legislation. It also included Association news like new officer lists and committee appointments, upcoming professional meetings, and personal notes about the career moves of state and federal conservationists. News briefs from the field ranged in subject from the Canadian Wildlife Service's efforts toward developing more humane trapping techniques to the $12 million meat value of the 1972

Texas deer kill, which was presented in contrast to projected drought-induced losses.[9]

Gottschalk urged the Association members to look beyond parochial concerns and become more involved in national and state political issues. Lobbying was not only respectable; it was crucial. Acting in the political arena as wildlife professionals, not politicians, conservationists must let their legislators know who they were, whom they represented, and what they thought about vital issues. Most members of Congress welcomed "expert knowledge presented in a professional way," he said, and they knew he would know. He also nudged them to work within their committees on a year-round basis, not just before conventions, to increase their knowledge and effectiveness.[10]

Meanwhile, the Washington-based Association initiated more efficient fiscal practices. Chester Phelps, in his new position as Secretary-Treasurer, reported in 1974 the hiring of certified public accountants to prepare the International's financial statements and a changeover to make the fiscal and audit years correspond with the calendar year. In 1974 the Association also moved its headquarters to the National Wildlife Federation building on 16th Street, Northwest, when NWF Executive Vice-President Kimball offered free rent. Even when that necessitated the purchase of $1,500 worth of furniture, the $4,200 rent savings was significant. Using a tape recorder instead of a court reporter to document convention transactions, curtailing the length and distribution of the published *Proceedings*, and limiting participation in legal cases to those of principles basic to all members represented further efforts to stretch thin dollars. Spiraling costs for printing, paper, and utilities that struck everywhere during this inflationary decade also shook the Association's viability just when the Washington office was getting under way.[11]

Once more the state conservationists had to consider assessing themselves more heavily for membership in the International. Proposals in 1974 to increase state dues to $1,500, other governmental memberships to $150, and associate memberships to $7.50 (from a recently raised $5) all passed, as did the establishment of a new category, Affiliated Organization Memberships, at $50 annual dues. The International was happy to approve the membership applications of three such conservation-related organizations in 1975, which modestly expanded its purse as well as its base of support. Income would finally exceed outgo in 1975, but the next ten years would see the necessity for doubling the state dues, not once but twice. Nevertheless, the Association was putting the machinery in place to play a larger role than ever before in national conservation matters, and the members were eager to get on with it.[12]

The Antihunting Menace

Unfortunately, one of conservationists' most pressing, frustrating problems was attitudinal and therefore one that offered only qualified hope of mitigation by official action. That problem was the mounting, increasingly virulent antihunting sentiment sweeping the country. The media sensationalized the already sensitive issue. In November 1969, for example, an NBC television program called "The Wolf Man" showed the slaughter of "our few remaining wolves" from low-flying aircraft. Assistant Interior Secretary Glasgow telegraphed Association President Woodward that his department had gotten nearly 4,000 letters from citizens revolted by this "callous and unsportsmanlike killing." No one in the International condoned hunting from planes, and indeed virtually all states had laws against it. Airings like this one, however, went beyond specific incidents to question all hunting, whether as a sport or a conservation tool. Glasgow appealed to the International for help in local public relations efforts and in promoting uniform state laws that would show hunters to be responsible, contributing citizens.[13]

Television struck again, on January 8, 1971, when NBC telecast the documentary "Say Goodbye" that included footage of the shooting from a helicopter of a female polar bear with cubs. The independent producer, Wolper Productions, had used film supplied by the Alaska Department of Fish and Game. By adroit cutting and splicing, however, it had created the impression that the bear was heartlessly killed and her cubs orphaned when in fact she had fallen from a tranquilizing shot administered in "a scientific and humane project designed to improve knowledge of polar bear." The sow later rejoined her offspring, none of them harmed, but the film did not show this, and public reaction was predictable.

The members of the International were furious. Chester Phelps, then President, fired off a press release and a letter to NBC in protest to "manipulations such as this" that "make no contribution to wildlife conservation," and indeed, "unfairly [undermine] public faith in federal and statewide wildlife officials." He asked the network to make a full investigation and report so he could inform the wildlife management agents who would have to respond to criticism leveled by misled viewers.

To its credit, NBC responded to Phelps through Vice-President Robert D. Kasmire within two weeks. Wolper had admitted to creating a composite scene by editing stock footage of the shooting of a male bear outside the territorial limits of the United States together with the Alaska film of the anesthetized female. The company justified its approach in order "to dramatize authenticated facts" concerning wildlife species threatened by human encroachment. Kasmire promised that the network would develop guidelines to prevent future misleading occurrences. And it did: "Where the program presents scenes of animal behavior or other scenes from nature as actualities, care must be taken to avoid giving the viewer mistaken impressions, and the use of staging, re-creation, reenactment, or dramatization must be disclosed." The Association had showed its clout and won concessions for the future, but of course that did little for the considerable damage already done to game managers' collective image.[14]

And it happened again. In 1975 CBS produced "The Guns of Autumn," a purported analysis of hunting and wildlife management. In the words of the Association's blistering resolution, the program "grossly misrepresented its subject matter" and "falsely portrayed and demeaned the successful effort of thousands" of state and federal officials legally responsible for North American wildlife. Further, it was "so lacking in balance, fairness and good taste as to suggest intentional distortion of natural resource management and hunting, thereby reducing broadcast journalism to an instrument of propaganda ultimately destructive of wildlife." The members instructed their officers and vowed themselves to protest the content and technique of "The Guns of Autumn" to CBS and the Federal Communications Commission as well as complain to local affiliates carrying the show. They did, but the program had already reached its audience.[15]

Other contemporary examples of the growing antihunting, antimanagement campaign included a spate of books that ranged from protectionism to a new emphasis on "animal rights," such as Cleveland Amory's 1974 *Man Kind? Our Incredible War on Wildlife*, in which the author featured photographs of trapped animals dying in protracted agony and used provocative section titles like "Support Your Right to Arm Bears" and "Real People Wear Fake Furs." The IAGFCC *Newsletter* reported in March 1974 that *Scholastic Magazine* had polled high school students for their views on a variety of subjects. The list itself was revealing: Watergate, President Nixon, hunting, mercy killing, and price controls. Forty-six percent of the students thought hunting should be banned as a sport; only 11 percent disagreed.[16]

The Association had already created a Promotion of Recreational Hunting Committee in 1970 to counter such attitudes. Its report the next year consisted of fourteen recommendations that ranged from educating the public about hunters' monetary contributions to wildlife to encouraging hunters to be safety conscious and sensitive to the ecological and sentimental concerns of other citizens. The Committee also strongly urged that the International undertake a professional study of the antihunting movement in order better to combat it.[17]

To learn more about antihunters, an introspective Association in 1972 heard a panel discuss the question, "Is Wildlife Management Responsive to Society's Concerns?" Justin Leonard of the University of Michigan gave a scholarly analysis of hunters and protectionists. Unhappy with how "Say Goodbye" had ascribed to sport hunters "almost undivided responsibility for destruction of non-game species, from the egret to the blue whale," he cited a Cleveland Amory interview in which the latter had admitted that only 3.6 percent of the people of California hunted. Yet, said Leonard, following the logic, "they somehow seemed to be leading the other 96.4 percent into all manner of reprehensible policies and practices." Leonard advised the game managers to pursue their educational efforts more vigorously.

John A. Hoyt, President of the Humane Society of the United States, predictably had a different message. He disputed that the licenses of "sport hunters" (quotation marks his) "carried the freight" of wildlife management any longer. He named Wisconsin, where he said licenses contributed no more than 15 percent of the state's natural resources budget; he had observed a "similar trend" elsewhere. "Don't be beguiled," Hoyt warned, "into believing that high powered and heavily financed house organs and lobbyists of the gun manufacturers accurately represent the increasing ecological and humane awareness of the American people." Professing to care more about the manner of killing than its fact, he suggested game management alternatives to hunting such as "reproductive inhibitors, live-trapping, redistribution of surplus animals, or the reintroduction of natural predators." If Hoyt would be no great help to the state conservationists' program, his was one of the more reasonable opposition voices.[18]

Wildlife managers were encouraged when President Nixon signed a Senate resolution to declare the fourth Saturday of each September "National Hunting and Fishing Day." In 1972 some 3,000 National Hunting and Fishing Day observances were held across the country, coordinated by the National Shooting Sports Foundation. The NSSF also issued inexpensive pamphlets reminding the public and hunters themselves about hunters' self-imposed excise tax that supported wildlife restoration to the tune of $40 million annually. The fact that out of 796 species of birds in America only seventy-four were hunted was also featured.[19]

The states also took the initiative in dealing with the "anti" movement. Several varieties of game remained plentiful in Ohio, for example, and with continuing high prices for fur, harvesting furbearers was an important economic activity. The antitrapping movement became a particular threat. The Ohio Wildlife Division undertook a massive educational campaign that included petitions against antitrapping petitions, film clips on positive wildlife management, well-timed testimony before the state legislature, and the solicitation of support of outdoor writers and businesses benefiting from hunting. The game interests beat the antitrapping bill in Ohio, but similar efforts elsewhere would fare differently.[20]

Every year the International Association of Game, Fish and Conservation Commissioners had to consider again the effects of antimanagement sentiment on the futures of state conservationists. In 1975 Gottschalk ran a lengthy newsletter column reviewing a Forest Service study on hunters and hunting. The researchers concluded that the state game agencies had to take the leadership role in promoting and implementing positive change, since they were the "fulcrum, balancing the concerns of sportsmen and landowners while being responsible for the welfare and health of game animals." The state wildlife managers should emphasize education and safety programs, sportsmanship, and a conservation ethic with hunters to improve their image. They should solicit hunter cooperation in law enforcement and deemphasize the killing of game among the many attractions of hunting.[21]

Management Vindicated, Nonhunters Accommodated

State game officials finally won not only vindication but grudging admiration for their management role in 1982 as a result of the well-publicized Everglades Deer Hunt. Colonel Robert Brantly, Executive Director of the Florida Game and Fresh Water Fish Commission, recapped the story for his Association colleagues. About 5,500 deer inhabited a two-sectioned, million-acre area in the Florida Everglades. But in May and June 1982, prolonged tropical storms and water diversion from other areas into this flood-control region caused water levels to rise from two to three feet. In six weeks the deer range was reduced by 90 percent. From past experience game managers knew a deer die-off was imminent, caused by the stress of excessive energy expenditure to find food. Moreover, disease transmitted by crowding and dirty water would further weaken the herd. Dead deer, including adults, were already documented. Immediate action being imperative, the state game commission recommended an emergency hunt of substantial proportions.[22]

In July, however, the Fund for Animals and other animal rights groups filed for an injunction to stop the hunt, contending that the deer had "rights," that shooting was inhumane, and that other endangered species would be harassed by the noise of airboats and other hunter traffic. They suggested the deer be captured and relocated, fed by air drop, or assisted with artificial islands.

The news media found a hot story. At one time more than 150 television reporters converged on the site or hovered in helicopters overhead. Soon the wildlife commissioners had to defend their actions in both state and federal courts. The International Association gave its immediate support, especially through attorney Lenzini, who got himself to Florida within hours to coordinate its legal defense. The state prevailed in both forums. While the scheduled hunt was delayed, however, the opposition forces convinced thousands of people that they could rescue 2,000 deer in eight days, or 250 a day. So Brantly shrewdly offered them two and a half days to capture and relocate 100 deer in exchange for an agreement not to seek the additional legal stay they had planned.[23]

The hunt proceeded in the southern section of the area while the rescuers went to work in the northern. The results were clear and instructive. Surveys showed a loss of 65.3 percent of the northern herd compared with 22.8 percent in the south, including the 723 taken by hunters. Meanwhile, the rescuers captured eighteen deer, half of whom died in the rescue attempt or soon after. Before it was over, public response became more friendly to the game managers. Florida headlines such as "Where are you now, Cleveland [Amory], that the deer need you?" did much to hearten the management proponents even though the national television cameras had already gone home.[24]

Could hunters and protectionists find any common ground? Stephen Kellert of Yale University's School of Forestry and Environmental Studies conducted several scholarly studies of changing attitudes toward wildlife during the 1970s. In a 1978 paper, "Attitudes and Characteristics of Hunters and Antihunters," he described holders of ten overlapping but separable attitudes toward animals, from naturalists who wanted their outdoors world unadulterated to scientists to aesthetes who saw beauty in wildlife. Not surprisingly, Kellert concluded that hunters tended to be dominionists wanting control or mastery over animals and utilitarians who emphasized animals' material value, while antihunters were more moralistic and humanistic in their opposition to exploitation and cruelty and their tendencies toward anthropomorphism. He also found the latter group to be disproportionately female, urban, and lacking in knowledge or experience with animals. But both of these opposing camps professed an ecological viewpoint, a primary concern for the environment. The dialogue should begin there, Kellert said. Moreover, the ecological attitude discouraged "antihunting sentiment based on anthropomorphic notions derived from intuitive emotion, and [opposed] hunting practiced without regard for the needs of game animals in their natural habitats." He suggested a multiple-use emphasis as well as the funding of research and recreation programs involving nongame wildlife.[25]

Indeed, many states consciously began adopting nongame programs. Oregon, for example, encouraged its citizens to support "Watchable Wildlife," finding in that phrase and a winsome raccoon logo, positiveness and "pizazz" not present in the negative connotations of "nongame." Missouri conservationists, after a systematic study of game and nongame needs as well as grim fiscal realities, proposed a comprehensive "Design for Conservation" to be funded through a tiny increase in the state sales tax. Missouri's citizens responded to a massive campaign for support and approved the required constitutional amendment. The earmarked fund thus created nearly doubled the state's conservation budget. The federal Fish and Wildlife Coordination Act, or "Nongame Act," of 1980 encouraged state programs for both game and nongame species by providing funding from general appropriations for projects identified through comprehensive planning. Perhaps wildlife advocates of all persuasions could agree on some constructive programs after all.[26]

State v. Federal Authority: The Marine Mammals

When John Gottschalk was asked to contribute a chapter to *Wildlife in America*, a Bicentennial book by top wildlife experts for the Council on Environmental Quality, on the topic "State v. Federal Authority over Wildlife," he chose instead to entitle it "The State-Federal Partnership in Wildlife Conservation." His often repeated philosophy that the feds and the states, each ineffective without the other, "must travel together into tomorrow," helped smooth the path of cooperation. But, while the overall jurisdictional climate was becoming more moderate and mutually accommodating, the partnership was not without tension. Continuing and new issues engaged the attention of both sides during the 1970s and beyond, with new legislation, topically significant in its own right, more often than not tipping the balance away from state autonomy and authority.[27]

The Marine Mammal Protection Act of 1972, which imposed a moratorium on the taking or importation of marine mammals or products made from them, was a broad-brush federal attempt at comprehensive marine mammal restoration and conservation programs. By the act the federal government preempted state authority over these animals "until such time as a state [prepared] a marine mammal management program consistent with the Act." The law, intended to be "neither purely protectionist nor purely exploitive," was exceedingly complex. Its exceptions for scientific research or public display purposes, harvest by natives for subsistence or folk craft manufacture, or takings incidental to commercial fishing all created numerous and varied difficulties. Jack Berryman called the enforcement machinery of the act an "administrative monstrosity," with responsibility for the various marine mammals divided between the Department of Interior and the Department of Commerce with an overlay of interference by an independent, scientifically expert, but in fact semipolitical Marine Mammals Commission.[28]

Gottschalk said the immediate practical effect of the law was to "divest most marine mammals of any protection," since what state regulations there were, admittedly few except in Alaska, were undercut by federal procedures too complicated to allow effective cooperation. For example, in Alaska coastal natives had for years depended upon the walrus for subsistence. They consumed the flesh and blubber, made leather of the hide, and created salable craft items from the tusks and other parts. Since statehood, Alaskan conservationists had with some success encouraged the Eskimos to protect pregnant cows and walrus young, but the state's efforts were halted by the explicit exemption for natives in the Marine Mammals Act. The Fish and Wildlife Service, understaffed and underfunded, could not even monitor the scattered walrus hunters. James Brooks, Alaska's Fish and Game Commissioner, spelled out the state's woes to the International at its 1975 convention. He called the results of Congress's "good intentions" and great effort "a resource conservation disaster." The congressional hearings, he said, had clearly established that Alaska's management program was successful, that marine mammal populations were, if not increasing, being sustained at high levels. Yet the new law disrupted ongoing practices that worked.[29]

Alaska, in 1973, petitioned for the return of its management jurisdiction over walrus under a complicated mechanism established by the Marine Mammals Act, but the confused executive departments really did not know how to proceed. They asked for an environmental impact statement and seemed to be stalling. Meanwhile, the nullified state conservation program was virtually helpless against wasteful but legal renewed killing of polar bear, seals, and walrus. Brooks closed with a plea to federal resource administrators to "take courage and make decisions that are appropriate to resource and environmental needs rather than manicuring them to avoid lawsuits by extremists' interests" and to "acknowledge that you do not have the awareness of local or regional concerns, the science, the money, the manpower or the moral mandate to justify or support further centralization of resource management authority in the federal bureaucracy." The Association, by resolution, repeatedly supported Alaska's position on marine mammals in particular and state management in general.[30]

Alaska regained authority over walrus and their harvest provisionally in 1975, but procedural tangles continued. Then, the natives, who insisted their exemption under the moratorium was still in effect, brought suit against the Interior Department, which had decreed the exemption rescinded when the state resumed management. When the Eskimos won, in People of Togiak v. United States, Alaska returned its jurisdiction over walrus to the federal government; under its constitutional prohibition of discrimination among its citizens, it could not legally give preferred hunting status to the natives. Meanwhile, federal officials, anticipating state takeover and unable to do much, did practically nothing to manage the animals. Finally, the law itself was overhauled in 1981 to be more clear and usable. It also "explicitly" overruled the Togiak decision so that Alaskan natives would be subject to state regulation. But Alaska, for political reasons, elected not to resume its authority. The controversy is quiescent, but nonmanagement continues. Ironically, the problem has become one of overabundance. Only natives can take walrus under the MMPA, and even though their kill increased threefold in the decade since 1972, the walrus population has exceeded the carrying capacity of its habitat. The situation remains in ecological as well as political disequilibrium.[31]

Endangered Species: More on Authority

Endangered species legislation represented another serious preemption of state authority. Preserving jeopardized classes of animals had become a popular cause as well as a major concern within the professional conservation movement. Federal efforts went back as far as early twentieth-century programs to save the bison and elk, but during the 1960s and 1970s interest and action intensified. The first Endangered Species Act of 1966 gave the Secretary of the Interior authority to fund studies and purchase lands for the support of endangered species. A supplemental law in 1969 authorized the Secretary to develop a list of species "threatened with worldwide extinction" and prohibit their importation in addition to increasing federal funding for land acquisition. Public pressure still increased, and in 1973 Congress passed a new act that further empowered the Interior Secretary (or the Commerce Secretary for marine species) to regulate the taking of animals in immediate endangerment or deemed to be threatened in the foreseeable future over all or a significant portion of their range. It was also designed to implement a new international treaty on endangered species.[32]

Testimony at the hearings for the 1973 Endangered Species Act included arguments that "the many efficient state management programs for the benefit of endangered species ought to be protected and not undercut by Federal legislation." The final act, a product of several combined bills and compromises in Conference Committee, charged the Department of Interior or Commerce, as appropriate, "to cooperate with the States to the maximum extent possible" and authorized the Secretary to provide financial assistance to any state with which it had a cooperative program to benefit an endangered species, up to three-fourths of the cost of an approved project. If state law were more restrictive than the federal, it would take precedence.[33]

The International Association of Game, Fish and Conservation Commissioners had applauded pro-state phrases in the legislation, but distrusted their practical application. Working hard with the 1973 Congress to establish protections for endangered species while preserving state authority, the Association had insisted that any preemption of state authority be balanced with a correspondingly strong federal program in the interests of the affected wildlife and their habitat. If the states were to be prevented from managing their animals, federal authorities must accept their responsibility to do so, the states declared. The resulting Section 7 of the act prohibited any federal agency from funding a project adversely affecting endangered species. For example, by this act the Department of Defense could not construct bombing ranges or channelize rivers that imperiled classes of animals (or plants).[34]

Section 7 of the Endangered Species Act became its "most potent weapon against the loss of species," but in a 1974 analysis, law student Rudy Lachenmeier predicted that Section 7 would prove "unworkable" since threatened or endangered species and their critical habitat were to be the "sole consideration" when agencies contemplated spending federal funds on environment-altering projects of any sort. In case of conflict, federal authorities had no power "to balance the impact on the species against the importance of the affected activity to the Nation." Lachenmeier suggested changes in the wording to favor the saving of a species "threatened with worldwide extinction" unless such an action required "an overriding and overwhelming risk to man." A copy of Lachenmeier's article in the Association's files contains penned marginal comments calling the author's conclusion "overly pessimistic" and noting that "this hypothesis assumes a totally inept administration of Section 7 and ignores the 'due process' aspects implied by the use of the term 'determination' of critical habitat!"[35]

History seemed to fulfill Lachenmeier's prediction when the tiny snail darter held up construction, already substantially completed, of the Tennessee Valley Authority's Tellico Dam in 1978. Only the most extreme protectionist could get overwrought over the insignificant little fish, which, in any case, subsequently appeared in other area rivers in thriving condition. But as Thomas Kimball of the National Wildlife Federation pointed out, the issue was larger than the snail darter. Unless a firm stand was taken against "politically-inspired exemptions" to the Endangered Species Act, the law would be weakened to practical worthlessness. The Supreme Court ultimately ruled that the law was clear and halted work on the dam. Congress thereupon amended the Endangered Species Act, establishing an Endangered Species Committee, or so-called God Committee, that was empowered to grant exemptions to the strictures of Section 7 if there were "no reasonable and prudent alternatives" to the agency's action, if the benefits of the project outweighed the benefits of available nonjeopardizing alternatives, or if the action were of regional or national importance. The Committee unanimously agreed that the dam failed to meet these criteria. Finally, in 1980, Congress assumed responsibility for the fate of the snail darter by exempting the Tellico Dam from federal law by a rider to another bill. If neither this particular dam nor the snail darter merited such costly attention, the basic lesson that biological assessment was essential and must occur prior to commencement of construction was clear.[36]

Meanwhile, the states on their own, and collectively through the International, prepared their own strategies for managing endangered species. Gottschalk devoted the bulk of his second IAGFCC *Newsletter* to the Endangered Species Act, calling particular attention to the "urgent need for the states to act promptly" to safeguard their management authority under the new law. He further implored the federal agencies to act expeditiously on preparing guidelines, approving state cooperative programs, and securing adequate funding.[37] Indeed, thirty-five states already had endangered species programs that included listings, prohibitions on taking, and habitat management. Furthermore, in 1973 the states had approximately 6,000 conservation agents to carry out such work compared with 158 federal officials, most of the latter located in ports of entry.

Yet, despite professed congressional intent to give the states a key role in implementing the new law and the inability of the federal government to act alone, the states found their work hampered by confused authority, lack of both state and federal money, complex procedural regulations, and, worst of all, the Secretaries' listing animals without consultation with the states. Such bowing to protectionist pressures often left the newly listed animal with no protection at any level.[38]

Difficulties with implementing the Endangered Species Act were exemplified by the problem of the eastern timber wolf, which had been listed as endangered under it. Perhaps it was imperiled elsewhere, but not in his state, protested Robert Herbst, Commissioner of Minnesota's Department of Natural Resources, in a September 1974 letter to Lynn Greenwalt of the Fish and Wildlife Service. Herbst asked Greenwalt to delist the timber wolf in Minnesota because the species met "none of the criteria" for endangerment enumerated in the Act. The wolves' habitat was not threatened except by natural forest maturation, which tended to drive deer away, but wolf protection would only increase depredation on the already low deer population. The timber wolf was not being overutilized; indeed, its current population was the highest ever reported along the North Shore of Lake Superior and its range was expanding despite limited predator control outside its main range. Disease was not a problem. The state management system was working well but needed continuing balance. Predator numbers were dependent upon prey numbers. If too many wolves killed too many deer, thereby destroying their own food supply, they would next stalk moose or beaver or livestock. Conflicts with residents would inevitably follow. Herbst pledged to manage wolves "according to a realistic appraisal of ecological factors" and to strive for a reasonable balance of all interests when human and wolf interest collided. But the federal machinery was not easily moved.[39]

The problem deteriorated to the point that Minnesota Congressman James Oberstar drew up a bill to allow people who had lost livestock to wolf depredation to lay claims for damages against the federal government. Gottschalk took a dim view of this approach despite the bill's specific disclaimer against precedent setting. Besides difficulties in validating charges, would not such a measure open the door of government responsibility for all manner of wildlife damages, from migratory birds devouring rice crops to alligators chewing children? Potential costs could be staggering. Gottschalk suggested that Minnesota's citizens would be better protected by placing the wolves under a responsible, realistic state-run management program that would control their numbers and whereabouts, thus making them tolerable to the residents. The wolf now, he said, "has become, at best, a symbol of federal indifference to local problems."[40]

Other states voiced similar complaints of losing control over successful management programs with unhappy results. Montana and Wyoming were capably restoring their grizzly bear populations, but federal edict under the Endangered Species Act arbitrarily curtailed hunting even though state officials recognized that habitat loss through land development was the real problem. Louisiana's alligators, having made, under a vigorous state conservation program, a healthy comeback from earlier overharvesting, almost became nuisances when federal law preempted state authority. Overly protective measures for alligators, in turn, led to danger for their furbearing prey and fears that landowners, unable to profit from the harvest of alligator hides, would drain their habitat for crop production. Kimball and others urged a broader view, but working out program details for such complex ecological problems daunted the most intelligent and well-intentioned professionals.[41]

International Trade and Endangered Species

At the same time that conservationists were trying to forge domestic programs, international aspects of endangered species management took center stage. As required by the 1969 law, the United States hosted in early 1973 a conference in Washington of wildlife experts from eighty nations. Its purpose was to create a system of international cooperation to ensure the survival of endangered wildlife and plants. The IAGFCC's John Gottschalk and many others participated on the United States team led by Russell Train, chairman of the Council on Environmental Quality. Three weeks of intense negotiation, under the diplomatic chairmanship of American ambassador Christian A. Herter, Jr., produced a unique and far-reaching document called the Convention on International Trade in Endangered Species of Wild Fauna and Flora (CITES).

Ambassador Wymberley Coerr, Advisor on Conservation Affairs in the State Department and U.S. delegation manager, related the work of the conference and the nature of the Convention to the International Association of Game, Fish and Conservation Commissioners at its 1973 annual meeting. The need, he said, stemmed from the danger to domestic wildlife of foreign demand. If, for example, European coat manufacturers, paying high prices for the furs of African leopards, encouraged poachers in Kenya, the cats could become threatened by inadequate local law enforcement on either continent. So preventing trade through internationally agreed-upon import and export controls, not the usual species or habitat management programs, provided the key to conserving endangered species worldwide. The Convention applied to both live animals and products made from them. A special section dealt with species inhabiting international waters. An international Secretariat within the United

Nations Environmental Program would serve as a coordinating organization, while each signatory country would establish a Management Authority, to issue import and export permits and monitor the affected trade, and a Scientific Authority, to provide independent scientific review of trade permit applications and advice on the status of particular species.

Three CITES appendices identified the animals, plants, or derivatives thereof, in the order of their degree of perceived endangerment and need for protection. Commercial trade in specimens of species listed in Appendix I, those threatened with extinction, was virtually eliminated. Appendix II listed species not imminently threatened but felt to be needing regulation to prevent endangerment as well as species requiring regulation in order to protect other threatened types, such as symbionts or look-alikes. Trade in Appendix II animals required an export permit based on the host country Scientific Authority's determination that trade would cause "no detriment" to the survival of the species. Any participating nation could list in Appendix III species it identified as being subject to regulation within its own jurisdiction and needing the cooperation of other countries to control its trade; for these species, an export permit was required.[42]

Ambassador Coerr reflected conservationists' general sense of optimistic anticipation over this treaty, which was the first one worldwide in both species application and participation, the first to pursue conservation through trade controls, and the first to utilize systematic scientific judgment for decision making on commerce in wildlife actually or potentially at risk. The United States quickly signed and ratified the Convention, which went into effect in 1975 when ten nations had approved it at Berne, Switzerland.[43]

High hopes soon turned to dismay for the American state game conservationists as the CITES agreement, like other protective laws before it, threatened their authority over their own wildlife. In 1976 twenty parties to the Convention (along with five nonparty nations and about twenty observer organizations) met at Berne for the first time since the initial negotiations to hammer out the mechanical details necessary to implement the treaty. Two actions taken there created consternation within the International Association. First, the attendees added all members of the family Felidae not already listed on Appendices I or III to Appendix II, in an apparent effort to protect the world's great spotted cats. William Huey, Secretary of New Mexico's Natural Resources Department, who reported to the Association in 1980, thought that this action had been "blessed with considerably more sentimental concern than biological knowledge." Then the international delegates developed what came to be known as the Berne Criteria, which identified procedures for adding or deleting species in the appendices. The criteria made it much more difficult to remove a species than to insert one. Further, the Berne Criteria for removal assumed that the standards for listing had been followed, which was not necessarily so.[44]

The proceedings at Berne put animals such as the American bobcat, lynx, and river otter on the CITES Appendix II. These species had enjoyed qualitative and quantitative health under state management, their harvest a significant economic pursuit in several states. The price of bobcat pelts in the latter half of the 1970s was up, the demand high. The Convention did not interfere with states in the taking of these animals, but it did regulate their international shipment. And the market was overseas.

Responsibility for advice on export permission lay with the Endangered Species Scientific Authority (ESSA), composed of representatives of six federal agencies and the Smithsonian Institution and accountable, as it happened, to no one. Its Executive Secretary, William Y. Brown, made no friends in the International Association when he spoke to its convention in 1977. In the absence of numerical population estimates and a tagging system for pelts, the ESSA would recommend that export be prohibited, he said. Most of the affected states were not counting bobcats. Not only was the task formidable, especially with limited resources, but without any reason to worry about their numbers, it seemed a waste of money. Already annoyed that bobcats were listed in the first place, the frustrated state wildlife managers argued that population trends should suffice to show lack of endangerment, but the ESSA insisted on a more rigorously based "no detriment" finding.[45]

The International Association went to work on several fronts to resolve the bobcat problem. In 1978 the *Newsletter* reported that the ESSA had convened a working group to discuss bobcats, lynx, and river otter. It concluded that blanket inclusions of these species on Appendix II was "inappropriate," and while the states should improve their research programs on the affected animals, they should also be consulted on international agreements that directly affected them.[46] That same year the Association resolved that whereas these animals had been "improvidently" and uninformedly listed, which "undermined the integrity of the Convention" and required state action directing "limited resources away from priority needs of other wildlife populations," and whereas they met the criteria for delisting, the Department of Interior should "take immediate and effective steps" at the upcoming CITES meeting in Costa Rica to achieve delistment.[47]

Huey attended the Costa Rica meeting and came away even more disillusioned. In addition to the thirty-four signatories (of the total of fifty-one) and sixteen nonparty nations, some fifty-six nongovernmental organizations participated in the negotiations, as was apparently acceptable under the terms of the Convention. Their active presence disturbed Huey, who felt they "exerted a significant, but improper influence" on the proceedings. Most of them were protectionist organizations—highly visible, well organized, and well financed. They did their main lobbying at parties and receptions they hosted. Huey noted their effect as several votes overrode the United States' position regardless of "sound biological principles." He was particularly distressed by defeats on issues involving species found only in North America and on which Canada, Mexico, and the United States were in agreement. He dryly observed that the nongovernmental organizations were quite willing, however, to let the United States bear the major financial burden of implementing the Convention. The New Mexico conservationist warned his colleagues that if they considered the states' role in wildlife management important to wildlife survival, they needed to give serious attention to the question of the nation's current and future involvement in international agreements. He had in mind a new treaty on migratory birds then being shaped in Bonn, Germany.[48]

Meanwhile, congressional oversight hearings in 1979 revealed that an "uncooperative and, on occasion, antagonistic relationship" between the Management Authority and the Scientific Authority had "caused a breakdown in the system for permitting trade, disrupted state wildlife management programs, and confused the respective roles of the two agencies." The International Association testified that the ESSA's lack of criteria and standards made its requests for biological data "impossible to fulfill" and its self-appointed task of assuring "optimum" populations beyond its charge of preventing endangerment. The ESSA had "transcended its fundamental purpose, to assure the scientific soundness of government decisions, and [attempted] to develop" for itself a trade restricting role "never intended by CITES" or authorized by the Endangered Species Act. Chairman Breaux of the oversight subcommittee laid the bulk of the blame to the "uniquely autonomous nature of the ESSA which allowed it to frustrate administrative guidance" and unilaterally "rewrite the treaty." The subcommittee proposed amending the Endangered Species Act to transfer the independent ESSA to a unit of the Fish and Wildlife Service. That would make the Interior Secretary accountable for both the Management Authority and the Scientific Authority and would establish the ESSA clearly as an advisory, not a regulatory, body.[49]

Gottschalk dispatched "URGENT" memoranda to all of the Association's governmental members in late September and early October 1979, pressing them to lobby their congressional delegations in support of Breaux's amendment. He reminded them that Breaux's proposal was "opposed vigorously by a coalition of 'environmental' groups led by the Defenders of Wildlife, who believe the Fish and Wildlife Service not to be trusted to make unbiased decisions" on CITES-listed species. The Association's Executive Committee, on the contrary, believed a more accountable ESSA would "produce a healthier atmosphere for cooperation between the states and the federal government" in administering CITES without jeopardizing any species legitimately covered by it. Canada had already combined its Scientific and Management Authorities, delegating their function to the provinces.[50]

The states responded promptly, vigorously, and in volume to Gottschalk's call for action. Robert Jantzen, Director of Arizona's Game and Fish Department, for example, sent a night letter to congressional leaders to urge the restoration of ESSA's intended advisory function within the FWS. The ESSA's arbitrary regulation of the export of bobcat pelts served "no useful end," he said, and had caused Arizona's trappers many problems. Minnesota Commissioner Joseph Alexander's letter made the point that overregulating nonthreatened animals "diverts needed public funds from authentic endangered species which deserve such attention."[51]

The resulting amendment, passed in December 1979, made the Secretary of the Interior both the Management Authority and the Scientific Authority under CITES and established a separate International Convention Advisory Commission (ICAC). The ICAC was organized like the old ESSA with one more member to represent the state wildlife agencies. Its advisory function was more clearly spelled out. The Secretary was not obligated to heed the Commission's advice but had to publish reasons when choosing not to do so.[52]

Despite the Association-supported appointment of Dr. Douglas Crowe, bobcat ecology expert from Wyoming, as the state fish and wildlife representative, it took little time for the ICAC to prove just as troublesome as the original ESSA. Legislative Counsel Wesley Hayden testified in December 1981 before the Senate Subcommittee on Environmental Pollution that the Association remained "strongly committed" to endangered species legislation and the CITES agreement, but they were not working as intended. The International Convention Advisory Commission, Hayden said, was meant to streamline implementation of the CITES agreement and provide accountable scientific advice to the Interior Secretary. It did neither. Interior's transfer of its CITES responsibilities to the ICAC only added an additional layer of bureaucracy and "compounded the entire problem." Worse, the ICAC had "fostered recommendations and policies inconsistent with sound wildlife and fishery management practices," Crowe's dissenting opinions notwithstanding. Let an expanded professional staff at the Fish and Wildlife Service do the job of the Scientific Authority, urged Hayden, through the "normal and accountable decision making process." Eliminating the ICAC, the Association's strong recommendation, would save the United States "upwards of $300,000 annually." The ESA Reauthorization Act of October 1982 did abolish the ICAC, much to the relief of the game managers and greater efficiency of future CITES-related decision making.[53]

The bobcat continued to be the centerpiece of state conservationists' difficulties in international and domestic endangered species management. While the Association worked for bobcat delistment, more workable export regulations, and legislation recognizing state authority, it also participated in litigation in order to protect the states' ability to function financially and administratively in wildlife management. The Endangered Species Scientific Authority had finally determined, on the basis of population-trend information and other scientific indicators supplied by the states, that the export of bobcat pelts, or parts, from a state's legal harvest during the 1979 and 1980 seasons would not be detrimental to the survival of the species in the United States. When the Management Authority then granted export permits to thirty-five states, the Defenders of Wildlife brought suit against the ESSA. Defenders argued that numerical population and harvest estimates were necessary to make a no-detriment finding; trend information would not do. Further, considering state data unreliable, they insisted the ESSA must generate its own numbers to support export conclusions. The International Association entered the case in support of the ESSA. The U.S. District Court for the District of Columbia threw out most of the plaintiff's challenge, but Defenders of Wildlife appealed. The U.S. Court of Appeals in Washington, D.C., reversed the lower court in part, holding that CITES required total bobcat population estimates for no-detriment findings. The lower court then issued an injunction enjoining further export of bobcat pelts. The Supreme Court denied the Association's petition for review of the case.[54]

Following disappointment in the courts, the Association once again sought remedial legislation. In October 1982 Congress responded by amending the Endangered Species Act to overrule legislatively the higher court's bobcat decision. The lawmakers made it clear that primary authority for the protection and management of a listed species such as the bobcat resided in the states, and therefore the Secretary's no-detriment findings were properly based on state agency-generated data. The Association and federal defendants (ESSA) then successfully applied to the district court to get the bobcat injunction lifted. Defenders of Wildlife appealed again, but this time the Court of Appeals ruled, as it had to, that the 1982 ESA amendments overrode its earlier opinion. Bobcat litigation had cost the International prodigious effort and more than $120,000, but winning that one major point, recognition of state authority, it believed, justified the expenditure.[55]

The Bonn Convention Rejected

As already mentioned, international efforts in wildlife management were broader than CITES in the 1970s. In 1978 the government of West Germany proposed a new treaty, eventually entitled the "International Convention for the Conservation of Migratory Species of Wild Animals," or, popularly, the "Bonn Convention." Its purpose was to guarantee strict protection for migratory wildlife considered in danger of extinction and to establish conservation programs for migratory species in general. Such programs would include the regulation of hunting and fishing and the protection of essential habitat. The convention itself would be an international framework for a series of multilateral agreements among "range states" (countries) that jointly provided habitat for a migratory species. The treaty proposal grew out of European conservationists' concerns over the impact of continued year-round exploitation of Eurasian and African migratory birds, but, as drafted, it would apply to any nonresident wildlife.[56]

By the time a second draft of the proposed Bonn Convention circulated among interested countries, the members of the International Association had serious doubts about it, even as they and the State and Interior Departments saw its need and approved the general concept. Mindful of ongoing frustrations with CITES, the Association would not go lightly into any new entanglements. Richard Yancey of the Louisiana Department of Wildlife and Fisheries, who chaired both the Association's International Treaties and Migratory Bird Committees and also served on the U.S. delegation to the treaty conferences, kept the Association informed. Several states had already pointed out that the treaty as proposed "paves the way for federal takeover" of management responsibility for numerous game and nongame species. Even United States jurisdiction would be threatened with international preemption. Furthermore, since the United States already participated in migratory bird treaties with Canada, Mexico, Japan, and the Soviet Union and had the Endangered Species Act, Marine Mammals Protection Act, and the CITES agreement to protect threatened wildlife, it had "really very little obvious or undiscovered need for a new convention." Meanwhile, the United States and Canada were quietly revising their migratory bird treaty to legalize but regulate natives' subsistence taking of certain migratory species and negotiating a treaty to cover the Porcupine caribou herd that ranged back and forth between Alaska and the Yukon Territory.[57]

Sixty-three nations attended the final signatory session for the new treaty in Bonn in June 1979, but by then the Association was certain of its opposition and grateful for the support of several other major wildlife organizations. The International objected to definitions of words like "migratory" that were "entirely too broad and imprecise" as well as to the hasty advancement of the proposal. Mostly it feared the Convention's potential for jurisdictional mischief and worked extensively to convince Congress and the executive departments of the treaty's shortcomings. In the end the United States, along with Canada, Japan, Australia, and the Soviet Union, declined to sign the Bonn Convention, much to the relief and credit of the Association. The state game managers had learned their CITES lessons well.[58]

The endangered species legislation, litigation, and international negotiations of the 1970s and early 1980s served to focus the Association's energies, demonstrate its clout, and pinpoint continuing problems. The state conservationists honed their skills and multiplied their commitment to the political process during this period, with the new central office in the national capital both a source of timely information and a prod. State administrative authority and technical ability finally achieved recognition on paper if not always in practice. Both the federal government and the states acknowledged that their mutual efforts and cooperation were essential, for if state conservationists lost their authority they also lost their capability for management on the land, where it mattered. The federal government was incapable of overseeing wildlife management nationwide even if it chose to do so.

Funding became the most pressing problem for endangered species programs in the states. Deliberate, across-the-board federal budget cutting in the 1980s made severe inroads in state wildlife programs. It was no wonder, wrote Wes Hayden in a 1982 discussion of "on-again-off-again" appropriations negotiations, that many people were convinced that "the excise tax approach is the only one that can be counted on to sustain a cooperative federal-state effort involving federal funding." Moreover, endangered species listings, national or international, dictated state spending priorities and placement of personnel, not always according to the judgment of conservation experts in the field. Overall, the endangered species program, however, became more workable and smoothly operating over the years, with increasing cooperation and commitment from all parties.[59]

Management in Court

The endangered species challenge would continue, but the Association engaged itself in numerous other issues as well. The court record of the International illustrates the breadth of its involvement; its success rate also indicates its influence and the care with which it selected cases for intervention. In December 1970 the Humane Society of the United States sued Interior Secretary Rogers Morton to enjoin him from allowing a public deer hunt in the Great Swamp National Wildlife Refuge in New Jersey, and in an amended complaint also in refuges at Eastern Neck, Maryland, and Chincoteague, Virginia. The Humane Society argued that the use of shotguns, bows and arrows, and muzzle-loading rifles by hunters not necessarily skillful was inhumane and incompatible with the purpose of the refuges and that necessary herd reduction should be accomplished by hired marksmen. The International Association intervened on behalf of the federal defendants, but the federal district court dismissed the complaint for failure of proof before its panel of experts could testify. When the Humane Society appealed, the U.S. Court of Appeals, D.C. Circuit, agreed with the lower court, saying that Congress had indeed authorized the use of national wildlife refuges for public hunting so long as such public recreation was not inconsistent with the refuges' primary objectives. The law did not require the Secretary to be "guided by considerations of humaneness." The case was an important victory for the use of hunting as a management tool under state control.[60]

The Association assisted the states of Montana and New Mexico in 1978 court challenges testing their right to charge different hunting license fees for residents and nonresidents. The Supreme Court ultimately said they could, holding that recreational hunting "is not a fundamental right of national citizenship," despite the plaintiffs' argument that the fee differentials, in these instances substantially higher for nonresidents, violated their rights of equal protection under the Constitution. The Court ruled, in two separate cases, that the states' preference for their own residents to enjoy an activity not available to all who might wish to participate in it was a "legitimate state interest." The states' citizens, after all, supported the high costs of producing and maintaining big game through taxes and "other economic penalties and forbearances." The Court did not, however, approve New Mexico's discriminatory allocation of resident and nonresident permits in limited permit hunts, since such distribution served no conservation purpose. The states would try again on allocation differentials, but these fee discrimination cases affirmed the states' management authority over their own resources.[61]

A benchmark in the confirmation of the primacy of state authority over wildlife resulted from three court actions in 1979 and 1980 involving a wolf reduction program initiated by the Alaska Department of Fish and Game on Bureau of Land Management lands. Association leaders had labored for four years on the Federal Land Policy and Management Act (FLPMA) of 1976, on which the court cases rested, to prevent federal agencies from obtaining the right to manipulate wildlife populations for land management objectives. This comprehensive policy for the use and management of national resource lands, expressly those of the BLM and also the national forests, as finally passed, generally satisfied the Association. In particular, section 302(b) reaffirmed state authority over fish and resident wildlife on these lands, reserving to federal managers closure authority over areas for limited, specified purposes, such as public safety.

The state authority provision of the FLPMA was tested almost immediately when Alaska agents began shooting wolves from aircraft to relieve pressure on the Western Arctic caribou herd, whose population had plummeted. Several animal welfare groups brought suit in the District of Columbia, not Alaska, against the Interior Secretary, not Alaska, to halt the hunt. They argued that the Secretary must close the area to hunting because no environmental impact analysis had been performed as required by the National Environmental Policy Act. Whether NEPA applied depended on whether the case involved a "federal action," which, in turn, depended on whether section 302(b) that imposed land management duties on the Secretary also imposed a supervisory duty over state wildlife activities.

The lower court in the District of Columbia thought it did and ordered the Interior Secretary to order Alaska to stop the wolf hunt. The IAFWA prevailed upon the Secretary to appeal even though the latter's lawyers felt that losing was likely. The Court of Appeals, D.C. Circuit, relying heavily upon an earlier Association amicus brief, thought otherwise and concluded that "far from attempting to alter the traditional division of authority over wildlife management, FLPMA broadly and explicitly reaffirms it." As for the Secretary's closure authority, Judge Carl McGowan, for the unanimous court, stated: "We are simply unable to read this cautious and limited permission to intervene in an area of state responsibility and authority as imposing such supervisory duties on the Secretary that each state action he fails to prevent becomes a 'Federal action.' A state wildlife-management agency which must seek federal approval for each program it initiates can hardly be said to have 'responsibility and authority' for its own affairs."

The Supreme Court declined the review requested by the protectionists' attorneys. Thus, this decision, a clear victory for the states, would prove extremely useful for future deliberations with federal agencies over fish and wildlife policy.[62]

Meanwhile, the 1971 Wild Free-Roaming Horses and Burros Act protected these animals on public lands as historic relics of the old West. But in 1974 the New Mexico Livestock Board removed and sold nineteen unbranded burros upon complaint from a rancher that the burros were molesting his cattle and eating their feed. The case went to court when the BLM belatedly reasserted its authority and demanded the return of the burros. In 1975 a federal district court ruled the Wild Horses Act unconstitutional as violating the state ownership doctrine, but the Supreme Court overturned that decision, upholding the constitutionality of the law and ruling that Congress, pursuant to the property clause, exercised complete control over the public lands, including the regulation and protection of wildlife living there.

The decision might have seemed a setback for state jurisdiction, but the Association noted that this particular case involved feral animals, not wildlife. Therefore, it accepted the property clause argument since the traditional state authority doctrines did not apply. As Legal Counsel Paul Lenzini put it to the Association members in 1975, "The doctrine of State ownership must be preserved," since not every problem was "susceptible to a quick federal fix," but it would not survive if "stretched to the limit." Finding grounds to yield gracefully in the case of wild horses and burros, about which the game managers had only qualified interest, was a winning move in the long run. Subsequent decisions in more significant cases granted the states the authority they claimed and needed for resource protection. The members of the International repeatedly expressed their gratitude for Lenzini's perceptive, articulate leadership, in 1976 presenting him with a plaque acknowledging his ten years of service to the Association.[63]

Finally, the Association helped thwart an effort by animal rights groups in 1978 to cut off funding for Pittman-Robertson projects. The Committee for Humane Legislation brought suit against Interior Secretary Cecil Andrus on the grounds that the Interior Department, which administered the P-R program, had not complied with NEPA requirements for environmental impact statements for either the overall Pittman-Robertson program or discrete state programs within it. More simply, according to International Association interpretation, the animal rights proponents opposed state-managed programs that benefited hunters and hunting. Legal jockeying went on for more than a year. Many of the 600 P-R funded projects were, technically, not in compliance with NEPA. The plaintiffs eventually "narrowed" their objections to 182 projects, which still involved virtually all states. Finally, Judge Charles Richey of the Federal District Court, District of Columbia, after earlier indications to the contrary, sent a signal from the bench that seemed to favor defendants' arguments on the importance of continued P-R funding. With that, the case proceeded to an immediate out-of-court settlement, the Fish and Wildlife Service agreeing to publish for comment notices of availability of no significant impact assessments. Project funding continued and serious problems were averted. "We pretty much won this one," said Jack Berryman, but the "close call" cost the Association about $100,000 and a dues raise. The potential for losing funding for hundreds of Pittman-Robertson projects encouraged the members to put their money where their priorities were; in 1979 the Association went $26,000 over budget to defend the "infamous P-R suit."[64]

The Association in Washington

Money for priorities came from dues, and members of the International Association proved themselves ready to dig deeper into their pockets when the need arose. At their Spring 1978 meeting in Phoenix, they approved (by a vote of 47 to 1) an increase in governmental members' dues to $3,000, mostly to reorganize the Washington office by adding a Legislative Counsel who would oversee affairs on Capitol Hill. Thus, two permanent staff members could give increased attention to legislative matters as well as the Association's other external activities and internal management. Associate member dues rose to ten dollars in 1980.

On January 1, 1981, governmental member dues of $6,000 went into effect (after a vote in March of 37 to 5). The Executive Committee had recommended this substantial increase in order to expand the Association's legal activities, pay for space, develop an operating reserve to stabilize dues for a five-year period, and raise employee salaries and benefits.

Specific Association programs benefited from the augmented income.

The staff increased communication with both the state members and the executive departments in Washington, with more frequent and effective political action a result. The Association established a Hunter Education Council in 1982 and an Aquatic Resource Education Council in 1984 to bring together disparate groups interested in these subjects to prepare educational materials. One example of the IAFWA's expanded international involvement was its cosponsorship of the first International Wildlife Symposium in Mexico City in 1985.[65]

Meanwhile, other changes were taking place in the organization. It changed its name. The International Association of Game, Fish and Conservation Commissioners became the International Association of Fish and Wildlife Agencies on January 1, 1977, after members agreed that their state roles were becoming broader than game conservation alone. Deleting the term "conservation" was difficult, but the concept was implicit in all they did. Bylaws amendments made the Regional Associations eligible for membership in the International in 1975. They had to apply, but there were no dues required. The Western Association was first, its President automatically becoming a nonvoting member of the Association's Executive Committee. The other Regional Associations soon followed. The 1980 bylaws changes that increased dues also made Canada and Mexico ex officio members of the Executive Committee, to involve them more actively and to comply with the recommendations of the International Union for the Conservation of Nature (IUCN) for international organizations.[66]

Finally, new faces appeared at IAFWA headquarters. Jack Berryman became the new Executive Vice President in 1979 when John Gottschalk moved over to become the Legislative Counsel. Berryman brought with him years of experience as a state wildlife specialist, federal aid coordinator, land grant university extension services professor, and U.S. Fish and Wildlife Service administrator. He saw the function of the Washington office as one "to catalyze, to mobilize, and focus the capabilities of the Association" and his own to orchestrate the total Association effort. In his first convention report he reiterated his pride in the unique, powerful organization and reminded his audience that "we must project a consistent image of professional integrity, of dependability, and intellectual honesty" as well as an "unwavering policy of balanced resource management." Gottschalk retired after about a year, retaining the specially created title "Counsel." "Dusty" Zaunbrecher took his position as chief lobbyist and legislative liaison with the states. He, too, stayed only a short time and was replaced in 1981 by Wesley Hayden, who came with extensive background in journalism and environmental affairs on Capitol Hill. Finally, in early 1986, upon Hayden's retirement, Gordon Robertson took over the Legislative Counsel's chair. He had worked with wildlife in two states and the Wildlife Management Institute.[67]

Members of the even more active and committed International Association expected much of their carefully chosen Washington office staffers and backed them fully. Together they worked against antihunters and for endangered species. They kept the United States free from an ominous international migratory bird convention while struggling to improve the unworkable aspects of the CITES agreement. They continued to press, with increasing success, for state authority in Congress and the courts. The Washington presence had proved its worth.

S ⋆ I ⋆ X

The Agenda Reviewed, A Future Agenda

The law locks up the man or woman,
who steals the goose from the common;
But the greater villain the law lets loose,
who steals the common from the goose.

ANONYMOUS
(seventeenth century)

MANY of the wildlife issues of the 1980s were long-standing concerns, but with the election of President Ronald Reagan the political climate in which they were debated and acted upon manifestly changed. Under Reagan's "New Federalism," emphasis shifted from federal control, with less federal money for local efforts as well. Continuing programs, like wildlife restoration under the Pittman-Robertson Act, proved their durability under varied challenges; others, like fish restoration, took on added dimensions. Persistent issues were reexamined, and some would appear near resolution. By mid-decade the Association achieved long-sought milestones in policy making and undertook a major internal study to target its goals for the future.

New National Priorities and Wildlife

The already beleaguered Interior Secretary James Watt laid out the new administration's priorities for the members of the International Association of Fish and Wildlife Agencies at their 1981 convention amid extraordinary security precautions, intrusive television cameras, and noisy, determined protestors of his environmental policies who circled just outside. Watt opened with reassuring words about balanced wildlife management ("I have faith in your profession and commitment to it"), the worth of hunters and anglers ("This Administration is going to be for the sportsman"), and state management of resident species ("Power is flowing back to the states" and "We believe in state governments"). The Administration, in favor of user fees, supported expansion of the Dingell-Johnson and Pittman-Robertson programs. Funding for wildlife would decrease within the intentional budget-cutting framework, but emphasis on maintenance, rather than new land acquisitions, represented sound management principles, the Secretary declared.[1]

Watt's speech was liberally sprinkled with details of state programs and the first names of their directors; he wanted his grasp of wildlife facts known and appreciated. The talk was also a piece of transparent partisan politics. Nevertheless, the Association's agenda prospered under Watt. The Secretary made promanagement, pro-state promises the members wanted to hear, and he kept them. For example, he secured White House support for the Dingell-Johnson Expansion Act in the face of an Office of Management and Budget steadfastly opposed to earmarked funding. It finally passed. He established a wetlands preservation task force (POWDR: Protect Our Wetlands and Duck Resources) of business, industrial, government, and conservation leaders, including Jack Berryman of the International Association, which provided the stimulus for current wetlands legislation. He successfully supported wildlife professionals for key positions in Interior over Administration-favored political candidates. And he brought forward the National Policy on Wildlife that had languished in the Interior Department for several years.[2]

Still, federal spending cuts hurt conservation. Funds for monitoring and research declined in all agencies at the same time that spending increased for minerals exploration and development. Wildlife habitat protection was thus doubly jeopardized. Association leaders, recognizing the inevitability of some budget reduction, attempted for a time to recommend to Congress areas where cuts would be least harmful to wildlife, but they found the lawmakers only too accommodating and soon reverted to reserving suggestions to positive promotion of issues of greatest need and highest Association priority. The states, meanwhile, reassessed their traditional roles and their determination to fulfill increased responsibility at a time of federal curtailment. But the budget situation was discouraging.[3]

The Sagebrush Rebellion

The so-called Sagebrush Rebellion of 1980–81 was another national issue affecting the state wildlife managers, this one placing them in the unusual position of opposing a states' rights movement. The Federal Land Policy and Management Act of 1976 increased the jurisdiction of the Bureau of Land Management and the U.S. Forest Service over public lands, most of them in the West, and mandated their management under principles of multiple use and sustained yield. The Sagebrush rebels in several western states, believing the federal agencies were mismanaging the land, overregulating its users, and ignoring local needs, sought to transfer the lands in question to state control. In 1979 the Nevada legislature simply passed a law declaring its public domain, almost half of its total area, to be under state jurisdiction. Soon ten other western legislatures introduced similar measures, and Utah's Republican Senator Orrin Hatch introduced a federal bill, the Western Lands Distribution and Regional Equalization Act, to deliver both BLM and Forest Service lands to state ownership. The LASER (League for the Advancement of States' Equal Rights) states published a public relations brochure asserting that "the West wants to be part of America upon an equal footing with the original states" and hosted a heavily attended federal lands policy conference in November 1980 to stimulate attention and support.[4]

There was clearly a good deal of support for the Sagebrush Rebellion among western politicians, ranchers, and mineral developers, but wildlife conservationists from all over the country responded with alarm. Daniel Poole, President of the Wildlife Management Institute, called the movement "not a rebellion, an ambush." He and others worried about degraded wildlife habitat under management by states committed first to "maximum economic return" and the loss of access to millions of acres by hunters, fishers, and other recreationists, whether the lands remained under state control or, worse, were sold to private parties. Neither alternative was very attractive.

The states had insufficient money, manpower, and legislative authority for diverse, balanced land management, in particular for the enhancement of wildlife values. Nevada, for example, the vanguard of the movement, had no state water laws that recognized wildlife or recreation as a beneficial use. Water, of course, was always at a premium. It had no wilderness laws to ensure undisturbed habitat for species such as mountain lion or bighorn sheep. Indeed, Nevada had no state land, having already sold it. Furthermore, the state could not possibly fund the management of the lands as the BLM had done; deficits and reduced services could be expected. As for the likely transfer to private ownership, who then would protect wildlife and the environment? Would corporations ensure access for public recreation? Could stockmen compete for purchase with mining interests? Who would take on the financial responsibility for game and nongame animals? Conservationists were more than skeptical about the rebels' plans.[5]

The state conservationists in the western states were in an awkward position. They could not publicly oppose their legislators or governors on the land takeover question, since their jobs derived from those very powers. On the other hand, they were responsible for the wildlife. The answer was to invoke the help of the International Association, which, as a body, could act where the individual state members could not. Nevada Fish and Game Commission Director Joseph Greenley, for example, quietly fed the Association staff facts on his state's current and past performance record and the legal background of its positions. So when the Sagebrush rebels convened in Salt Lake City in 1980, IAFWA Executive Vice-President Jack Berryman went there to represent all of the members. He was careful to begin his testimony with the statement that "we do not presume to speak for any individual state, nor to interfere in its internal processes. Rather, we present the collective views of our member agencies on those issues where there is a consensus." Thus, in a sentence he took the heat off the uncomfortable western state directors and put the force of national agreement among conservationists behind his remarks, even though at that meeting he was a "lone voice" against divestiture.[6]

Berryman, himself a product of the West and a spokesman for a states' rights organization, made clear the International Association's firm opposition to large-scale land transfer from federal to state control. But he did this within a context of acknowledging widespread frustrations with the present federal land management system and attempting to find common ground for problem solving. "Our mutual objective," he said, "*always* must be to satisfy society's increasing demands in such a way that we never reduce this Nation's productive capacity and capability." A "healthy, dynamic federalism," with "vigorous state and federal governments each operating within their proper spheres" would promote the land policy goals of the conference. Berryman also reminded his audience that the Association spoke from the authority of its detailed 1971 study, *Public Land Policy Impact on Fish and Wildlife*, and the ongoing work of its land resources committee.[7]

Land problems were many, to be sure. Federal shortcomings included allowing overgrazing and overharvesting of timber on federal lands, failing to provide a responsible animal damage control program, and being unable to develop clear policies for riparian habitat or jurisdiction for fish and wildlife management. In general, the federal government had shown itself too anxious to intrude on state authority. However, the western lands in question belonged to all of the people; they had never been under state ownership. The needs of all users must be respected when formulating policy for public lands. The unrest had justification, but a successful Sagebrush Rebellion would only polarize interests and make matters worse, and not just in the West. "The goal should be to improve not to destroy an established system of land and resource management, which, despite known and mainly minor deficiencies, has been and is the envy of the world," Berryman concluded.[8]

But the western land ownership controversy persisted. The 1982 Association convention voted, once again, to oppose a proposed large-scale sale or transfer of federal lands. The delegates reiterated that multiple users by the millions, including all manner of recreation seekers as well as those exploiting timber, edible vegetation, water, and minerals, enjoyed benefits from and access to these lands. But now, despite congressional intent to "retain most of these lands for the enjoyment of future generations," the present Administration was seeking to raise revenue by selling "unneeded public lands and waters," without public input or concern with National Environmental Protection Act regulations. The Association insisted that public lands be transferred to private ownership only if they contained "no significant fish, wildlife, historical or recreational values or similar benefits," that lands in the public domain be managed according to protective federal law, and that the affected states be consulted in connection with any disposal plans.

The federal government did indeed dispose of some of its land, but not as much as feared or under unacceptable conditions. The BLM, under Secretary Watt's "good neighbor" policy, adopted more workable policies and streamlined procedures to mollify unhappy state officials and land users. In the end, the Sagebrush Rebellion, having indirectly achieved much of the change it sought, quietly died away.[9]

Fifty Years of Pittman-Robertson

The state conservationists continued to cultivate their time-tested cooperative relationship with the federal government on the Pittman-Robertson program, which neared its fiftieth anniversary of providing money for state-run wildlife restoration efforts. Federal excise taxes on hunting equipment to the tune of some $1.5 billion had been matched in a 75–25 percent ratio by more than $500 million in state funds, chiefly from hunting license receipts. These user fees continued to be used to purchase and develop habitat and conduct wildlife research to restore and maintain numerous species, both game and nongame. For a half-century, only hunters paid the tax and funded the projects, but all manner of wildlife and those who enjoyed it benefited from the dependable, earmarked income that allowed long-range program planning and implementation. Those whose livelihood derived from outdoors pursuits reaped economic gain, and managers enhanced their professional credentials with augmented training and knowledge from P-R project spinoffs.[10]

The Pittman-Robertson program withstood legal challenge from protectionists in the late 1970s. To prevent recurrence of harassment from antihunters, Congressman Pat Williams, Democrat of Montana, introduced a bill in the fall of 1979 that would require P-R projects to carry an environmental impact statement, as the protectionists had demanded, but would forestall a court from halting or limiting funding of a project while a lawsuit was pending. The bill never emerged from committee, though the need for it dissipated, at least so far as state wildlife agencies were concerned, with the settlement of the P-R litigation. Williams's effort demonstrated, however, that the friends of Pittman-Robertson were prepared to take whatever action seemed necessary to protect this vital law.[11]

The Pittman-Robertson program expanded to include financing of hunter education programs, which reached some 700,000 people per year and were required by thirty-six states. The Association successfully deflected a congressional effort to further divert part of the proceeds from the tax on handguns to compensate victims of crime, since that would have curtailed funds available for the management and educational programs intended by the original act.

The importance of the continuing Pittman-Robertson program to the general health and abundance of wildlife in America could not be overstressed. Nor could the importance of the hunter, whose willing subsidy made it possible. Said Interior Secretary Don Hodel in celebration of the golden anniversary of the passage of the Pittman-Robertson Act, "Many Americans are surprised to learn that hunters have been the mainstay of wildlife conservation over the last half-century."[12]

Dingell-Johnson: New Identity, More Money

Fish restoration, like wildlife restoration, had long enjoyed special angler-supported federal funding, but by the late 1970s Dingell-Johnson revenues proved inadequate to the tasks of providing sufficient fish habitat and fishing opportunities. "D-J Expansion" became a rallying cry for the Association and fishing-enthusiast allies. Association correspondence going back to 1977 expressed the need for additional income and proposed to include under the 10 percent excise tax all tackle not already covered and to add a 3 percent tax on boats and motors, excluding boats less than twenty-five feet long, hydroplanes, kayaks, sailboats, and boating equipment. Senators Jennings Randolph (D-WV) and Russell Long (D-LA) introduced a bill in October 1979 with these provisions. While virtually all major conservation and sport fishing organizations supported the bill, budget officials, who never approved of earmarked funds, and boat manufacturers, who feared losses in sales, stoutly opposed it. The Boating Industry Association argued, for example, that anglers, not boaters, should pay the tax. But conservationists pointed out that 70 to 80 percent of boaters engaged in fishing and, after all, the rest did get to use the maintained lakes.[13]

This unsuccessful bill was only the beginning of an all-consuming effort by the International Association in league with other like-minded groups to increase fish restoration funding. The Association collected a pile of documents almost a foot high on this one issue. The American League of Anglers established a *D-J Expansion Bill Newsletter* in 1979, to which John Gottschalk among others contributed, and every state appointed a D-J Coordinating Committee chair by the end of that year. Articles on D-J expansion in sports magazines proliferated. In 1981 Dominique's Restaurant in Washington, which served a wide variety of exotic fresh fish and game, hosted a lobbying reception for congressional staff. The Association coordinated coalition efforts and presented testimony again and again. Finally, the manufacturers reassessed their position. Hydra-Sports Incorporated of Nashville, for example, announced that, having taken a "responsible, long-term view," it would support the then pending bill and indicated that the marine industry was "not united in opposition" to the proposed excise tax on boats and motors. Finally, in December 1984 the Wallop-Breaux bill, encompassing all of the features suggested since 1979, became law, with funding to begin with fiscal year 1986. Sport fishing and recreational boating enhancement projects could expect an increase in funding to at least $125 million annually, about triple that available under the thirty-five-year-old Dingell-Johnson program, which the new act supplanted. It was a hard-won, sweet victory. Users would still financially sustain their own recreation as well as that of others.[14]

Continuing Concerns

Association action persisted across the broad spectrum of its historical concerns. Duck stamp revenues, the third type of federal funding for wildlife, continued to support the acquisition of wetlands and refuges for migratory wildfowl with the proceeds from the stamp's annual purchase price of $7.50. In addition, the federal government influenced land-use decisions through financial incentives to private landowners, enforcement of regulations, and the direct purchase of land. The International Association supported waterfowl efforts through its own committees and the international and regional flyway councils, where its leadership was central. The flyway councils were particularly concerned about the Midwest prairie pothole region and the coastal swamps, where some progress was being made to preserve and restore vital wetlands through Water Bank programs, farm legislation, and the Wetlands Loan Act of 1961, which allowed the Fish and Wildlife Service to draw on future duck stamp income to purchase habitat. Unfortunately, in the budget-reduction climate of the 1980s, only a fraction of the authorized funds for wetlands acquisition under the loan program was spent. Wetlands continued to disappear.[15]

The IAFWA organized and conducted a Worldwide Furbearer Conference in Frostburg, Maryland, in August 1980, attended by representatives of eighteen countries. Its printed *Proceedings* and the publication of *The North American Furbearers: A Contemporary Reference* were tangible, useful products of the IAFWA Fur Resources Committee's efforts. The Association also encouraged research on more efficient, humane trapping methods and worked to oppose antitrapping legislation. It pressed for amendments to the CITES agreement to improve regulations for its implementation, especially regarding bobcats and other furbearers of economic importance to Americans.[16]

The Marine and Estuarine Committee led Association efforts to enhance the aquatic environment for fisheries and recreation through legislation and direct action. Its promotion of a national plan to develop obsolete offshore petroleum platforms as artificial reefs to encourage fisheries was just one example of its varied activity. The Association supported national legislation to extend U.S. fisheries' offshore jurisdiction to 200 miles to protect dwindling resources even though regional management would preempt state authority. Animal damage control and the use of toxicants never stopped commanding attention. In all cases the chief problem for fish and wildlife managers boiled down to that of habitat loss, the challenge being to prevent or restore environmental depravation.[17]

A proliferating array of conservation organizations stood ready to help, or hinder, the International Association of Fish and Wildlife Agencies in its historical and current efforts to meet the environmental challenge. Groups ranging from hunter-oriented users like the National Rifle Association to animal-rights protectionists such as the Friends of Animals added their specialized, contradicting perspectives to the cacophony of wildlife voices. They dominated one another by turn, cancelled each other out, and sometimes worked together. The Association established networks or temporary coalitions with most of them at one time or another and opposed the same ones on other occasions.

Media Ventures

It seemed, however, in the late 1960s and on into the 1970s, that organizations opposing the International Association's management philosophy increasingly commanded popular support and sympathetic media attention. To counter the protectionists and their allies, who also claimed the sobriquet "conservationists," the Association, fresh on the national scene with its recently established Washington office, sought to tap the mass media market.

In 1972 the Executive Committee proposed that the International establish a specialty magazine, a type newly in vogue, for a limited but committed audience of wildlife conservationists. The publication was to satisfy both financial and nonfinancial goals. As a paying business enterprise, a successful magazine would "support policy and information requirements" of the Association and its cosponsoring organization, the American Association for Conservation Information. It would also fuse a following of outdoors lovers to support responsible wildlife management policies. As an antidote to an increasing public interest in "unnecessarily restrictive firearm legislation, a growth in anti-hunting sentiment, and an apparent defection of the young to other pursuits than hunting and fishing," all of which affected state agency funding for wildlife, the latter goal could also be considered financial. But *The American Outdoors*, an effort of wildlife professionals who were magazine amateurs, could not attract sufficient financial or technical support and was never published.[18]

Two years later the International Association pursued national television. As antihunting, antitrapping, and antimanagement "misinformation" mounted, a special Conservation Television Committee proposed a plan for four one-hour specials that would present, in prime time, a balanced, nonemotional, factual documentation of American wildlife resource conservation. The Committee envisioned programs of top quality that would be entertaining as well as educational. Finding sponsors with the resources and interest to fund the $300,000 project, however, proved impossible. "Say Goodbye" and its ilk would have no rebuttal from the resource management community in 1974.[19]

The Association attempted to spread its message twice more via television and once through print. A commercially produced wildlife series called "American Outdoors," funded primarily by the Fred Bear Sports Club, achieved limited distribution in 1976; plans for a second phase of the series got as far as a favorably reviewed IAFWA pilot film on the sea otter in 1977. In the early 1980s TV producer Glen Lau offered free short-segment coverage of wildlife management topics on his nationally broadcast "Sports Afield" and "Coors Western Outdoorsmen" programs. He requested, in exchange, state-provided ideas and assistance with research and filming. A few dozen clips resulted, and some 6 million people viewed eight shows in 1982, but too few stretched state agencies were able or willing to contribute material. Lau faced bankruptcy in 1983. Meanwhile, a final magazine effort also failed. *Earth One*, in 1977, was to have been a quarterly "learned journal" for "decision makers in the fields of wildlife conservation, natural resources, and the environment" that would analyze pressing issues in depth. But some wildlife managers feared the journal would be "more of the same" and might compete with the forty or so excellent state conservation magazines already published. Again, there was no money.[20]

The International formed the AWARE (America's Wildlife Association for Resource Education) Foundation in 1977 as a tax-exempt legal entity to receive financial donations to keep its television and other educational projects going, but the overall dollar response was insufficient to sustain a major media effort.[21]

These failures at popular communication disappointed Association members who wanted to go public with the resource management message, especially when the other side was so successfully exploiting the media. In March 1985, when the Executive Committee met to discuss the future of the International Association and ways to improve its effectiveness, the Communications Committee and its supporters pressed for the addition of a staff public relations expert to enhance Association visibility and responsiveness in the ongoing public debate over antimanagement.

But Jack Berryman and others did not favor public relations as a priority activity. In August 1985 Berryman argued in a memorandum to the Executive Committee that the Association's influence "should not be redirected to the general public. We are not a membership or grassroots organization." With unique strength in members having direct contact with the state and national political systems as well as representing most of the professional wildlife expertise in the country, the Association "should do more of what we do best," that is, influence public policy, in a "dependable, low-profile" way. The states should develop their own public relations and educational programs, since the state agencies did represent the grassroots, Berryman said. In order to pursue intensified lobbying efforts the Association should more efficiently organize its committees, perhaps by specific legislative topic, and more closely orchestrate their work. That would require additional professional and support personnel in the Washington office. The Association agreed with Berryman's position and in September 1986 hired Dr. Laura Manning, a political scientist with experience and expertise in endangered species and marine fisheries issues.[22]

Thus, the Association finally solved its media dilemmas by making the deliberate decision to let other organizations better equipped for public relations occupy the limelight and to render its own influence quietly but forcefully with the decision makers in the halls of government.

The Native American Rights Controversy

Two other deep-rooted concerns of the Association eluded resolution over the years. The question of Native American rights as to the use of fish and wildlife resources has been conspicuously divisive and is unlikely to find solution in the near future. The controversy over the adoption of nontoxic shot, on the other hand, appears near closure at last.

For two decades conflicts between Native Americans and state conservation authorities raged, particularly in the courts, over hunting and fishing rights on and near reservation lands. These began at a time of general Indian unrest that brought claims for unmet treaty conditions; rights to wildlife were a convenient focus for broader issues of sovereignty. The story was complicated at every stage. Different arrangements made by different tribes for priority resource use on reservation and nonreservation lands made general accord and legal precedent-setting difficult. The judicial basis for decision making rested with treaties negotiated between the various tribes and the United States at least a century ago. Such treaties, considered binding agreements between two sovereign nations but long forgotten by most Americans, remained the supreme law of the land according to Article VI of the Constitution. Furthermore, as federal lawyers pointed out, treaties were not a grant of rights *to* the Indians but rather a grant of rights *from* them, with the Indians reserving to themselves those rights not granted. Most Indians, by tradition and habit, were hunters and fishers and arguably had a right to remain so and to use their "usual and accustomed hunting and fishing grounds and stations," even if off the reservation. Under treaty this was a right superior to that of non-Indians, who possessed only fishing "privileges." Sympathetic observers held that America's Indians had been badly, even dishonorably, treated over the course of history. Protecting these traditional rights to game seemed a paltry and decent thing to do for a long-aggrieved people.[23]

That was one side of the story. State game managers charged with conserving their state's natural resources saw another and were appalled at the mischief such interpretations of law wreaked. Native Americans apparently had no legal obligation to be responsible takers of game and fish. On reservations, state law had no force or effect. Off the reservation, on the Indians' "usual and accustomed grounds," the state could regulate Indian harvest only to the minimum extent "necessary for the preservation of the resource." State authorities faced with preferential and uneven enforcement of regulations found their ability to regulate at all jeopardized. They were helpless to stem the resource diminishment. The governing treaties, negotiated in times of resource plenty, were now being applied in times of relative scarcity. The only remedy was national legislation to clarify or modify the treaty provisions, but Congress would have none of this highly emotional issue.[24]

In 1974 a distressed Indian Relations Committee reported to the Association on Indian rights problems in almost two dozen states and provinces. They varied in all possible respects, but a single case illustrates the general difficulties. In February 1974, U.S. District Court Judge George H. Boldt confirmed, in United States v. Washington, that Native Americans had uncontested fishing rights in the coastal streams of western Washington, based on legitimate treaty provisions. A U.S. court of appeals upheld Boldt's ruling in 1975. The Association *Newsletter* wrote that Boldt's decision realized "the worst fears of states in which Indians comprise a substantial portion of the population." Adding to the state conservationists' dismay, the article continued, Indians were exempt from laws applicable to anadromous fish and could take an unlimited harvest for personal or ceremonial use even off the reservation. The judge did decide that Indians' rights to nonreservation fishing were "non-exclusive," so that opportunities at the catch must be equally shared with non-Indians. But what that meant to Boldt was a fifty-fifty split of the harvest; that is, the relatively few Indians were entitled to the same amount as the vastly larger non-Indian population. That did not sound like equality to state administrators. And where would enough fish come from? The Association urged the Congress of the United States in 1974 to effect changes in Indian treaties such as would "achieve the goal of equal rights for all its citizens and to insure protection of the fish and wildlife resource." In 1979 the U.S. Supreme Court affirmed the Northwest Treaty Tribes' right to up to 50 percent of the salmon catch in Washington. That was that.[25]

Other cases involving other tribes, locations, and issues surfaced during this period of Indian activism. They were all over, says Jack Berryman, "like a terrible rash." New York Cayugas laid claim to prime deer hunting country. In North Carolina the Cherokees asked the courts to forbid the state from requiring non-Indians to purchase state licenses to fish in reservation waters. And so on. Sometimes decisions favored state law and regulation of resources, often not. With Congress and the courts reluctant to address the very real conservation issues below the surface of the sensitive one of minority rights, wildlife managers will not likely see the resolution of the Native American problem soon.[26]

Lead Poisoning and Steel Shot

Lead poisoning of animals, chiefly waterfowl ingesting pellets from spent shotshells, emerged in the 1960s as a serious wildlife management issue. Few people then knew that the problem had been identified a century earlier or that it would embroil the conservation community in one of its most divisive scientific and political conflicts ever. Fortunately, this story appears to be nearing a happy ending.

In February 1894 George Bird Grinnell introduced American sportsmen to the dangers of lead poisoning to waterfowl on the front page of *Forest and Stream*. Grinnell described the scenario of hunters' fallen lead collecting on ducks' feeding grounds and their eating it for grit. Their gizzards ground the pellets down into fine dust easily acted upon by the gastric juices, with disastrous results. He wrote, "The [poisoned] birds are dumpy, stupid and stagger in their walk, and have little control over themselves." They also suffered respiratory problems, vomiting, convulsions, and fever. Grinnell did not mention their imminent deaths, but even today most ducks dead from lead poisoning are not readily found. They tend to expire in the marshes and disappear or are devoured. Nor was

Grinnell first to note the toxic effects of lead on animals. He cited an 1852 article in the Edinburgh *Medical Journal* in which Dr. G. Wilson reported detecting lead in the organs of animals that had died from drinking lead carbonate-impregnated water from a nearby factory.[27]

In 1919 Alexander Wetmore, Assistant Biologist with the Bureau of Biological Survey, pursued both field observation and scientific experimentation to establish the relationship between ingestion of lead shot and lead poisoning in waterfowl. He learned that even two or three swallowed shot pellets could be fatal, while six invariably were. Usually from fifteen to forty pellets were found in contaminated ducks; one bird had seventy-six. Wetmore also worried about the survivors of lead poisoning. Would the "well-known" fact that lead induced abortions in female mammals apply to waterfowl? Scientists had recently determined that lead administered to male domestic fowl had a "powerful effect" on their virility and the vitality of their offspring. Would the same symptoms affect wild birds? Wetmore also proved that lead was the toxic agent in the shot and that the marshes popular with hunters were full of the pellets, which disintegrated only slowly over time. In wetlands areas where gravel was scarce, waterfowl quickly swallowed shot when found. Wetmore's studies were rigorously conducted and sound in their judgments, but in 1919 he could only describe the problem, not even suggest a solution. He had successfully treated some affected birds with magnesic sulphate but concluded that the process was too time-consuming and uncertain of outcome to be practical.[28]

Numerous other scientific investigations, appearing sporadically over the years, verified and expanded Wetmore's findings. Frank Bellrose of the Illinois Natural History Survey became a leading authority on lead poisoning of waterfowl by the 1950s. Noting that different species seemed to vary in their susceptibility to plumbism, Bellrose concluded that their diverse eating habits, not their universal need for grit, were the primary determinants. For example, redheads, ring-necked ducks, and canvasbacks, which dove and dug for seeds and aquatic tubers in shoal water areas, consumed more poison than open-water, deep-diving waterfowl or foliage eaters such as scaup or baldpate varieties. In any case, the ducks kept dying, by the 1980s more than 2 million per year.[29]

Finally, in 1965, the Mississippi Flyway Council, in a study entitled "Wasted Waterfowl," formally urged that a substitute for lead shot be sought that was not toxic to waterfowl when ingested and also acceptable to the arms industry and hunters. The flyway council was not the first to propose an alternate shot material, and there also had been efforts of various types, not surprisingly unsuccessful, to discourage waterfowl from alighting in pellet-infested areas. In 1936 researchers R. G. Green and R. L. Dowdell proposed lead and magnesium pellets that would disintegrate in water, or gizzards, but the resulting shot did not perform well and, in fact, all tested lead alloys proved toxic. Gradually, scientific evidence accumulated that showed nontoxic steel (actually soft iron) pellets to be the only feasible substitute for lead.[30]

Whether steel shot would work or not seemed to depend on who was being asked, but by 1970 the International Association of Game, Fish and Conservation Commissioners was convinced that it would. In that year the Association recommended, by unanimous resolution, that the Bureau of Sport Fisheries and Wildlife take "immediate steps" to "bring about an orderly transition from the use of toxic to nontoxic shot for all hunting of migratory birds" and that, absent a "compelling reason by the industry," regulations prohibiting toxic shot should be in place by the 1973 waterfowl hunting season. The National Wildlife Federation petitioned the Interior Department for similar regulations in 1972, and the Fish and Wildlife Service promised it would seek "an early solution" to the problem. Assistant Interior Secretary Nathaniel P. Reed formed a Steel Shot Coordinating Committee composed of representatives from ammunition manufacturers, flyway councils, and conservation organizations to evaluate further the extent of waterfowl poisoning and the effectiveness of steel shot.[31]

But the transition to nontoxic shot was to be neither orderly nor early. Hunters who had never seen a lead-poisoned duck were not convinced of the problem and resented inconvenience imposed by distant bureaucrats. Steel shot was more expensive than lead, had somewhat different ballistics characteristics, and was not always locally available. Early problems with performance and potential or real damage to gun barrels had been largely eliminated, but hunters in the field might not know that or be willing to grant second chances with their egos as marksmen or their prized firearms on the line. The Missouri Conservation Commission conducted an experiment with hunters who were given unmarked boxes of iron or lead shotshells. The study showed that both groups of hunters bagged similar numbers of birds and in this case the steel shot users left fewer cripples behind. But the controversy was only beginning.[32]

In 1973 the Association heard a lengthy session devoted to the nontoxic shot issue. Ralph Bitely of the Maryland Wildlife Administration gave a grim report of lead-induced waterfowl mortality ("no longer tolerable," he said) in the Chesapeake area and concluded that following a year of voluntary compliance, his agency would move forward with a state regulation prohibiting the discharge of a firearm loaded with lead within 100 yards of the important waterfowl-habitat waters of Maryland. Bitely urged the states to support a ban on lead shot in one flyway in 1974 and nationwide in 1975. Yet when the Interior Department conducted public hearings in each of the flyways on substituting steel shot for lead, Maryland was among the majority of states that opposed the Fish and Wildlife Service's proposed regulation by flyway, its legislature having decided that Maryland "should be no more progressive than the rest of the states" and "could be no more restrictive than Federal regulations provide."[33]

The IAGFCC *Newsletter* revealed the Association's growing internal dissension on the issue. The wildlife agencies of Massachusetts, Vermont, Georgia, Virginia, and Maryland in the Atlantic Flyway opposed the proposed federal regulation as did the Lead and Zinc Institute and the National Rifle Association. The International Association itself put forward at the hearings its 1974 resolution that called for local, not flyway-wide, application of steel shot through state-federal cooperation—a backing off from its earlier position. The National Wildlife Federation, several generally protectionist conservation groups, steel manufacturers, and Herbert Doig of New York, alone among the state fish and wildlife chiefs of his region, appeared on the list of those approving the immediate substitution of steel.[34]

The nontoxic shot issue had become one of states' rights, echoing the sounds of turn-of-the-century states unwilling to impose migratory bird shooting restrictions on their own hunters only to give neighboring states with more liberal laws more targets. The Association's debate on the 1974 resolution revealed members' reluctance to endure political hardship for an unpopular cause when their particular states had no significant lead poisoning problem. No one mentioned migratory birds as a national and international resource, and Bitely's stance for a nationwide ban on lead shot was conspicuously lonely. In the end the frustrated, patience-tried delegates passed a resolution, amid a chorus of "No" votes, whose wording no one was sure of. When finally printed it read that "a nation-wide or flyway-wide prohibition of the use of lead shot is unnecessary and undesirable."[35]

The Fish and Wildlife Service in 1976 began implementing a steel shot requirement anyway, first in heavily hunted Atlantic Flyway areas only, to be later expanded. By 1978 there were steel shot rulings covering parts of thirty-two states. And there were some unhappy, resisting hunters and game officials. But in 1978 Congress took a hand in the matter, passing the "Stevens Amendment" to the Interior Department's appropriation bill. It prohibited the Fish and Wildlife Service from spending federal funds to implement or enforce a nontoxic shot program in a state unless it had the state's consent, and in those states only in areas identified by the state. Basically, that put the issue back in the hands of the states, where it pitted wildlife managers against fierce local opposition to regulation. The national government, which first had tried to impose restrictions with heavy-handed lack of consideration for state input, now abdicated its responsibility to a national resource. The International Association of Fish and Wildlife Agencies opposed the Stevens Amendment, by resolution in 1978, as a political impediment to biological decision making by the Fish and Wildlife Service in cooperation with the states. But some state officials, who did not see the lead poisoning problem as a national one, favored the Stevens Amendment.[36]

The controversy swirled and touched down like a tornado at intervals for the next several years. Lead versus steel shot became a prevalent topic in contemporary outdoors literature. One of the most persuasive contributions was Steve Grooms's editorial article, "The Steel Shot Controversy," which appeared in Minnesota's *Fins and Feathers* in 1980. The "debate" was over, if there ever was one, in Grooms's view. "The jury is in, and they have found steel to be biologically necessary and ballistically effective." A misinformed failure to act on nontoxic shot gravely threatened the future of waterfowl, the future of waterfowl hunting, and the future of hunting itself, according to Grooms. Ducks and geese, a "mobile, shared resource," he said, could be managed fairly and intelligently only through a federal framework. Actions such as the Stevens Amendment put game management in the hands of "politicians with no special commitment to either hunting or natural resources." With antihunting sentiment growing, it made no sense to appear to promote poisoning ducks and give animal-rights politicians and lawyers a case for shutting down waterfowling all over. Hunters could ill afford a "to hell with the resource" attitude; it was neither ethical nor sportsmanlike to poison birds unnecessarily.[37]

The International Association, especially its Migratory Bird Committee, continued to grapple with the steel shot stumbling block. In response to an obvious need of professional wildlife personnel, conservation boards and commissions, and hunters, twenty-three states representing all four flyways, two industrial members, and the National Wildlife Federation organized a cooperative lead poisoning control information program under the leadership of Tom Roster, ballistics consultant. He conducted seminars and shooting clinics with nontoxic shot. Meanwhile, in the view of Texas game manager and IAFWA Migratory Bird Committee chairman Ted Clark, the Fish and Wildlife Service maintained "minimal" visibility, carrying out only partially its policy of conducting research and serving as an information clearing house. Regulation on toxic shot it left to the states.[38]

While lead versus steel became an increasingly polarized political issue, waterfowl mortality continued. When a few bald eagles, not only a national symbol but an endangered species, died, secondary victims of their poisoned waterfowl prey, the controversy intensified dramatically. The National Wildlife Federation sued the Department of Interior for implementation of a mandatory nontoxic shot program by 1987, arguing that lead shot "is a technological anachronism and lead poisoning is an indefensible waste of valuable wildlife resources." Convinced that the courthouse was the least satisfactory place to resolve the controversy, IAFWA Executive Committee chairman Robert Brantly, President Russell Cookingham, and Jack Berryman met with the litigating parties in Washington in an attempt to mediate the issue. But neither side would compromise. The mediation effort collapsed. Tensions ran high.[39]

In the meantime, despite the setback, the International Association of Fish and Wildlife Agencies was working hard to develop a nontoxic shot policy that would enjoy internal consensus and be both possible and palatable within the conservation, political, munitions manufacturing, and hunter communities. After several iterations the Association approved a position statement in March 1986 that called for a mandatory but gradual phase-in of nontoxic shot nationwide by 1991, starting with the counties or areas of greatest hunting intensity.[40]

Suddenly the smoke cleared. The gradual phase-in approach was a workable compromise for those who wanted nontoxic shot immediately and those who wanted it not at all. Beginning the phase-in where lead was most concentrated promised the best possible remedy for the threatened waterfowl. The Interior Department adopted the Association's policy as its own in June 1986, and the U.S. District Court, Sacramento, dismissed the National Wildlife Federation's suit as "premature." The Federation declared a victory in light of the federal government's acceptance of the IAFWA phase-in policy. In 1984 Durward Allen, emeritus professor of wildlife ecology at Purdue University, had grumbled that "we have known about lead in the marshes for 90 years. It is time we made our move." The move that worked was finally made in 1986, led by the International Association.[41]

Resource Policies: Consensus at Last

Several other long-standing efforts at broad policy making within the conservation community also came to fruition in the 1980s. Both the Departments of Agriculture and Interior, taking up business never quite finished despite considerable exertion in earlier decades, worked on perfecting national fish and wildlife policies that would guide decision making and future directions. In particular, they both managed to delineate the state-federal relationship to the satisfaction of state conservationists in binding statements of principle adopted in 1982 and 1983, respectively. That is to say, the executive departments recognized the states' primary authority over resident fish and wildlife.[42]

The International Association also renewed its determination to draft a statement of philosophy and positions on a broad range of traditional resource management concerns. The special Policy Development Committee, chaired by Glenn Bowers, started with the seventeen policy statements drafted and redrafted during the early 1970s but never adopted. The Committee updated these and added new ones to create a comprehensive compilation, "Resource Policies of the IAFWA." Its opening articulated the Association's basic premise since 1902: "Fish and wildlife resources are held in trust by the individual states and, for certain species, by the United States for the enjoyment, appreciation, economic and scientific benefit of present and future generations." One specific policy that had to be developed from scratch surprised everyone: the Association had never previously formulated a formal statement on hunting! The membership approved the Resource Policies document in 1983, reserving editorial privilege to the Executive Vice-President and Legal Counsel to eliminate any lingering historical or technical inconsistencies.[43]

The state and federal agencies finally had official references to guide their individual work as well as their interactions, most importantly on matters of jurisdictional boundaries. An ad hoc states' rights committee as late as 1981 had recommended that the Association draft a bill to confirm states' primary authority and responsibility over fish and wildlife. The Western and Southeastern Associations agreed that the time had come "to resolve once and for all" that basic question of sovereignty. Berryman deflected these proposals out of concern for "timing and strategy." Demanding a final, definitive victory seemed an unnecessary risk. (The 1964 Solicitor's opinion was not too old to remember.) The policy statements of 1982 and 1983, then in the works, would prove a practical alternative.[44]

And finally, in May 1986, continental wildlife managers rejoiced at the signing of a North American Waterfowl Management Plan by U.S. Interior Secretary Don Hodel and his Canadian counterpart, Environment Minister Thomas McMillan. Almost unraveling at the last moment, this agreement was a major international achievement, outranked only by the Migratory Bird Treaty of seventy years earlier between the same two countries. The Management Plan, like other broad policies, also stemmed from long-standing though intermittent efforts to formalize long-range cooperative plans for managing international waterfowl resources and, especially, their habitats. It established goals and strategies through the year 2000 for restoring declining migratory bird populations. The plan was to be reviewed every five years and implemented at the flyway, national, provincial, territorial, state, and private levels. It did not commit the purse of either country for the plan's total cost or for expenditures beyond its borders. It carried a strong emphasis on public-agency and private contribution. Mexico was not included, but both signatories encouraged its future participation. So in rather short order (if at long last) state, national, and international wildlife managers had clear policy tools with which to manage more effectively the resources in their charge.[45]

In sum, the intense 1980s saw both frustration and achievement. The Association proved unable to resolve the persistent Indian rights controversy or harness the media. But the Sagebrush Rebellion was deflected, and fish and wildlife programs won new funding and respect in an era of reduced federal support. The International Association scored major victories in nontoxic shot implementation and international water fowl management. Its own house was in order.

In Retrospect

A retrospective look at the societal context within which the International Association of Fish and Wildlife Agencies has carried out its mission shows undulating, shifting currents of thought and action. Within the scope of this study, the conservation, or, later, environmental, movement has known three distinguishable crests of popular support. Outdoorsman Theodore Roosevelt was responsible for the first. Under Roosevelt's dynamic personal and presidential leadership, Gifford Pinchot and others first articulated the need for wise use of natural resources. The second wave of conservation interest crested during the presidency of Franklin D. Roosevelt, who pragmatically linked his own lifelong engagement with the natural world to the economic needs of the desperate 1930s. Programs he promoted, such as the Civilian Conservation Corps, served the dual purpose of benefiting the environment and providing jobs for the most vulnerable resource of all, people. World War II demanded different priorities, and it was not until the 1960s that conservation interest peaked again. President John F. Kennedy lent his personal magnetism to the cause and encouraged it through imaginative, articulate leaders such as Interior Secretary Stewart Udall. This third wave persisted through the 1970s, though for wildlife conservationists the movement significantly changed its character with the rise of antimanagement advocacy groups. The Association's fortunes, as seen, have ridden these three waves.

While the Association has remained remarkably stable in its goals and purposes over the years, its principal opposition has shifted ground. During the early days of the century, a "frontier mentality" that assumed everlasting, unlimited resources still commonly prevailed. Game commissioners gathered together to promote policies of limited, intelligent hunting and fishing practices to preserve the wildlife from extinction at the hands of shortsighted or unscrupulous "game hogs" and market hunters. The conservationists cooperated to put these thoughtless shooters out of business, but in recent years wildlife managers have been more severely challenged by protectionists and even more radical animal-rights proponents who oppose the killing of animals at any time for any reason regardless of scientific opinion or the consequences for either animal or human society.[46]

Another change observable over time is the training and status of individual state fish and game managers. The earliest of these officials were usually patronage appointees with skimpy education, if any, in resource management and little administrative or enforcement power. Money was scarce and tied to political vagaries; scientific research was scarcer. Gradually, professionalism increased as colleges established formal programs in fish and wildlife management and directors were chosen for their technical knowledge and skill. The creation of the Cooperative Wildlife Research Units at land grant colleges in the 1930s marked a turning point for educational training. The Pittman-Robertson and Dingell-Johnson Acts, which required trained personnel to administer restoration programs in the states, in effect mandated improved education and directed the development of curricula at these colleges, now numbering twenty-two. They are still the training grounds for the vast majority of wildlife professionals. Currently, the field seems to be undergoing a new period of politicization and rapid turnover, which inhibits program continuity and erodes morale. Yet, even political replacements today are likely to be professionally qualified.

Availability of financial support has ebbed and flowed, but funding has ever been a challenge. States are now looking to nontraditional sources of revenue to support game and nongame programs to supplement historical efforts such as those funded by the Pittman-Robertson and Wallop-Breaux Acts.[47]

The state-federal relationship, a dominant theme in the history of the International Association, has ever been dynamic and fraught with the tension of jurisdictional clashes. Overall, the states have seen their authority eroded by national and international law. Yet the present time marks a high point in mutual trust and cooperation among resource leaders representing the two levels of government, to the benefit of fish and wildlife.

The mid-1980s have proven to be a satisfying point from which to review the achievements of the International Association of Fish and Wildlife Agencies. Long-standing programs have been confirmed and now possess assured futures; many loose ends from the past have been tied up. A strong, confident, respected organization has decided its future goals and direction. Knowing its past will help judge the wisdom of its future choices. The International Association has known disappointment, failure, even embarrassment. But its history has been a success story.

Appendix A
Chronology of Major Developments in the History of Fish and Wildlife Management

1629	The West India Company granted hunting privileges to persons planting colonies in New Netherlands.
1647	Massachusetts Bay colonial ordinance contained provisions regarding the "right of hunting."
1694	Massachusetts established the first closed season on deer.
1708	The first closed season on birds was designated, in certain New York counties, for heath hen, grouse, quail, and turkey.
1739	Massachusetts established the first game warden system. New York followed in 1741.
1776	The first federal game law required closed seasons on deer in all colonies except Georgia.
1782	The bald eagle became recognized as the national emblem.
1789	The U.S. Constitution established federal authority over treaty making, federal land policy, and interstate commerce. It did not specifically mention wildlife, but these provisions have been cited ever since in matters of jurisdiction over various wildlife issues.
1802	The U.S. Army Corps of Engineers was formed.
1812	General Land Office was established within the Department of the Treasury to administer sales and surveys of public land.
1818	Massachusetts enacted the first law protecting nongame birds, declaring a closed season on larks and robins.
1832	The United States established its first national park, in Hot Springs, Arkansas.
1836	The Bureau of Indian Affairs was established.
May 20, 1844	The New York Sportmen's Club, the first conservation organization in the United States, met for the first time in New York City. In 1873 it became the New York Association for the Protection of Game.

Appendix A

1846	Rhode Island enacted the first law against spring shooting. It forbade the killing of wood duck, black duck, woodcock, and snipe.
March 3, 1849	The Department of Interior was established, assuming management of the General Land Office and Bureau of Indian Affairs, along with other federal agencies.
1852	California established the first closed season on antelope and elk.
May 20, 1862	Congress passed the Homestead Act, promoting westward agricultural expansion.
1864	Idaho passed the first game law seasonally protecting bison, along with deer, elk, antelope, mountain sheep, and mountain goats.
c. 1865	Massachusetts established a Commission of Fisheries and Game, probably the first state game commission.
1870	The American Fisheries Society was formed.
1871	Congress established the U.S. Fisheries Commission to redistribute, propagate, and introduce desirable game and food fishes (16 Stat. 593). Dr. Spencer Baird was the first Commissioner of Fisheries.
March 1, 1872	Congress established Yellowstone National Park (17 Stat. 32).
1872	Maryland passed the first law providing rest days for waterfowl hunting.
1873	New Jersey passed the first nonresident hunting license law, although several states had earlier laws restricting or prohibiting nonresident hunting.
1873	Charles Halleck founded *Forest and Stream*, a weekly conservation and sportsmen's journal.
1875	Arkansas established the first law prohibiting the market hunting of waterfowl.
1875	The American Forestry Association was organized.
1878	Iowa limited its hunters to twenty-five prairie chickens per day, the first bag limit law in the country.
March 3, 1885	Congress created the Bureau of Biological Survey within the Department of Agriculture for the purpose of collecting specimens of certain species, especially birds, and researching their relationship to agriculture. Until 1896 this agency was called the Division of Economic Ornithology and Mammalogy; it became the U.S. Fish and Wildlife Service in 1940.
December 1887	Theodore Roosevelt organized the Boone and Crockett Club to promote the interests of big game conservation and hunting.
1887	George Bird Grinnell helped found New York's Audubon Society, the nation's first.
March 3, 1891	The Forest Reserve Act permitted the President to set aside forest reserves (later national forests) on the public domain.
1892	President Benjamin Harrison by proclamation prohibited hunting and

	fishing on Alaska's Afognak Island, thus creating the first national wildlife refuge (Proclamation No. 39, 27 Stat. 1052).
May 7, 1894	The Yellowstone Park Protection Act protected all wildlife, timber, and minerals within the park from molestation. The Act prohibited hunting but allowed hook and line fishing (28 Stat. 73).
1894	George Bird Grinnell first warned Americans about the dangers of lead poisoning to waterfowl from ingesting spent shot pellets.
1895	Michigan and North Dakota passed the first laws requiring all hunters to purchase a license from the state.
1896	In Geer v. Connecticut, the U.S. Supreme Court affirmed the concept of state ownership of game, ruling that a Connecticut law that forbade the shipment of game birds out of the state did not preempt Federal prerogative over interstate commerce (161 U.S. 519).
1897	G. O. Shields and New York sportsmen founded the Camp Fire Club, which gained national influence after it formed a conservation committee in 1909.
January 18, 1898	R. P. Lydecker and G. O. Shields organized the League of American Sportsmen in New York City to assist in the enforcement of existing game laws and promote conservation awareness. It lasted until 1908.
May 25, 1900	Congress passed the Lacey Act to prevent interstate transportation of game killed in violation of local laws (31 Stat. 187).
July 20, 1902	William F. Scott, the Game Commissioner for Montana, convened the first meeting of the National Association of Game and Fish Wardens and Commissioners at Mammoth Hot Springs in Yellowstone National Park.
1903	Theodore Roosevelt, by presidential proclamation, established Pelican Island, Florida, as a bird sanctuary and the first of what became the National Wildlife Refuge System.
December 1904	Congressman George Shiras (R-PA) introduced the first federal migratory bird bill in Congress.
January 24, 1905	Congress authorized the President to set aside areas in the Wichita Forest Reserve, Oklahoma, for the protection of game animals and birds (33 Stat. 614).
February 1, 1905	The U.S. Forest Service supplanted the Division of Forestry in the Department of Agriculture to administer the national forests. Gifford Pinchot was its chief.
1905	The National Association of Audubon Societies was formed.
June 8, 1906	The Antiquities Act authorized the President to set aside as national monuments areas of historical, archaeological, or scenic significance. Theodore Roosevelt used this act to preserve many wildlife ranges.
June 28, 1906	Congress prohibited the hunting of birds on wildlife refuges except under the regulations of the Secretary of Agriculture (34 Stat. 536).
1906	The National Association of Game and Fish Wardens and Commis-

	sioners adopted its first constitution and elected its first Honorary Life Member, Dr. T. S. Palmer.
1907	Gifford Pinchot, as described in his autobiography *Breaking New Ground*, developed the concept of the interrelationship of forests, soils, waters, fish, wildlife, minerals, and other natural resources. WJ McGee coined the term "conservation" to describe it.
May 1908	Theodore Roosevelt was host of the first White House Governors' Conference on the subject of conservation, including the conservation of wildlife resources.
February 18, 1909	President Roosevelt convened the first North American Conservation Conference in Washington, D.C., attended by representatives from the United States, Canada, Newfoundland, and Mexico.
April 21, 1910	Congress passed an act for the protection and utilization of fur seals, sea otters, and other furbearers in Alaska. The Act established a special reservation on the Pribilof Islands and forbade the killing of fur seals in the Pacific Ocean (36 Stat. 326).
July 7, 1911	An international convention between the United States, Great Britain, Japan, and Russia prohibited pelagic sealing in the North Pacific Ocean (37 Stat. 1542).
1911	Firearms manufacturers organized the American Game Protective Association.
1911	Congress passed the Weeks Act, making possible the purchase of land to establish national forests in the East.
August 1912	The National Association of Game and Fish Commissioners, meeting in Denver, adopted its first bylaws and printed the proceedings of its annual meeting in book form.
March 4, 1913	The Weeks-McLean Migratory Bird Act declared all migratory game and insectivorous birds to be "within the custody and protection of the government of the United States" through the Department of Agriculture (37 Stat. 828, 847).
July 1, 1914	Congress appropriated the first federal funds for predatory animal control in national forests and on other public lands in order to protect livestock.
September 1, 1914	The last passenger pigeon died in captivity in the Cincinnati Zoo, making the species extinct.
August 16, 1916	The United States and Canada (through Great Britain) signed a treaty for the protection of migratory birds by prohibiting or regulating their hunting (39 Stat. 1702).
August 25, 1916	Congress established the National Park Service "to conserve the scenery and the natural and historical objects and the wildlife" of national parks, monuments, and reservations.
1917	The first Crown Game Preserve in Ontario was established by order-in-council.
1917	The National Association of Game and Fish Commissioners became

	the International Association of Game, Fish and Conservation Commissioners. The change in name reflected the Association's interest in full cooperation with Canada. Dues were set at twenty-five dollars per year for state members.
July 3, 1918	Congress passed the Migratory Bird Treaty Act, authorizing U.S. compliance with the Migratory Bird Treaty of 1916 (40 Stat. 755).
April 19, 1920	The U.S. Supreme Court, in the case of Missouri v. Holland, upheld the constitutionality of the Migratory Bird Treaty of 1916, ruling that federal treaty-making powers overrode state ownership of game and permitted federal regulation (252 U.S. 416).
January 1922	Representatives from seven western states met in Salt Lake City to form the Western Association of State Game Commissioners for the purpose of promoting western conservation interests.
1922	The Izaak Walton League, a private conservation organization, was formed.
June 7, 1924	With an appropriation of $1.5 million for land acquisition, Congress established the Upper Mississippi River Wildlife and Fish Refuge (43 Stat. 650).
1924	The first National Conference on Outdoor Recreation was held in Washington, D.C.
1924	Congress passed the Clarke-McNary Act, which extended federal ability to buy lands for inclusion in the national forest system and provided for private, state, and federal cooperation in forest management.
January 13, 1925	The Alaska Game Law created an Alaska Game Commission under the Bureau of Biological Survey and established bird and mammal protection equivalent to state laws in the United States (43 Stat. 739).
May 20, 1926	The Hawes Act prohibited interstate shipment of black bass when state law forbade their import or export (44 Stat. 576).
April 23, 1928	Congress established the Bear River Migratory Bird Refuge in Box Elder County, Utah (45 Stat. 448).
1928	The U.S. Supreme Court ruled, in the Kaibab deer control case Hunt v. United States, that the United States could protect its lands and property notwithstanding state law.
1928	The IAGFCC spearheaded the creation of the National Committee on Wild Life Legislation. The Committee was composed of one member each from the IAGFCC, the Western Association of State Game Commissioners, American Forestry Association, the Izaak Walton League, and the National Association of Audubon Societies; and five at-large members selected by these representatives.
February 18, 1929	The Migratory Bird Conservation Act (Norbeck-Andreson) established a Migratory Bird Conservation Commission and authorized the acquisition of waterfowl refuge land subject to state consultation (45 Stat. 1222).

Appendix A

December 2, 1929	President Herbert Hoover advocated consolidating the federal government's eight agencies in five departments for the conservation of natural resources into one. It never happened.
April 17, 1930	The U.S. Senate formed a Special Committee on the Conservation of Wild Life Resources.
June 17, 1930	Congress removed import duties on live game birds used for stocking purposes as the National Committee on Wild Life Legislation had recommended.
1930	The National Park Service created a Wildlife Division, which assumed responsibility for wildlife resource management, biological research, and the study of problems arising from the joint use of wilderness areas by animals and humans, within the National Parks.
July 14, 1932	Congress passed the District of Columbia Refuge Act (S. 3792), making migratory bird hunting illegal in the District.
1932	J. N. "Ding" Darling led the effort to establish a training school in game management at Iowa State College. It became the model for the Cooperative Wildlife Research Unit Program.
March 31, 1933	Congress established the Civilian Conservation Corps (CCC) as part of Roosevelt's New Deal effort to create employment as well as promote forest conservation (48 Stat. 22).
May 12, 1933	In order to relieve unemployment through forestry and other conservation measures, Congress, with the strong support of President Roosevelt, passed the Federal Emergency Relief Act (48 Stat. 55).
May 18, 1933	Congress established the Tennessee Valley Authority (48 Stat. 58).
January 1934	President Roosevelt appointed a Wildlife Restoration Committee (Thomas Beck, Jay N. "Ding" Darling, and Aldo Leopold) to make policy recommendations such as rehabilitating submarginal lands for game development.
March 10, 1934	The Coordination Act authorized the Secretaries of Agriculture and Commerce to cooperate with federal, state, and other agencies to develop a nationwide program of wildlife conservation and rehabilitation and to recommend remedial measures for water pollution and unwise water impoundments (48 Stat. 401).
March 10, 1934	Congress passed the Joseph T. Robinson National Forest Refuge Act, establishing fish and game sanctuaries in national forests upon the approval of the states containing the forests.
March 16, 1934	The Migratory Bird Hunting Stamp ("Duck Stamp") Act, the first federal statute creating a fund exclusively for wildlife conservation, required the takers (age sixteen and over) of migratory waterfowl to purchase a one-dollar federal hunting stamp annually. Proceeds would be used to acquire and manage waterfowl refuges (48 Stat. 451).
March 29, 1934	The Department of Agriculture issued Regulation G-20-A, investing the Secretary of Agriculture with broad powers to regulate hunting

	and fishing within national forests. State game officials vigorously protested the regulation as a usurpation of state jurisdiction.
June 28, 1934	The Taylor Grazing Act provided for the protection of public lands from overgrazing and soil erosion by regulating their use and occupancy (48 Stat. 1269).
December 1934	The State Park Division of the National Park Service created a wildlife section to protect fauna and flora in the state parks.
1934	The number of migratory waterfowl crossing the continental United States, which had been steadily declining since 1925, dropped to its lowest point because of drought, swamp drainage, overshooting, and inadequate enforcement of the Migratory Bird Treaty Act.
1934	The International's Committee on Model Game and Fish Law, under the chairmanship of the Hon. Harry B. Hawes, submitted a model organizational bill for the creation of state fish and game commissions, along with supplemental suggestions for additional sections to existing game codes.
April 27, 1935	The Soil Conservation Act created the Soil Conservation Service within the Department of Agriculture for the control and prevention of soil erosion (49 Stat. 163).
June 15, 1935	In addition to providing a payment of 25 percent of the gross receipts from wildlife refuges to counties for use on schools and roads, Congress authorized the addition of land to wildlife refuges by exchange of (1) land, timber, or other materials in wildlife refuges or (2) of unreserved nonmineral lands on an equal value basis (49 Stat. 378, 382).
August 14, 1935	The American Wildlife Institute was formed to promote and assist in the coordination of the wildlife conservation, restoration, and management work of existing agencies in the Western Hemisphere. Through a Federated Council, the Institute proposed to function as a larger-scale version of the National Committee on Wildlife Legislation. It launched research and training programs in game management at nine land grant colleges.
1935	The Cooperative Wildlife Research Unit Program, to conduct wildlife research and provide academic training in professional wildlife management, was initiated at nine land grant colleges.
February 7, 1936	The United States and Mexico signed a treaty for the Protection of Migratory Birds and Game Mammals, modeled in part on the 1916 treaty between the United States and Canada. It limited hunting of migratory birds, endorsed "refuge zones" in which hunting was forbidden, and prohibited hunting from aircraft.
February 1936	Franklin Roosevelt was host of the first North American Wildlife Conference, to consider wildlife restoration and conservation.
June 16, 1936	Wildlife management on Indian reservations was placed under the jurisdiction of the Division of Forestry and Grazing in the Bureau of Indian Affairs.

Appendix A

June 20, 1936	Congress passed the enabling act for the Convention on wildlife between the United States and Mexico, giving the Secretary of Agriculture regulatory responsibility (49 Stat. 1555).
1936	The U.S. Forest Service established a Division of Game Management. Formerly the Division of Grazing handled wildlife management responsibilities.
1936	Congress considered the Kleeberg Bill, which proposed to consolidate in the Department of Agriculture all federal activities relating to wildlife. It did not pass.
1936	The National Wildlife Federation was founded.
September 2, 1937	President Roosevelt signed the Pittman-Robertson Federal Aid to Wildlife Restoration Act which apportioned proceeds from excise taxes (10 percent) on arms and ammunition to the states according to a formula based on total area and number of hunters, for wildlife restoration projects.
1937	The Wildlife Society was organized.
May 11, 1938	Congress authorized the Secretary of Commerce to carry out measures to protect migratory fish (salmon) from irrigation projects (52 Stat. 345).
May 9, 1939	Reorganization Plan No. 2 transferred the Bureau of Fisheries, formerly in the Department of Commerce, and the Bureau of Biological Survey, formerly in the Department of Agriculture, to the Department of Interior. The Secretary of Interior became the chairman of the Migratory Bird Conservation Commission (53 Stat. 1431, 1433).
April 2, 1940	Reorganization Plan No. 3 created the U.S. Fish and Wildlife Service in the Interior Department by consolidating the Bureau of Fisheries and the Bureau of Biological Survey (54 Stat. 1231, 1232).
August 30, 1940	The U.S. Court of Appeals, Fourth Circuit, ruled against the state of North Carolina in the Pisgah National Forest case, Chalk v. United States, noting that on ceded lands the federal administrators could reduce the deer population to protect its lands from injury. The Supreme Court declined to review the decision.
October 12, 1940	A convention between the United States and other American republics committed the signatories to take appropriate steps to protect nature and wildlife in their respective countries (56 Stat. 1354).
April 1941	The Secretary of Agriculture, working with Association leaders, repealed Forestry Regulation G-20-A and replaced it with Regulation W-2, which recognized state authority and encouraged state-federal cooperation in the maintenance of desirable wildlife populations on national forest lands.
June 1, 1942	As a continuation of the 1911 Fur Seal Convention, the United States and Canada signed the Provisional Fur Seal Agreement that increased Canada's share of the take at the Pribilof Islands from 15 to 20 percent (58 Stat. 1379).

Appendix A

1942–1945	The IAGFCC refrained from holding annual meetings in response to wartime restrictions on travel.
May 16, 1946	The General Land Office and the Grazing Service were combined to create the Bureau of Land Management in the Department of Interior (60 Stat. 1097, 1099).
May 1946	The Wildlife Management Institute was created to promote the public activities of the American Wildlife Institute, which later continued as the North American Wildlife Foundation.
July 24, 1946	An amendment to the Wildlife Restoration Act of 1937 revised the apportionment of funds so that any one state could receive no less than one-half of 1 percent and no more than 5 percent of the total amount apportioned while the federal government could support up to 25 percent of the maintenance costs of completed wildlife restoration projects (60 Stat. 656).
August 8, 1946	Congress directed the Fish and Wildlife Service to conduct "vigorous" programs to eliminate sea lamprey from the Great Lakes (60 Stat. 930).
August 14, 1946	An amendment strengthened the Coordination Act of 1934 by requiring all new federal water projects to include provisions to prevent or minimize damage to fish and wildlife (60 Stat. 1080).
December 2, 1946	The United States and fourteen other nations signed a convention to establish an International Whaling Commission to investigate and regulate whaling practices (62 Stat. 1716).
1946	The Association first discussed the possibility of establishing a national office in Washington.
1947	The Fish and Wildlife Service administratively created the Atlantic, Mississippi, Central, and Pacific Flyways to better administer hunting regulations for migratory birds.
1947	The Association increased state member dues to forty dollars.
May 19, 1948	The Wherry-Burke Act authorized the transfer of surplus war property to the states for use in wildlife conservation purposes other than for migratory birds or to the Secretary of Interior if the land had particular value for migratory bird management (62 Stat. 240).
June 30, 1948	The Water-Pollution Control Act (Taft-Barkley Act) authorized federal appropriations to aid states and municipalities in the implementation of programs for stream population abatement (62 Stat. 1155).
February 8, 1949	The United States and ten other countries signed a convention to establish an International Commission for the Northwest Atlantic Fisheries with investigative and regulatory responsibilities (64 Stat. 1067).
August 12, 1949	A new Duck Stamp Act increased the price of the hunting stamp to two dollars (63 Stat. 599).
August 9, 1950	The Dingell-Johnson Federal Aid to State Fisheries Act provided federal aid to the states for fish restoration and management projects, with money from excise taxes on fishing equipment (64 Stat. 430).

Appendix A

May 9, 1952	A Convention among the United States, Canada, and Japan established the North Pacific Fisheries Commission with authority to conduct investigations and make recommendations to protect the respective countries' interests in the fisheries of the North Pacific (68 Stat. 698).
1952	The regional flyway councils and National Waterfowl Council were all operating.
August 1955	The Bible-Price-Young Act allocated the $13.5 million surplus in Pittman-Robertson funds to the states over a five-year period. Further amendments to the Pittman-Robertson Act allowed expenditures for management of wildlife areas and resources under a broad definition that excluded little except law enforcement and public relations activities (69 Stat. 698).
1955	The United States and Canada established the Great Lakes Fishery Commission to control the parasitic sea lamprey.
1955	Crossley, S-D Surveys, Inc. of New York conducted the first National Survey of Fishing and Hunting under contract to the Fish and Wildlife Service.
1955	The Fish and Wildlife Service was divided into the Bureau of Commercial Fisheries and the Bureau of Sport Fisheries and Wildlife.
July 9, 1956	The Federal Water Pollution Control Act strengthened the Taft-Barkley Act with tougher enforcement, increased appropriations for municipal sewage treatment plant construction, and a Water Pollution Advisory Board (70 Stat. 498).
1958	A new Fish and Wildlife Coordination Act stipulated that wildlife conservation receive equal consideration and be coordinated with other features of water resource development programs.
1958	The Association first convened a Legal Committee.
1958	Congress established an Outdoor Recreation Resources Review Commission to inventory resources and recommend policies and programs for future needs.
1958	Congress raised the Duck Stamp fee to three dollars.
1958	The Engle Act confirmed that state game and fishing laws, regulations, and maintenance responsibilities applied to federally controlled or owned military lands.
1960	Sikes Military Reservation Act authorized funds for wildlife improvement on military lands and protected the state's jurisdiction over wildlife and licensing thereon.
1961	The United States and Canada established an International Migratory Birds Committee representing agricultural and wildlife interests in lieu of an acceptable convention on waterfowl management.
1961	The Association of Conservation Engineers was formed to promote sound engineering practices in fish, wildlife, and recreation project development.

Appendix A

1961	The Wetlands Loan Act allowed the Fish and Wildlife Service to draw upon future duck stamp revenues to purchase habitat.
May 1962	President John F. Kennedy was host of the Third White House Conference on Conservation, which focused on environmental quality.
1963	The Bureau of Outdoor Recreation was established in the Interior Department to coordinate federal recreational programs.
March 1964	Association President Nelson Cox appointed an ad hoc committee on the "Federal Invasion of State Rights."
September 3, 1964	The Land and Water Conservation Fund Act created a user fee-generated, earmarked fund to develop outdoor recreational facilities in the states (78 Stat. 897).
December 1, 1964	The Interior Department's Deputy Solicitor Edward Weinberg declared that the United States had constitutional power, superior to state power, to control and protect its lands and resident wildlife thereon.
1964	The Wilderness Act established a National Wilderness Preservation System.
1964	Congress established the Public Land Law Review Commission to examine and suggest improvements in policies, laws, and regulations affecting federal lands, their resources, and their uses.
July 9, 1965	The Federal Water Project Recreation Act promised "full consideration" to outdoor recreation opportunities and fish and wildlife enhancement during the planning and implementation of federal water projects (79 Stat. 213).
1965	The Association established a Public Land Law Review Committee "to assist and keep abreast of" the Public Land Law Review Commission's proceedings.
1965	The Bureau of Sport Fisheries and Wildlife, through the Department of Interior Library, contracted with the Denver Public Library to collect, index, store, and make available for reference use all existing and future Pittman-Robertson and Dingell-Johnson published and unpublished reports. The program was called the Wildlife Reference Service or simply "the Library."
1965	The Federal Water Quality Control Act established a federal Water Pollution Control Administration to provide research and development grants and increased municipal sewage treatment plant grants. It also required the establishment of water quality standards for interstate waters (79 Stat. 903).
1965	The Anadromous Fish Conservation Act (PL 89-304) directed the Interior Secretary to make studies and recommendations to conserve and enhance anadromous fishery resources (79 Stat. 1125).
November 3, 1966	The Clean Water Restoration Act further improved the Water Pollution Control Act with grant aid for pollution abatement studies and programs in basin areas (80 Stat. 1246).

Appendix A

1966	The first Endangered Species Preservation Act authorized the Secretary of Interior to fund studies and acquire lands for habitat for imperiled species using the Land and Water Conservation Fund. The Act made no provision for the restriction of hunting, selling, or otherwise taking designated species (80 Stat. 926).
1966	The Association retained Paul Lenzini as Legal Counsel.
1969	The U.S. Court of Appeals, Tenth Circuit, in the state-federal authority case New Mexico State Game Commission v. Udall, reversed a lower court and held that Carlsbad Caverns National Park administrators had the power, under the Constitution's property clause, to protect federal lands from deer degradation without state interference.
1969	The Endangered Species Conservation Act, supplementing and expanding the 1966 Act, authorized the Interior Secretary to generate a list of species threatened with worldwide extinction and banned their importation except for limited purposes (83 Stat. 275).
April 22, 1970	Environmentalists celebrated the first Earth Day.
September 1970	The Department of Interior issued a regulatory statement that recognized the legitimacy of state authority over resident wildlife and encouraged cordial state-federal relationships.
1970	The National Environmental Policy Act (NEPA) required an environmental impact statement (EIS) for any federal action significantly affecting the quality of the human environment. The Act did not specifically provide for the protection of wildlife, but subsequent court decisions implicitly assumed wildlife to be a part of the "human environment." The Environmental Protection Agency was formed.
1970	The Association authorized the establishment of a full-time Washington office; no immediate action was taken. Dues were raised to $1000.
1970	The Association presented its first Seth Gordon Award for "inspired leadership and distinguished services in natural resources management" to Seth Gordon.
December 1971	The Association issued its "Public Land Law Policy Impact on Fish and Wildlife" in response to the Public Land Law Review Commission's "One-Third of the Land," of 1970.
1971	The Wild Free-Roaming Horses and Burros Act directed the Secretary of Interior, or Agriculture, as appropriate, to protect these animals on public lands as historic relics of the old West.
April 1, 1972	Russell Neugebauer became the Association's first full-time Executive Vice-President.
September 1972	President Nixon declared the first National Hunting and Fishing Day, to be an annual observance on the fourth Saturday of September.
1972	The Marine Mammal Protection Act imposed a moratorium on the taking or importation of marine mammals or products made from

	them, with certain exceptions such as harvest by natives, and preempted state authority over these animals (86 Stat. 1027).
1972	The Association proposed its first magazine venture, *The American Outdoors*, with the cosponsorship of the American Association for Conservation Information. It was not published.
May 1, 1973	John Gottschalk was appointed Executive Vice-President, filling the vacancy caused by Neugebauer's death on December 16, 1972.
November 1973	The *IAGFCC Newsletter* was inaugurated.
1973	The Endangered Species Act prohibited the taking of species listed as "endangered," protected "look-alikes" or species threatened over only part of their range, and designated "critical habitats" that must be preserved. The Interior Secretary could fund up to 75 percent of the cost of a cooperative program with a state to benefit an endangered species (87 Stat. 884).
1973	The United States ratified the Convention on International Trade in Endangered Species, which went into effect in 1975 upon signature by ten nations.
February 1974	A U.S. district court decision, upheld on appeal, in United States v. Washington, gave Native Americans uncontested fishing rights in certain western Washington coastal streams and the right to half the off-reservation catch. These rights, based on treaties, were affirmed by the U.S. Supreme Court in 1979.
July 8, 1974	U.S. Court of Appeals, District of Columbia Circuit, ruled in the Great Swamp case (Humane Society of the United States v. Morton) that public hunting was an authorized use of a national wildlife refuge, thus recognizing hunting as a legitimate management tool under state control.
1974	The Sikes Act Extension formally endorsed cooperative measures between the Secretaries of Interior and Agriculture and the states for conservation and rehabilitation programs, under state jurisdiction, on military lands. It required habitat restoration and protection for endangered species.
1974	The Association dues for state members increased to $1,500.
1975	The regional associations became eligible for IAGFCC membership, their presidents automatically becoming members of the Executive Committee.
June 17, 1976	The Supreme Court, in Kleppe v. New Mexico, ruled that Congress exercises complete control, under the property clause, over public lands including the power to regulate and protect wildlife living there.
1976	The Federal Land Policy and Management Act recognized state authority over fish and resident wildlife on national resource lands, reserving to federal authorities limited, specified controls.
January 1, 1977	The International Association of Game, Fish and Conservation Commissioners changed its name to the International Association of Fish and Wildlife Agencies.

Appendix A

1977	The Association's Magazine Subcommittee initiated start-up funding efforts for a proposed management magazine, to be entitled *Earth One*. The project was dropped in 1979 when fund raising failed.
1977	IAFWA established America's Wildlife Association for Resource Education (AWARE) Foundation to raise funds for its television and magazine projects.
March 1978	The Association raised state member dues to $3,000.
1978	The International Convention for the Conservation of Migratory Species of Wild Animals ("Bonn Convention") was drafted and accepted in West Germany. The United States did not sign.
1978	The U.S. Supreme Court affirmed a state's right to charge unequal hunting license fees for residents and nonresidents (Terk v. Gordon, Baldwin v. Montana).
1978	Congress passed the "Stevens Amendment" which forbade the Fish and Wildlife Service to expend federal funds to impose a nontoxic shot program in a state unless it had the state's consent.
January 1, 1979	Jack Berryman became the Association's Executive Vice-President.
1979	The Association created the new position Legislative Counsel for the Washington office, naming to it John Gottschalk.
1979	The case Committee for Humane Legislation v. Andrus, which threatened funding of Pittman-Robertson projects because of their failure to include Environmental Impact Statements, was dismissed, but the court required notice of availability of environmental assessment reports.
August 1980	The IAFWA sponsored a World Furbearer Conference in Frostburg, Maryland.
1980	Association bylaw amendments made Canada and Mexico ex officio members of the Executive Committee.
January 1, 1981	State Member dues increased to $6,000.
July 20, 1982	The Department of Agriculture approved a Policy on Fish and Wildlife.
1982	Amendments to the Endangered Species Act and the Bobcat II case (Defenders of Wildlife v. Endangered Species Scientific Authority) lifted the requirement of population estimates to reach no-detriment findings for export of animals or pelts under CITES and recognized the primary authority of the states.
March 18, 1983	The Department of Interior released a Fish and Wildlife Policy: State-Federal Relationships.
September 1983	The Association approved a statement of principles, "Resource Policies of the IAFWA," in draft, at its convention in Milwaukee.
1983	The IAFWA initiated a State Associate program, bringing a state conservationist to Washington for a year of research and training.
December 1984	The Wallop-Breaux Act supplanted the Dingell-Johnson program for

	fish restoration and increased its income by adding a 3 percent tax on boats and motors.
March 1986	The IAFWA proposed the gradual but mandatory phase-in of non-toxic shot, beginning in areas of greatest hunting intensity, to be completed by 1991. The Interior Department accepted these guidelines in June 1986.
May 1986	The United States and Canada signed the North American Waterfowl Management Plan to restore declining waterfowl populations and improve habitat.

Appendix B
Presidents of the International Association of Fish and Wildlife Agencies

Name	*Years Served*	*State*
* W. F. Scott	1902–1907	Montana
* T. Gilbert Pearson	1910–1912	New York
* Joseph Acklen	1912–1913	Tennessee
* George H. Graham	1914–1916	Massachusetts
* M. L. Alexander	1916–1918	Louisiana
* J. Quincy Ward	1918–1919	Kentucky
* W. E. Barber	1919–1921	Wisconsin
* Honore Mercier	1921–1922	Quebec
* William C. Adams	1922–1923	Massachusetts
* Lee Miles	1923–1924	Arkansas
* J. B. Harkin	1924–1925	Ontario
* E. Lee LeCompte	1925–1926	Maryland
* F. C. Walcott	1926–1927	Connecticut
* I. T. Quinn	1927–1928	Alabama
* David H. Madsen	1928–1929	Utah
* Hoyes Lloyd	1929–1930	Ontario
* Llewellyn Legge	1930–1931	New York
* William J. Tucker	1931–1932	Texas
* Ross L. Leffler	1932–1933	Pennsylvania
* Guy Amsler	1933–1934	Arkansas
* James Brown	1934–1935	Vermont
Elliott S. Barker	1935–1936	New Mexico
* Charles F. Thompson	1936–1937	Illinois
* Frank B. O'Connell	1937–1938	Nebraska
* Arthur L. Clark	1938–1939	Missouri
* J. D. Chalk	1939–1940	North Carolina
* Seth Gordon	1940–1941	Pennsylvania
* P. J. Hoffmaster	1941–1946	Michigan
* I. T. Bode	1946–1947	Missouri

Appendix B

Name	*Years Served*	*State*
* Lester Bagley	1947–1948	Wyoming
* R. P. Hunter	1948–1949	Connecticut
* Dr. Harrison F. Lewis	1949–1950	Ontario
* Cleland N. Feast	1950–1951	Colorado
George W. Davis	1951–1952	Vermont
Chester S. Wilson	1952–1953	Minnesota
* Harry D. Ruhl	1953–1954	Michigan
Howard D. Dodgen	1954–1955	Texas
* Bruce F. Stiles	1955–1956	Iowa
* Dr. W. J. K. Harkness	1956–1957	Ontario
John A. Biggs	1957–1958	Washington
* A. D. Aldrich	1958–1959	Florida
Clyde P. Patton	1959–1960	North Carolina
P. W. Schneider	1960–1961	Oregon
* Hayden W. Olds	1961–1962	Ohio
Frank W. Groves	1962–1963	Nevada
* Nelson Cox	1963–1964	Arkansas
L. P. Voigt	1964–1965	Wisconsin
William E. Towell	1965–1966	Missouri
* Melvin O. Steen	1966–1967	Nebraska
Walter T. Shannon	1967–1968	California
W. Mason Lawrence	1968–1969	New York
Harry Woodward	1969–1970	Colorado
Chester F. Phelps	1970–1971	Virginia
* Ralph A. MacMullan	1971–1972	Michigan
Carl N. Crouse	1972–1973	Washington
O. Earle Frye, Jr.	1973–1974	Florida
Kenneth H. Doan	1974–1975	Manitoba
John E. Phelps	1975–1976	Utah
Charles D. Kelley	1976–1977	Alabama
Russell W. Stuart	1977–1978	North Dakota
Glenn L. Bowers	1978–1979	Pennsylvania
Robert A. Jantzen	1979–1980	Arizona
Larry R. Gale	1980–1981	Missouri
E. Charles Fullerton	1981–1982	California
Dr. James Timmerman	1982–1983	South Carolina
C. D. Besadny	1983–1984	Wisconsin
Russell A. Cookingham	1984–1985	New Jersey
Gary T. Myers	1985–1986	Tennessee

* Deceased

Appendix C
Dates and Places of Annual Meetings, International Association of Fish and Wildlife Agencies

Year	*Place*	*Dates*
1902	Yellowstone National Park, Wyoming	July 20
1904	Columbus, Ohio	February 11
1906	St. Paul, Minnesota	January 25–27
1907	Yellowstone National Park, Wyoming	August 9–10
1910	New Orleans, Louisiana	February 5–7
1912	Denver, Colorado	August 22–September 2
1913	Boston, Massachusetts	September 12
1914	Washington, D.C.	September 19–October 3
1915	San Francisco, California	September 7–9
1916	New Orleans, Louisiana	October 12–14
1917	St. Paul, Minnesota	August 27–29
1918	New York, New York	September 12–13
1919	Louisville, Kentucky	October 6–7
1920	Ottawa, Ontario, Canada	September 23–24
1921	Allentown, Pennsylvania	September 8–9
1922	Madison, Wisconsin	September 4–5
1923	St. Louis, Missouri	September 20
1924	Quebec, Canada	September 8–9
1925	Denver, Colorado	August 20–21
1926	Mobile, Alabama	September 20–21
1927	Hartford, Connecticut	August 11–12
1928	Seattle, Washington	August 27–28
1929	Minneapolis, Minnesota	September 12–13
1930	Toronto, Ontario, Canada	August 25–26
1931	Hot Springs, Arkansas	September 24–25
1932	Baltimore, Maryland	September 19–20
1933	Columbus, Ohio	September 21–22
1934	Montreal, Quebec, Canada	September 10–11
1935	Tulsa, Oklahoma	September 12–13
1936	Grand Rapids, Michigan	August 31–September 1

Appendix C

Year	*Place*	*Dates*
1937	Mexico City, Mexico	August 26–27
1938	Asheville, North Carolina	June 20–21
1939	San Francisco, California	June 29–30
1940	Toronto, Ontario, Canada	September 2–3
1941	St. Louis, Missouri	August 28–29
1946*	St. Paul, Minnesota	September 9–11
1947	Denver, Colorado	September 8–10
1948	Atlantic City, New Jersey	September 15–17
1949	Winnipeg, Manitoba, Canada	September 12–13
1950	Memphis, Tennessee	September 14–15
1951	Rochester, New York	September 10–11
1952	Dallas, Texas	September 11–12
1953	Milwaukee, Wisconsin	September 14–15
1954	Seattle, Washington	September 16–17
1955	Augusta, Georgia	September 12–13
1956	Toronto, Ontario, Canada	September 13–14
1957	Las Vegas, Nevada	September 9–10
1958	Philadelphia, Pennsylvania	September 11–12
1959	Clearwater, Florida	September 14–15
1960	Denver, Colorado	September 15–16
1961	Memphis, Tennessee	September 11–12
1962	Jackson Lake Lodge, Wyoming	September 13–14
1963	Minneapolis, Minnesota	September 9–10
1964	Atlantic City, New Jersey	September 17–18
1965	Portland, Oregon	September 20–21
1966	Kansas City, Missouri	September 14–16
1967	Toronto, Ontario, Canada	September 11–13
1968	Tucson, Arizona	September 12–13
1969	New Orleans, Louisiana	September 8–10
1970	New York, New York	September 16–18
1971	Salt Lake City, Utah	September 13–15
1972	Hot Springs, Arkansas	September 13–15
1973	Disney World, Florida	September 10–12
1974	Honolulu, Hawaii	September 11–13
1975	Las Vegas, Nevada	September 8–10
1976	Dearborn, Michigan	September 23–24
1977	Vancouver, British Columbia	September 12–14
1978	Baltimore, Maryland	September 10–13
1979	West Yellowstone, Montana	September 10–11
1980	Louisville, Kentucky	September 24–26
1981	Albuquerque, New Mexico	September 14–16
1982	Hilton Head Island, South Carolina	September 19–22
1983	Milwaukee, Wisconsin	September 10–14
1984	Juneau, Alaska	September 8–11
1985	Sun Valley, Idaho	September 11–14
1986	Providence, Rhode Island	September 14–18

*Meetings Postponed, 1942–1945

Appendix D
Honorary Life Members of the International Association of Fish and Wildlife Agencies

Dr. T. S. Palmer was made the Association's first honorary life member in 1906.

1906 - Dr. T. S. Palmer

The next mention of Honorary Members occurred in the 1912 *Proceedings*. The first bylaws of that year allowed the Association to "elect as honorary members ex-presidents and other persons who have rendered distinguished service in the cause of wild bird, game and fish protection."

1912 - Charles E. Brewster*
S. F. Fullerton, Minnesota
D. C. Nowlin, Wyoming
Dr. T. S. Palmer, District of Columbia
T. Gilbert Pearson, New York
Col. John Pitcher
W. F. Scott, Montana

In 1916 three new honorees were listed, but not the previous ones.

1916 - Edward A. McIlhenny, Louisiana
Mrs. Edward A. McIlhenny, Louisiana
Mrs. Russell Sage, New York

The *Proceedings* were silent on Honorary Life Memberships for many years, but the newly revised bylaws of 1947 contained the earlier provision for electing Honorary Life Members for "distinguished service in the cause of conservation administration." The Association, on a motion of Seth Gordon, awarded such membership to Ray P. Holland for serving twenty-seven years as its Secretary-Treasurer.

*The state was sometimes not given.

Appendix D

1947 - Ray P. Holland

The next listing of Honorary Life Members appeared in the 1961 *Proceedings*. The election dates of the five designees were not given, although Holland was included and all of the conservationists listed had made their major contributions long before that year. The earlier honorees disappeared altogether.

1961 - Elliott Barker, New Mexico
Ray P. Holland, Vermont
Dr. Harrison F. Lewis, Nova Scotia
Hoyes Lloyd, Ontario
Carl D. Shoemaker, Washington, D.C.

This same roster was reprinted every year until 1966, when Seth Gordon's name was added, without recorded ceremony.

1966 - Elliott Barker, New Mexico
Seth Gordon, California
Ray P. Holland, Vermont
Dr. Harrison F. Lewis, Nova Scotia
Hoyes Lloyd, Ontario
Carl D. Shoemaker, Washington, D.C.

In 1969 Shoemaker's name was inexplicably dropped and in 1970 those of I. T. Quinn and Verne Joslin added.

1970 - Elliott Barker, New Mexico
Seth Gordon, California
Ray P. Holland, Vermont
Verne E. Joslin, Minnesota
Dr. Harrison F. Lewis, Nova Scotia
Hoyes Lloyd, Ontario
I. T. Quinn, Alabama

This list of seven was augmented in 1971 with two additions, Lester Bagley and Cleland Feast.

But in 1972, even with the addition of Guy Amsler, the honor roll was reduced to eight, with the unexplained deletions of Holland and Quinn.

1972 - Guy Amsler, Arkansas
Lester Bagley, Wyoming
Elliott Barker, New Mexico
Cleland Feast, Colorado
Seth Gordon, California
Verne E. Joslin, Minnesota
Dr. Harrison F. Lewis, Nova Scotia
Hoyes Lloyd, Ontario

This tally held until 1975, when only six were named—Bagley, Barker, Feast, Gordon, Lloyd, and Amsler. Apparently the names of the recently deceased were eliminated.

The next year the list of honorees changed considerably, with several additions.

1976 - Guy Amsler, Arkansas
Lester Bagley, Wyoming
Elliott Barker, New Mexico
Albert M. Day, Pennsylvania
Cleland Feast, Colorado
Ira N. Gabrielson, Virginia
Seth Gordon, California
C. R. Gutermuth, Washington, D.C.
Thomas L. Kimball, Virginia
Hoyes Lloyd, Ontario
James W. Webb, South Carolina

In 1977 Holland, Joslin, Lewis, and Quinn were resurrected, and this register of fifteen continued until 1983, when three new honorees were added: John Gottschalk, Mason Lawrence, and Lester Voigt.

Robert Jantzen, Merrill Petoskey, and Daniel Poole were made Honorary Life Members in 1984. The honor was accorded to Chester Phelps, John Phelps, and Glenn Bowers in 1985 and Wesley Hayden in 1986, so that the current roster of honorees reads:

1986 - Guy Amsler, Arkansas*
Lester Bagley, Wyoming*
Elliott Barker, New Mexico
Glenn L. Bowers, Pennsylvania
Albert M. Day, Pennsylvania*
Cleland Feast, Colorado
Ira N. Gabrielson, Virginia*
Seth Gordon, California*
John S. Gottschalk, Virginia
C. R. Gutermuth, Virginia
Wesley F. Hayden, Virginia
Ray P. Holland, Vermont*
Robert Jantzen, Virginia
Verne E. Joslin, Minnesota*
Thomas L. Kimball, California
Mason W. Lawrence, New York
Harrison F. Lewis, Nova Scotia*
Hoyes Lloyd, Ontario*
Merrill Petoskey, Michigan
Chester F. Phelps, Georgia
John E. "Bud" Phelps, Utah

Appendix D

Daniel Poole, Maryland
I. T. Quinn, Alabama*
Lester P. Voigt, Wisconsin
James W. Webb, South Carolina*

The Association would welcome information on Honorary Life Members, especially from the earlier years, whose records have been apparently lost.

*Deceased

Appendix E
Recipients of the Seth Gordon Award

The International Association presented its first Seth Gordon Award to Seth Gordon in 1970 "for a half century of inspired leadership and distinguished service in natural resources management." Since then the award has been given annually to an individual exemplifying similar long-standing qualities of leadership and service in wildlife conservation administration. The honoree must also have worked with a governmental agency affiliated with IAFWA and shown a sustained interest in its programs and purposes. The Seth Gordon Award is the Association's highest.

The first Seth Gordon Award was an owl cast in lucite, but the material proved unsatisfactory, so the Association had it and subsequent statuettes executed in Steuben glass. The owl is mounted on a wood base with a bronze citation panel.

Seth Gordon Award Recipients

1970 - Seth Gordon
1971 - I. T. Quinn
1972 - Dr. Leslie L. Glasgow
1973 - Michigan Department of Natural Resources in recognition of its late director, Dr. Ralph A. McMullan. Accepted for the department by Charles D. Harris.
1974 - Hoyes Lloyd
1975 - John S. Gottschalk
1976 - Dr. W. Mason Lawrence
1977 - Carl N. Crouse
1978 - Lester P. Voigt
1979 - Chester F. Phelps
1980 - John E. "Bud" Phelps
1981 - O. Earle Frye, Jr.
1982 - Glenn L. Bowers
1983 - Charles D. Kelley
1984 - Larry R. Gale
1985 - Jack H. Berryman

Appendix F
Recipients of the Ernest Thompson Seton Award

The International Association of Fish and Wildlife Agencies presents the Ernest Thompson Seton Award annually to the state, provincial, or federal agency which has best promoted to the public the need for scientific management of wildlife resources. The selection committee seeks particularly an educational or public relations effort on an issue with political risk or high public impact. The individual deemed most responsible for the success of the program is also honored.

Woodstream Corporation, manufacturer of outdoor equipment, sponsors the Ernest Thompson Seton Award, which is a framed, numbered, wildlife print for both the agency and the individual.

Seton was a turn-of-the-century author and artist who produced practical, popular guides to understanding nature for young readers. He also cofounded the Boy Scouts of America.

Ernest Thompson Seton Award Recipients

1977 - Michigan Department of Natural Resources
Individual: Oscar Warbach

1978 - Ohio Department of Natural Resources
Individual: Dale L. Haney

1979 - Tennessee Wildlife Resources Agency
Individual: Michael O'Malley

1980 - Canadian Wildlife Federation
Individual: Kenneth Brynaert

1981 - Missouri Department of Conservation
Individual: Clarence E. Billings

1982 - Idaho Department of Fish and Game
Individual: Jerry M. Conley

1983 - Florida Game and Fresh Water Fish Commission
Individual: Robert M. Brantly

1984 - New York Department of Conservation
Individual: Herbert Doig

1985 - Georgia Game and Fish Division
Individual: Leon A. Kirkland

Appendix G
Digest of the Resource Policies of the International Association of Fish and Wildlife Agencies[1]

Fish and wildlife resources are held in trust by the individual states and, for certain species, by the United States for the enjoyment, appreciation, and economic and scientific benefit of present and future generations.[2]

Jurisdiction Over Fish and Wildlife

In the United States, primary authority and responsibility for the management and protection of fish and resident wildlife reside in the several states. The resulting right to regulate the taking and possession of fish and resident wildlife is independent of the ownership of land or waters on or in which fish or resident wildlife may be found.

Professional Resource Management

All renewable natural resources—air, water, forest, and range, as well as fish and wildlife—should be managed in accordance with sound scientific principles which are predicated upon the sustained-yield concept and, when possible, allow for restoration of those resources that have been degraded.[3]

1. From Resource Policies of the IAFWA, approved in draft by the membership September 1983, Milwaukee, Wisconsin, with subsequent updates. The Policy Statements are not necessarily in priority order.
2. For the purpose of this text: Fish and wildlife includes all existing native and desirable non-native populations of wild mammals, fish, birds, reptiles, and amphibians; including species not sought for food, fur, hide, or sport.
3. Fish and wildlife management is a human effort to manipulate scientifically the natural resources to produce the desired numbers and kinds of animals for the overall best interests of fish and wildlife and humans.

Appendix G

Hunting, Fishing, and Trapping

The Association recognizes properly regulated hunting, fishing, and trapping as necessary techniques of sound fish, wildlife, and habitat management which allow utilization of valuable natural resources and provide legitimate wholesome and healthful types of recreation. The Association supports complete protection of fish and wildlife when necessary to preserve breeding stocks or when species are threatened or in danger of extinction.

Weather Modification

Weather modification practices should be undertaken only after thorough studies of all potential effects upon the plant and animal communities indicate that the public benefits will outweigh the disadvantages.

Native American Rights

The Association opposes preferential hunting and fishing rights for Native Americans, as granted by courts interpreting treaty provisions, in the interests of preserving fish and wildlife resources, the states' historical authority over such resources, and the states' responsibilities to all citizens. The Association urges the Executive Branch to appeal to Congress, not the courts, where meaningful compromise is not possible, to provide a comprehensive basis and the stable funding necessary for durable native programs to protect and manage fish and wildlife resources.

Use of Steel Shot

The Association supports federal-state cooperation for the implementation of the mandatory but gradual phase-in of nontoxic shot nationwide by 1991, beginning with the counties or areas of greatest hunting intensity, as proposed by the International Association of Fish and Wildlife Agencies and adopted by the Department of Interior in 1986.

Agricultural Lands

The Association supports programs which provide long-term protection for agricultural lands and urges the development of incentives to keep prime farmlands in agricultural production. It urges the adoption of soil and water conservation practices, including those providing fish and wildlife habitat, which reduce erosion and the subsequent siltation of streams, lakes, and estuaries. The Association opposes the development of marginal lands for the production of crops already in surplus and for speculative incentive.

Appendix G

Habitat Protection

The Association calls upon officials at all levels of government, representatives of industry, developers, landowners, and private citizens to join in a concerted effort to protect and enhance the natural habitat in fields and forests, prairies and grasslands, deserts, wetlands, islands, lakes and streams, and oceans, bays, and estuaries for the benefit of fish and wildlife resources.

Natural Beauty

The Association supports national legislation embracing what is commonly termed a "bottle bill" to enhance the beauty of the natural environment and the quality of outdoor recreational experiences.

Energy

The Association urges industries and governmental officials at all levels to recognize the need to protect environmental values in the development and use of energy resources. Further, the Association recommends that high priority be accorded to a national effort to encourage research and development of non-polluting, renewable sources of energy, such as solar, wind, geothermal, and tidal power, as well as means of encouraging energy conservation.

Hunter, Trapper, and Angler Education

The Association endorses vigorous programs of hunter, trapper, and angler education that emphasize ecological interrelationships, environmental quality, and management principles. The Association encourages the widespread adoption of improved ethics and patterns of behavior, which will make outdoor recreational practices conform to conservation principles acceptable to property owners and the public at large.

Management of Public Lands

The Association supports the concept of multiple use of public lands, where fish and wildlife management, timber management, and grazing of domestic livestock are coordinated and integrated according to accepted scientific practices for the greatest benefit to the greatest number of people. The Association urges the respective federal and state agencies to support actively forage rehabilitation efforts on lands that are currently below their potential. It opposes the blanket transfer of large amounts of federal land to the states or to private ownership if such transfers would result in a substantial decrease in production or public use of fish and wildlife resources. The Association encourages state fish and wildlife agencies to draft and propose state organic acts under which they will manage all state lands not designated individually for single or limited purpose use.

Appendix G

Exotics

The Association supports strong and vigorous controls over the importation of exotic fish and wildlife, including those that are threatened or in danger of extinction. Responsible agencies should permit such importations only after ascertaining that these species are free of disease and will not constitute a menace or nuisance to humans, native fish and wildlife, or domestic livestock and poultry, if liberated.

International Affairs

The Association recognizes the value of international agreements as means of promoting fish and wildlife conservation on a continental, hemispheric, and world basis, and will actively support such agreements, provided that it can be demonstrated that such agreements will be beneficial to resources in North America and will not be disruptive to existing agreements in the Western Hemisphere or to existing state programs.

Wild and Scenic Rivers

The Association encourages the preservation of designated wild and scenic free-flowing rivers for fish and wildlife habitat and enhancement of recreational opportunities through federal, state, and provincial legislation.

Commercial Shooting Preserves

The Association supports the operation of properly regulated shooting preserves as management tools to provide natural-like hunting opportunities for a segment of the public and reduce pressure on wild populations.

Firearms Control

The Association opposes any efforts to infringe upon, restrict, modify, or further derogate, by legislation, rule, or order, the Constitutionally guaranteed right of U.S. citizens to lawfully own and use firearms.

Fish and Wildlife and Human Population

The Association supports programs that encourage understanding of human ecology and the realization that humans share, with all other biological organisms, a dependence upon the environment. The Association encourages people to value, enjoy, and utilize the world's plant and animal resources but also to develop an attitude of stewardship and responsible management for those resources. It seeks to minimize, within the context of human needs, all types of human contamination and mass alteration of the environment and to foster the concept that the human population can and must be maintained within the limits of the world's resource base. The Association supports programs that allocate space of sufficient quality and quantity to sustain healthy fish and wildlife populations for food and recreational needs.

Federal Aid Funds

The Association recognizes the seminal importance of the Federal Aid in Wildlife Restoration Act, the Federal Aid in Fish Restoration Act, the Anadromous Fisheries and Conservation Act, and the Commercial Fisheries Research and Development Act for resource enhancement and scientific management. The Association advocates periodic updating of these laws to meet the needs of the states but vigorously opposes any withholding, reduction, or diversion of federal aid funds, or any attempt to encompass funds into block grants to the states for general revenue purposes.

Stocking of Hatchery-Reared Fish

The Association prefers the maintenance, enhancement, and/or rehabilitation of native fish communities under natural conditions but approves the stocking of hatchery-reared fish to improve the quality and quantity of public fishing opportunities. Hatchery operations should be conducted with concern for the risks of transmitting diseases or parasites to other populations. Stocking of hatchery-reared fish is warranted to place suitable species in new waters to establish a fishery; introduce additional predator or food fishes where the need for such remedial management has been demonstrated; supplement natural production or maintain a fishery in the absence of natural production; restock restored waters where fish life has been eliminated and will not be naturally repopulated within a reasonable time.

Environmental Pollution

The Association recognizes the need to comprehend the environmental requirements and interdependence of all organisms and biological communities of the earth and encourages the search for ways to discourage and control environmental pollution and to reclaim degraded ecosystems. The Association encourages the use of all available knowledge of the physical environment and the adverse effects of pollution in planning human activities to maintain a physically and aesthetically diverse as well as biologically sufficient environment.

Cooperation between United States, Canada, and Mexico in Wildlife Management

The Association supports continued and expanded cooperation among the wildlife agencies of the United States, Canada, and Mexico in biological research and species and habitat management for consumptive and nonconsumptive wildlife use.

Appendix G

Pesticides

The Association recognizes the value of properly used chemical pesticides in crop and resource production, protection, and management but urges the use of biological and nonchemical controls wherever feasible in preference to chemical controls. Only the most selective, least hazardous, and least persistent chemicals, in the smallest effective concentrations, should be applied in the safest possible manner to avoid injury to fish, wildlife, humans, and the environment.

Standards for use of chemical pesticides by governmental agencies should be exemplary. All large-scale pesticide applications should be evaluated, with necessary costs borne by the agency making the application.

The Association encourages research centered on biological controls and new selective pesticides that are less hazardous and less likely to contaminate the environment.

Endangered Species of Fish and Wildlife

To provide for the conservation, protection, propagation, restoration, and management of threatened and endangered species of fish and wildlife, as defined and listed under the U.S. Endangered Species Act of 1973, the Convention on International Trade in Endangered Species of Wild Fauna and Flora (CITES), and by member states, provinces, and countries, the Association supports all biologically sound programs of research, education, and habitat preservation. It supports programs of public information and private organizations dedicated to the conservation, within biologically sound principles, of endangered and threatened species.

The Association encourages the continuing improvement of international, federal, provincial, and state endangered fish and wildlife programs, and the laws, regulations, and processes that implement them. It supports worldwide efforts to oppose illegal traffic and commerce in endangered or threatened animals or any part, products, eggs, or offspring thereof. The Association encourages adjacent member states and/or provinces to develop plans and action programs to protect threatened and endangered fish and wildlife that may move to, from, or within their respective jurisdictions.

To achieve greater integrity in the existing listing of endangered and threatened species, particularly in the appendices to the CITES agreement, the Association urges the early removal or reclassification of species or subspecies that are improperly listed and the listing of deserving species.

Animal Damage Control

The Association, recognizing that wild animals may have both negative and positive social and economic values, supports prevention or control of damages to surrounding plant and animal resources or endangerment to public health and safety as an integral part of wildlife management. The Association encourages the use of techniques known to be of value in counteracting damage without threatening the survival of the offending species, including exclusion or mechanical protection, use of repellent chemicals or devices, environmental or biological control of the offending animals, and reduction of the number of offending animals through transfer or lethal control. It encourages control methods that are as efficient, safe, economical, humane, and selective as possible, with minimum lethal control. The Association promotes continuing research in animal ecology and methods of damage prevention and control and thorough planning of control programs with justification, implementation, and evaluation on the basis of total social benefits. It encourages self-help or extension-type programs with technical assistance rather than full service programs when possible.

Fish and Wildlife Aspects of Public Works Projects

The Association supports construction of public works and federally financed or sanctioned private projects when, and only when, adequate measures for protecting fish and wildlife resources and other environmental values are assured in advance by the sponsor or construction agency. These measures and associated costs must be included as project cost and incorporated into the cost/benefit analysis early in the planning process. Full mitigation and compensation for damages, preferably with replacement in kind, must be determined and funded by project proponents, preferably under the direction/guidance of fish and wildlife agencies whose coordination is assured throughout the planning, development, and operational phases of the project.

To accomplish these objectives, the Association urges practical application of the National Environmental Policy of 1969 with active input and participation by state and federal natural resource agencies. This practice should be extended to large state and local projects not covered by federal policy.

Nonreimbursable Fish and Wildlife Enhancement on Federal Reservoirs

In order that federal agencies constructing dams may develop recreation opportunities on the impounded waters, the Association supports enactment of federal laws that will provide, as part of the project costs in all reservoirs, a minimum fish and wildlife conservation pool and wildlife management development consistent with the resource potential and the public interest. Such determination should be made by the U.S. Fish and Wildlife Service and the fish and wildlife agencies of the affected states.

Transfer of Surplus Federal Lands to Fish and Wildlife Agencies

The Association requests an impartial study of each parcel of surplus federal land under consideration for sale, barter, exchange, or gift to determine its value as fish and wildlife habitat. If the area provides important habitat or facilities for fish or wildlife, the Association urges the federal agency to transfer said land to an appropriate state or federal fish and wildlife agency for management.

Wilderness Management

The Association supports management of lands within the National Wilderness Preservation System that is directed toward maintenance of all existing native and desirable non-native fish and wildlife, with emphasis on the preservation of endangered or threatened species. To this end the Association encourages the implementation of Forest Service and Bureau of Land Management policies and guidelines based on the 1976 wilderness management negotiations between these agencies and the IAFWA.

Road Management

The Association calls for federal and state public land management agencies, when planning roads, to work cooperatively with the state wildlife agencies to consider carefully the needs of wildlife and possible dangers from the proposed transportation system. Such plans should include a system for managing access, including road closures, that will fully protect wildlife from the associated hazards.

Water Allocations

The Association advocates water allocation measures which ensure that sufficient waters are retained in water bodies to maintain spawning and rearing habitats of fish, allow migration of fish, and maintain riparian and wetland communities. Prior to making water allocation decisions, the possible effects of major water withdrawals, impoundments, or alterations on fish and wildlife resources should be determined. Alternatives to a water diversion should be considered if the proposed change in instream flows or lake water levels will negatively affect fish and wildlife populations. Water resources should be managed to allocate water, both diversionary and instream, equitably among all users in a way that promotes the viability of fish and wildlife populations and accommodates human demands.

Protection of Riparian Habitats

The Association supports the protection and restoration of water courses and associated riparian ecosystems for the benefit of fish and wildlife and the people who use and enjoy these resources.

Notes

Abbreviation: *Proc.*: *Proceedings* of the annual convention of the International Association of Game, Fish and Conservation Commissioners.

The Association was organized in 1902 as the National Association of Game and Fish Wardens and Commissioners. In 1910 it appeared as the National Association of Game Commissioners and Game Wardens, although this could have been journalistic imprecision rather than a name change. From 1914 through 1916 the name National Association of Game and Fish Commissioners (or Fish and Game Commissioners) was used. In 1917 a bylaw amendment to allow the inclusion of Canada formally changed the name to International Association of Game, Fish and Conservation Commissioners. This designation continued until 1977 when the current name International Association of Fish and Wildlife Agencies was adopted.

Introduction

1. Factual material for this chapter is taken in large part from Jack Berryman's summary address, "The International Association: Its Importance to the Fish and Wildlife Resource Worker," delivered before the 39th Conference of the Southeast Association of Fish and Wildlife Agencies, Lexington, Kentucky, on October 28, 1985. Other sources include recent issues of the IAFWA *Newsletter*; Berryman, "Report of the Executive Vice President," Association Convention, Sun Valley, Idaho, September 11, 1985; Paul Lenzini, "Summary of Association Participation in Litigation," September 1984; IAFWA Constitution and Bylaws, August 1980; IAFWA promotional brochure, "Project Wild," IAFWA *Proc.* 1983, pp. 59–73; correspondence from regional associations; and telephone interviews with Berryman and Lenzini.

1. "From This Little Meeting"

1. Montana Department of Fish, Wildlife & Parks, *Annual Report*, 1980, pp. 4, 6.

2. "Wardens in Convention," *Forest and Stream: A Weekly Journal of the Rod and Gun* 59 (August 2, 1902):81.
3. Ibid.; T. Gilbert Pearson, "When Our Association Was Young—An Historical Sketch," *Proc.* 1934, pp. 19–20.
4. "Game and Fish Interests," *Forest and Stream*, August 9, 1902, p. 105; see also *Proc.* 1934, p. 19.
5. "Game and Fish Interests," August 9, 1902, p. 105; see also *Proc.* 1934, p. 19.
6. "Game and Fish Interests," August 9, 1902, pp. 106–7; *Proc.* 1934, p. 20.
7. "Game and Fish Interests," August 9, 1902, p. 107; 161 U.S. 519 (1896); Michael J. Bean, *The Evolution of National Wildlife Law*, rev. ed. (New York: Praeger Publishers, 1983), pp. 16–17.
8. U.S. Department of Agriculture, Bureau of Biological Survey, *Chronology and Index of the More Important Events in American Game Protection, 1776–1911*, by T. S. Palmer, Bulletin no. 41 (Washington, D.C.: Government Printing Office, 1912), p. 13; James B. Trefethen, *Crusade for Wildlife: Highlights in Conservation Progress* (Harrisburg, Pa.: Stackpole, 1961), p. 118; Clark Walsh, "The Good Old Days: A Review of Game and Fish Administration in Oregon, Part I," *Bulletin of the Oregon State Game Commission*, December 1959, p. 5; Roderick Nash, ed., *The American Environment: Readings in the History of Conservation* (Reading, Mass.: Addison-Wesley, 1968), pp. ix–xi.
9. Lacey Act, Ch. 553, 31 Stat. 187 (1900).
10. U.S., Congress, House, *Congressional Record*, 56th Cong., 1st sess., 1900, 33, pt. 6:4874–75, 5704.
11. "Wardens in Convention," August 2, 1902, p. 81, and "Game and Fish Interests," August 9, 1902, p. 106.
12. Frank Graham, Jr., *Man's Dominion: The Story of Conservation in America* (New York: M. Evans, 1971), p. 14; David Cushman Coyle, *Conservation: An American Story of Conflict and Accomplishment* (New Brunswick, N.J.: Rutgers University Press, 1957), p. 229.
13. Trefethen, *Crusade for Wildlife*, pp. 15–18.
14. Gifford Pinchot, *Breaking New Ground* (New York: Harcourt, Brace, 1947), pp. 322–26; Nash, *American Environment*, pp. 40–41; J. Leonard Bates, "Fulfilling American Democracy: The Conservation Movement, 1907 to 1921," *Mississippi Valley Historical Review* 44 (June 1957):33–36.
15. Bates, "Fulfilling American Democracy," p. 42; see also, Gifford Pinchot, *The Fight for Conservation* (Seattle: University of Washington Press, 1967).
16. T. S. Palmer, "Lest We Forget," *Bulletin of The American Game Protective Association* 14 (January 1925):11–12.
17. Ibid.; "Absolute Prohibition of Traffic in Game," *Forest and Stream*, February 10, 1894, p. 1; *National Cyclopaedia of American Biography*, 1943 ed., s. v. "Grinnell, George Bird."
18. *Proc.* 1934, pp. 14–19.
19. U.S. Department of Agriculture Bulletin no. 41, *Chronology and Index of the More Important Events in American Game Protection, 1776–1911*, by T. S.

Palmer (Washington, D.C.: Government Printing Office, 1912), pp. 9–16; U.S.D.A. Bulletin no. 16, *Digest of Game Laws for 1901*, by T. S. Palmer and H. W. Olds (Washington, D.C.: Government Printing Office, 1901), pp. 13–14; U.S.D.A. Bulletin no. 19, *Hunting Licenses: Their History, Objects and Limitations*, by T. S. Palmer (Washington, D.C.: Government Printing Office, 1904), pp. 12–19; and U.S.D.A. Bulletin no. 1049, *Game as a National Resource*, by T. S. Palmer (Washington, D.C.: Government Printing Office, 1922), pp. 26–29. See also Aldo Leopold, *Game Management* (New York: Charles Scribner's Sons, 1933), pp. 13–15.

20. T. Gilbert Pearson, "Wildlife Protection in the United States," *Proc.* 1938, p. 61.

21. "Game and Fish Interests," August 9, 1902, p. 105.

22. *Proc.* 1934, p. 20.

23. "Notes," *The American Field* 61 (February 20, 1904):169; also cited in *Proc.* 1980, p. S-3.

24. "Game Wardens in Conventions," *Forest and Stream* 66 (February 20, 1906): 183; also cited in *Proc.* 1980, pp. S-4 to S-6.

25. *National Cyclopaedia of American Biography*, 1930 ed., s. v. "Palmer, Theodore Sherman"; "National Association of Game Commissioners and Game Wardens," *The American Field* 73 (February 19, 1910):169; cited in *Proc.* 1980, p. S-11.

26. "Annual Meeting, National Association of Game and Fish Wardens and Commissioners," *The American Field* 68 (August 31, 1907):184–85; cited in *Proc.* 1980, pp. S-7 to S-8.

27. "National Association of Game Commissioners and Game Wardens," February 19, 1910, p. 169; cited in *Proc.* 1980, p. S-13.

28. "Annual Meeting, National Association of Game and Fish Wardens and Commissioners," August 31, 1907, p. 185, and "National Association of Game Commissioners and Game Wardens," February 19, 1910, p. 169; cited in *Proc.* 1980, pp. S-10, S-12 to S-13; *Proc.* 1912, pp. 26–40.

29. Trefethen, *Crusade for Wildlife*, p. 164.

30. H.R. 15601; "Federal Protection of Wildfowl," *Forest and Stream*, December 10, 1904, p. 1.

31. Trefethen, *Crusade for Wildlife*, pp. 165–68.

32. The name was shortened from the original unwieldy designation American Game Protective and Propagation Association.

33. Graham, *Man's Dominion*, pp. 216–17; Trefethen, *Crusade for Wildlife*, p. 168.

34. See *Bulletin of The American Game Protective Association*, beginning in 1912.

35. T. Gilbert Pearson, "Our Bird Treaty with Canada," *Proc.* 1935, p. 14; U.S. Congress, Senate, *To Protect Migratory Game and Insectivorous Birds of the United States*, S. Report no. 675 to accompany S. 6497, 62nd Cong., 2nd sess., 1912, p. 1; U.S., Congress, House, *Protection of Migratory and Insectivorous*

Birds of the United States, Report no. 680 to accompany H.R. 36, 62nd Cong., 2nd sess., 1912, pp. 2–3.

36. S. 6497 supplanted S. 6478. U.S., Congress, Senate, *Congressional Record*, 62nd Cong., 2nd sess., 1912, 48:5167, 5248; *Proc.* 1935, p. 14; see also Trefethen, *Crusade for Wildlife*, p. 169.

37. U.S., Congress, House, *Congressional Record*, 62nd Cong., 3rd sess., 1913, 49:2725.

38. U.S., Congress, House, *Congressional Record*, 62nd Cong., 3rd sess., 1913, 49:4330; *Proc.* 1935.

39. U.S., Congress, Senate, *Congressional Record*, 62nd Cong., 3rd sess., 1913, 49, pt. 2:1494.

40. Migratory Bird Law, 37 Stat. 847; *Proc.* 1935, pp. 14–15.

41. *Proc.* 1935, pp. 15–16.

42. Association records for 1913 have not survived. Acklen's speech, "Federal Migratory Bird Law," delivered at the 1913 convention, was read into the record at the 1922 convention. *Proc.* 1922, pp. 52–54.

43. U.S., Congress, *Congressional Record*, 63rd Cong., 1st sess., 1913, 50:3530, 2339–40; Trefethen, *Crusade for Wildlife*, pp. 170–72; *Proc.* 1935, pp. 16–17.

44. Trefethen, *Crusade for Wildlife*, pp. 172–73; *Proc.* 1935, pp. 17–21.

45. U.S. Department of Agriculture, Bureau of Biological Survey, *Migratory-Bird Treaty-Act Regulations and Text of Federal Laws Relating to Game and Birds*, Service and Regulatory Announcements—B.S. 75, April 1931, pp. 8–10. The complete text of the treaty was published in the *Bulletin of The American Game Protective Association* 5 (October 1, 1916):1–3.

46. U.S., Congress, House, *Congressional Record*, 64th Cong., 2nd sess., 1917, 54:1377; Ch. 128, 40 Stat. 755 (1918).

47. Trefethen, *Crusade for Wildlife*, p. 173; *Proc.* 1935, pp. 17, 21; Bean, *National Wildlife Law*, pp. 20–21.

48. E. W. Nelson, "Co-operation between the Federal Government and the States in the Enforcement of the Enabling Act," *Proc.* 1918, pp. 15–17.

49. *Proc.* 1918, p. 59.

50. Ibid., pp. 17, 39, 56, 107–8, 110.

51. Graham, *Man's Dominion*, p. 201; Trefethen, *Crusade for Wildlife*, pp. 206, 208; *Proc.* 1917, p. 39. J. Leonard Bates also discusses the problem of wartime profiteering in the name of patriotism as it affected a broad range of natural resources, not including wildlife. "Fulfilling American Democracy," pp. 49–51.

52. *Proc.* 1918, pp. 5–6, 72–76; Graham, *Man's Dominion*, pp. 200–201.

53. *Proc.* 1918, pp. 111–19, 125.

54. William T. Hornaday, "Does the Supply of Game Justify any Relaxation in the Laws that Regulate its Taking?" *Bulletin of The American Game Protective Association* 7 (April 1918): 24; Graham, *Man's Dominion*, pp. 202–6; Trefethen, *Crusade for Wildlife*, pp. 208–28; see also William T. Hornaday, *Our Vanishing Wild Life: Its Extermination and Preservation* (New York: Charles Scribner's Sons, 1913). No IAGFCC Model Game Law has surfaced. Trefethen

might have been referring to the American Game Policy developed under Aldo Leopold's leadership in 1930 by the American Game Protective Association.
55. Herbert Hoover, "United States Food Administration Memorandum on the Use of Game as Food," *Bulletin of The American Game Protective Association* 7 (April 1918):26.
56. "Meeting of National Association of Fish and Game Commissioners," *The American Field* 86 (October 28, 1916):507–8; cited in *Proc.* 1980, p. S-18 to S-20.
57. *Proc.* 1912, p. 5; *Proc.* 1917, cited in *Proc.* 1980, p. S-22; *Proc.* 1918, p. 109.
58. *Proc.* 1917, cited in *Proc.* 1980, p. S-22; *Proc.* 1918, pp. 119–20; *Proc.* 1919, p. 13.
59. *Proc.* 1916, cited in *Proc.* 1980, pp. S-19 to S-20; *Proc.* 1919, pp. 13, 28–30.
60. *Proc.* 1918, pp. 12, 60–62.

2. Building Game Management, Building an Association

1. Seth Gordon, "Then and Now—With a Few Thoughts for the Future," *Proc.* 1961, p. 167.
2. Aldo Leopold, "Ten New Developments in Game Management," *American Game* 14 (July 1925):7–8, 20; Aldo Leopold, *Game Management* (New York: Charles Scribner's Sons, 1933), pp. 15–21.
3. *Proc.* 1918, pp. 33–39; U.S. Department of Agriculture Bulletin no. 1049, *Game as a National Resource*, by T. S. Palmer (Washington, D.C.: Government Printing Office, 1922), pp. 42–43.
4. U.S.D.A., *Game as a National Resource*, pp. 42–44; Leopold, *Game Management*, p. 15.
5. Leopold, *Game Management*, pp. 195–96.
6. Ibid., pp. 15–16, 125; Ira N. Gabrielson, *Wildlife Refuges* (New York: Macmillan Co., 1943), pp. 6–9; U.S.D.A., *Game as a National Resource*, pp. 31–33; "Meeting of National Association of Fish and Game Commissioners," *The American Field* 86 (October 28, 1916):506, cited in *Proc.* 1980, p. S-20.
7. U.S.D.A., *Game as a National Resource*, p. 1.
8. *Bulletin of The American Game Protective Association*, January 1925, p. 6; Gabrielson, *Wildlife Refuges*, pp. 11–14.
9. Frank Graham, Jr., *Man's Dominion: The Story of Conservation in America* (New York: M. Evans, 1971), pp. 217–20; Donald C. Swain, *Federal Conservation Policy, 1921–1933* (Berkeley: University of California Press, 1963), pp. 36–38; William T. Hornaday, *Thirty Years War for Wild Life: Gains and Losses in the Thankless Task* (New York: Charles Scribner's Sons, 1931).
10. Frank E. Smith, *The Politics of Conservation* (New York: Pantheon Books, 1966), pp. 165–66. Smith was a Democratic congressman from Mississippi during the 1950s. Swain, *Federal Conservation Policy, 1921–1933*, pp. 36–38. See also Jenks Cameron, *The Bureau of Biological Survey: Its History, Activities and*

Organization (Baltimore: The Johns Hopkins Press, 1929), for a sympathetic, even defensive, treatment of the Bureau during the 1920s.
11. Swain, *Federal Conservation Policy, 1921–1933*, pp. 160–63.
12. See, for example, *Proc.* 1920, p. 33; James B. Trefethen, *Crusade for Wildlife: Highlights in Conservation Progress* (Harrisburg, Pa.: Stackpole, 1961), p. 252.
13. Trefethen, *Crusade for Wildlife*, p. 254; U.S., Congress, House, *Congressional Record*, 67th Cong., 1st sess., 1921, 61, pt. 4:3310. The bills were S. 1452 and H.R. 5823.
14. *Proc.* 1921, pp. 40–49, 81.
15. *Proc.* 1922, pp. 63–65.
16. *Proc.* 1923, pp. 20–22.
17. *Bulletin of The American Game Protection Association*, January 1925, p. 10.
18. Ibid.; Graham, *Man's Dominion*, pp. 221–23.
19. Hornaday, *Thirty Years War for Wild Life*, pp. 190–91; *Proc.* 1925, pp. 76–98; for Burnham's version of the story see Maitland De Sorno, *John Bird Burnham—Klondiker, Adirondacker and Eminent Conservationist* (Saranac Lake, N.Y.: Adirondack Yesteryears, Inc., 1978), pp. 198–200.
20. *Proceedings, Western Association of State Game Commissioners*, 1924, pp. 17–28.
21. *Proc.* 1925, pp. 100–101; see also, *Proc.* 1926, pp. 116, 121; Trefethen, *Crusade for Wildlife*, p. 259.
22. Hornaday, *Thirty Years War for Wild Life*, pp. 144–45; *Proc.* 1929, p. 17. The Committee ceased functioning in 1938. See Supplemental Sketch for *Who's Who in America*, Seth Gordon Papers, University of Wyoming Archives.
23. *Proc.* 1926, pp. 114–40, passim.
24. *Proc.* 1927, p. 69.
25. Graham, *Man's Dominion*, p. 222.
26. Bird banding studies over the years, especially during the 1920s, had established that migratory waterfowl tended to confine their transcontinental flights to fairly well-defined geographical regions. Four north-south routes became apparent: the Atlantic, Mississippi, Central, and Pacific Flyways. For example, see Albert M. Day, *North American Waterfowl* (New York: Stackpole and Heck, 1949), pp. 71–76.
27. *Proc.* 1928, pp. 26–29; Gabrielson, *Wildlife Refuges*, p. 14.
28. Hornaday, *Thirty Years War for Wild Life*, pp. 236–40.
29. Migratory Bird Conservation Act, 45 Stat. 1222; *Proc.* 1929, pp. 17–18; Trefethen, *Crusade for Wildlife*, p. 259.
30. Graham, *Man's Dominion*, pp. 222–23.
31. Gordon had just finished serving on the American Game Association's committee, under Aldo Leopold's chairmanship, that had produced the American Game Policy of 1930, so taking a long view supported with specific proposals for action would have been much on his mind. American Game Association, "American Game Policy," *Transactions of the Seventeenth American Game Conference*, 1930, pp. 281–89; *Proc.* 1931, pp. 40–41, 48–53.

32. *Proc.* 1929, pp. 21–25.
33. *Proc.* 1930, pp. 106–9; *Proc.* 1932, p. 98; *Proc.* 1933, pp. 39–40, 142.
34. Gabrielson, *Wildlife Refuges*, p. 19; see also *Proc.* 1934, p. 22.
35. U.S.D.A., *Game as a National Resource*, pp. 2–5, 28–29.
36. Guy Amsler, interview with John C. Sunderland, June 27, 1985, pp. 21, 23.
37. See Trefethen, *Crusade for Wildlife*, pp. 230–37.
38. Ibid., pp. 237–38; *Proc.* 1931, p. 43.
39. Cameron, *Bureau of Biological Survey*, p. 191n; Gordon cited in *Proc.* 1926, p. 21.
40. Cameron, *Bureau of Biological Survey*, p. 191.
41. The case was Hunt v. United States. Michael J. Bean, *The Evolution of National Wildlife Law*, rev. ed. (New York: Praeger Publishers, 1983), p. 22; *Proc.* 1931, p. 48.
42. *Proc.* 1931, pp. 42–48; *Proc.* 1936, p. 21.
43. *Proc.* 1918, pp. 33–39; *Proc.* 1919, pp. 45–52; Hornaday, *Thirty Years War for Wild Life*, pp. 65–67; Cameron, *Bureau of Biological Survey*, pp. 48–52; Graham, *Man's Dominion*, pp. 274–78.
44. Trefethen, *Crusade for Wildlife*, pp. 247–50; Cameron, *Bureau of Biological Survey*, p. 49; see also Susan L. Flader, *Thinking Like a Mountain: Aldo Leopold and the Evolution of an Ecological Attitude Toward Deer, Wolves, and Forests* (Columbia: University of Missouri Press, 1974), especially chap. 1.
45. Whitney R. Cross, "Ideas in Politics: The Conservation Policies of the Two Roosevelts," *Journal of the History of Ideas* 14 (June 1953):435–36.
46. Gabrielson, *Wildlife Refuges*, pp. 17–18.
47. The American Wildlife Institute in 1935 superseded the American Game Association, which was successor to the American Game Protective Association. It proposed to function like an enlarged National Committee on Wildlife Legislation and promoted programs in research and training at land grant colleges. In 1946 it became known as the Wildlife Management Institute. See *Proc.* 1935, pp. 76–77.
48. Gabrielson, *Wildlife Refuges*, pp. 17–19; Trefethen, *Crusade for Wildlife*, pp. 264–72; Edgar B. Nixon, ed. & comp., *Franklin D. Roosevelt and Conservation, 1911–1945*, vol. 1 (Hyde Park, N.Y.: Franklin D. Roosevelt Library, National Archives and Records Service, 1957), pp. 347–48.
49. *Proc.* 1934, pp. 21–23.
50. Ibid., pp. 24–27.
51. *Proc.* 1935, pp. 30–33.
52. Ibid., pp. 37–57; see esp. pp. 40–41.
53. Ibid.; Elliott Barker, interview with Jesse Williams, October 21, 1983.
54. *Proc.* 1935, pp. 90–91.
55. U.S., Congress, Senate, Special Committee on Conservation of Wildlife Resources, *Proceedings of the North American Wildlife and Natural Resources Conference called by President Franklin D. Roosevelt, February 3–7, 1936* (Washington, D.C.: Government Printing Office, 1936), pp. v–xi; H. P. Sheldon,

Chief, Division of Public Relations, Bureau of Biological Survey, to William D. Hassett, Special Assistant to Stephen T. Early, September 26, 1936, in Nixon, *FDR and Conservation*, vol. 1, p. 580.

56. Nixon, *FDR and Conservation*, vol. 1, pp. 581–82.

57. Leopold, "Ten New Developments," *American Game*, July 1925, p. 7; Trefethen, *Crusade for Wildlife*, pp. 268–69; A. S. Hawkins, R. C. Hanson, H. K. Nelson, and H. M. Reeves, eds., *Flyways: Pioneering Waterfowl Management in North America* (Washington, D.C.: U.S. Department of Interior, Fish and Wildlife Service, 1984), pp. 359–60; "The Cooperative Wildlife Research Unit Program" (Washington, D.C.: Wildlife Management Institute, 1970), pamphlet. The Wildlife Management Institute has provided research unit grants for fifty years. Today there are programs at twenty-two colleges.

58. *Proc.* 1937, p. 31; Trefethen, *Crusade for Wildlife*, p. 259.

The literature on the passage and implementation of the Pittman-Robertson Act is voluminous in both primary and secondary sources. One of the most useful accounts is Robert M. Rutherford's *Ten Years of Pittman-Robertson Wildlife Restoration* (Washington, D.C.: Wildlife Management Institute, 1949). Rutherford was chief of the Federal Aid Branch of the Fish and Wildlife Service in 1949.

59. *Proc.* 1936, pp. 59–60. The bills were S. 2670 and H.R. 7681, respectively. U.S., Congress, *Congressional Record*, 75th Cong., 1st sess., 1937, 81:5856–57, 6490.

60. U.S., Congress, Senate, *United States Aid to States in Wildlife Restoration Projects*, S. Rept. 868, 75th Cong., 1st sess., 1937, pp. 2–3; U.S., Congress, House, *Aid to States in Wildlife Restoration Projects*, H. Rept. 1572, 75th Cong., 1st sess., gave the same information.

61. Pittman-Robertson Act, Ch. 899, 50 Stat. 918 (1937); Rutherford, *Ten Years of Pittman-Robertson*, p. 11.

62. U.S., Congress, *Congressional Record*, 75th Cong., 1st sess., 1937, 81:8583–85, 9460–61; Henry A. Wallace, Secretary of Agriculture, to Daniel W. Bell, August 26, 1937, in Nixon, *FDR and Conservation*, vol. 2, p. 119. The International Association never used its customary policy of endorsement by resolution on this bill. Action proceeded too quickly.

63. *Proc.* 1937, p. 32.

64. Wallace to Bell, August 26, 1937, and Bell to Marvin H. McIntyre, August 30, 1937, in Nixon, *FDR and Conservation*, vol. 2, pp. 117–21.

65. Nixon, *FDR and Conservation*, vol. 2, p. 119, n.3.

66. Rutherford, *Ten Years of Pittman-Robertson*, p. 10.

67. *Proc.* 1938, pp. 28–30; U.S. Department of Agriculture, *The Wildlife Restoration Program under the Pittman-Robertson Act of 1937*, by Albert M. Day, Misc. Publ. no. 350, May 1939, p. 1.

68. *Proc.* 1938, pp. 32–33; Rutherford, *Ten Years of Pittman-Robertson*, pp. 10–11; U.S.D.A., *Wildlife Restoration Under Pittman-Robertson*, pp. 5–6.

69. Refusing states were Nevada, Montana, Georgia, Florida, and Louisiana. *Proc.* 1939, pp. 34–40.

70. U.S., Department of the Interior, *Annual Report of the Secretary of the Interior, Report of the Bureau of Biological Survey*, 1940, pp. 256–57. For an overview of wildlife restoration projects, see the *Pittman-Robertson Quarterly* for specific years beginning in 1938. It gives statistics on apportionment, abstracts of state quarterly reports, titles of project publications, and lists of projects newly approved.
71. *Proc.* 1936, p. 51; Barker interview, October 21, 1983, p. 1.
72. *Proc.* 1936, pp. 27, 28.
73. Ibid., pp. 48–55.
74. *Proc.* 1939, p. 68.
75. Ibid., pp. 122–23.
76. *Proc.* 1940, pp. 90–109.
77. U.S., Congress, House, Select Committee on Conservation of Wildlife Resources, *Conservation of Wildlife*, H. Rept. 3112, 76th Cong., 3rd sess., 1941, pp. 45–64; citations from pp. 47, 64.
78. Chalk v. United States, 114 F.2d 207 (4th Cir. 1940), cert. denied, 312 U.S. 679 (1941). Paul Lenzini to author, May 1, 1986.
79. Cited in D. N. Graves, Report of the Executive Committee, *Proc.* 1941, pp. 17–18; *Proc.* 1941, pp. 13–14; *Proc.* 1964, p. 26. See also Lloyd Swift, oral history interview, March 6, 1986, for the federal perspective on the state-federal controversy. Swift, here and in correspondence of March 10, 1986, emphasized the "major role" of the Association in the drafting of Regulation W-2.
80. U.S., Congress, *Congressional Record*, 75th Cong., 1st sess., 1937, 81:8584. Joel Bennett "Champ" Clark was a Democrat. James F. Keefe, Missouri Department of Conservation, to author, July 8, 1985. See also Robert H. Connery, *Governmental Problems in Wild Life Conservation*, chap. 8: "The Organization and Functions of the State Conservation Departments" (New York: Columbia University Press, 1935), pp. 177–202.
81. *Proc.* 1938, p. 13. There were forty-seven official members in both 1940 and 1941 but not quite the same ones. *Proc.* 1940, p. 10; *Proc.* 1941, p. 10. See reports of the Secretary-Treasurer in the *Proceedings*, by year, for detailed figures. *Proc.* 1934, p. 138.
82. See, for example, *Proc.* 1912, pp. 42–46.
83. *Proc.* 1921, p. 90; Barker interview, p. 5; Seth Gordon, "Being President Isn't Always Fun!" *Proc.* 1963, p. 126; *Proc.* 1938, p. 49.
84. *Proc.* for years named.
85. *Proc.* 1926, pp. 132–33; Bean, *National Wildlife Law*, pp. 69–72.
86. Barker interview, pp. 14–15; *Proc.* 1937, passim.
87. *Proc.* 1926, p. 29; Senator Harry Hawes, Democrat of Missouri, an ardent sportsman and longtime friend of the Association, wrote popular books on conservation issues.
88. See Swain, *Federal Conservation Policy, 1921–1933*, pp. 45–48.
89. *Arkansas Deer* almost immediately was rechristened the *Arkansas Conserva-*

tionist. Outdoor Writers' Association, *America's Great Outdoors*, n.p., from Arkansas Game and Fish Commission files, 1985.
90. *Proc.* 1940, p. 44.
91. *Proc.* 1918, p. 11; *Proc.* 1932, p. 51.

3. Wildlife Is Big Business

1. *Proc.* 1940, p. 13.
2. Ibid., pp. 13–14; Frank Henry Buck was a Democratic representative from California.
3. Ibid., pp. 46–50.
4. Ibid., pp. 29, 35.
5. A. S. Hawkins, R. C. Hanson, H. K. Nelson, and H. M. Reeves, eds., *Flyways: Pioneering Waterfowl Management in North America* (Washington, D.C.: U.S. Department of Interior, Fish and Wildlife Service, 1984), p. 360.
6. *Proc.* 1938, pp. 113–15. See, for example, comments of P. J. Hoffmaster, Director, Michigan Department of Conservation, *Proc.* 1941, pp. 103–9.
7. Aldo Leopold, "The State of the Profession," *Journal of Wildlife Management* 4 (July 1940):343–46.
8. *Proc.* 1921, p. 79.
9. Frank E. Smith, *The Politics of Conservation* (New York: Pantheon Books, 1966), pp. 262–63.
10. Letter of Transmittal, *Annual Report of the Secretary of the Interior, 1941*, pp. xii–xiii.
11. Ibid.
12. *Proc.* 1963, p. 126.
13. *Proc.* 1941, pp. 89–91; *Proc.* 1946, p. 9.
14. *Proc.* 1946, pp. 9, 16–17.
15. Ibid., pp. 17–20.
16. Ibid., pp. 162–63.
17. Ibid., pp. 166–73.
18. Ibid., p. 15.
19. Gordon used the term "Transactions" throughout, but he undoubtedly was referring to the annual convention "Proceedings." *Proc.* 1947, pp. 119–21.
20. *Proc.* 1947, pp. 119–22, 130.
21. Ibid., pp. 123–24, 126.
22. Ibid., pp. 124–26; *Proc.* 1922, p. 13.
23. *Proc.* 1947, pp. 126–30; *Proc.* 1948, p. 260.
24. *Proc.* 1946, p. 19.
25. Ibid., pp. 18–19.
26. Ibid., pp. 204–5; Smith, *The Politics of Conservation*, p. 263; Michael J. Bean, *The Evolution of National Wildlife Law*, rev. ed. (New York: Praeger Publishers, 1983), p. 182. Robertson's bill was H.R. 6097.
27. Bean, *Evolution of Wildlife Law*, pp. 181, 184–85.

28. *Proc.* 1946, pp. 24–31.
29. Ibid., pp. 181–200.
30. Ibid., pp. 187–93, 196–99.
31. Ibid., pp. 203–7; J. N. Darling, I. N. Gabrielson, and I. T. Bode, *Proposed Dams on Missouri River Watershed* (Washington, D.C.: National Wildlife Federation, 1945), p. 4.
32. Ira N. Gabrielson, "Concepts in Conservation of Land, Water, and Wildlife," *Smithsonian Report for 1948*, Publication no. 3965 (Washington, D.C.: Government Printing Office, 1949), p. 289.
33. *Proc.* 1948, p. 87; see also Albert M. Day, "The Status of Waterfowl," *Proc.* 1946, pp. 80–90.
34. *Proc.* 1946, pp. 18, 22, 165.
35. *Proc.* 1948, pp. 74–84; see esp. pp. 81–82.
36. *Proc.* 1962, p. 151; *Proc.* 1957, p. 161; *Proc.* 1964, p. 81.
37. S. 1155 and H.R. 4018 became Public Law No. 537. See *Proc.* 1947, pp. 20, 62, 139; *Proc.* 1948, pp. 98, 107.
38. *Proc.* 1948, pp. 146–64, 262.
39. *Proc.* 1949, pp. 150–51.
40. Robert M. Rutherford, *Ten Years of Pittman-Robertson Wildlife Restoration* (Washington, D.C.: Wildlife Management Institute, 1949), p. 15.
41. *Proc.* 1946, pp. 131–41.
42. Rutherford, *Ten Years of Pittman-Robertson*, p. 10; *Annual Report of the Secretary of the Interior*, Fish and Wildlife Service, 1943, p. 237.
43. Rutherford, *Ten Years of Pittman-Robertson*, p. 10; *Proc.* 1946, p. 162; *Proc.* 1947, p. 139; *Proc.* 1951, p. 178.
44. *Proc.* 1949, p. 142; see also *Proc.* of early 1950s, legislative and resolutions committee reports; *Proc.* 1954, pp. 80–81.
45. Ch. 861, 69 Stat. 698; also cited in Bean, *Evolution of Wildlife Law*, p. 219; *Proc.* 1955, pp. 84, 155; *Annual Report of the Secretary of the Interior, Fish and Wildlife Service*, 1956, pp. 293–94.
46. *Annual Report of the Secretary of the Interior, Fish and Wildlife Service*, 1958, p. 355; see also Interior Department *Annual Report* for other years of the 1950s.
47. *Proc.* 1937, p. 51; *Proc.* 1941, p. 147.
48. This bill was H.R. 1746. Carl Shoemaker, "Flash—Dingell-Johnson Bill Vetoed—Flash," *Conservation News* 14 (October 15, 1949):1; *Proc.* 1947, pp. 133–34, 140; *Proc.* 1948, p. 261; *Proc.* 1949, p. 141.
49. U.S., Congress, House, *Providing that the United States Shall Aid the States in Fish Restoration and Management Projects*, H. Rept. 2327, 81st Cong., 2d sess., 1950, pp. 2–3; U.S., Congress, Senate, *Aid to States in Fish Restoration and Management Projects*, S. Rept. 2029, 81st Cong., 2d sess., 1950, pp. 1–3. H.R. 6533 became Public Law 681; see Ch. 658, 64 Stat. 430.
50. H. Rept. 2327, 81st Cong., 2d sess., 1950, pp. 2–3; S. Rept. 2029, 81st Cong., 2d sess., 1950, pp. 1–3.

51. Ch. 658, 64 Stat. 430; see also Bean, *Evolution of Wildlife Law*, p. 226.
52. *Annual Report of the Secretary of the Interior, Fish and Wildlife Service*, 1952, pp. 338–40; *Annual Report*, 1955, pp. 322–23; *Annual Report*, 1956, pp. 292–93. For a comprehensive overview of fish restoration projects, see the *Dingell-Johnson Quarterly*, for specific years beginning in 1951, for statistics on apportionment, abstracts of state quarterly reports, titles of project publications, and lists of projects newly approved.
53. *Proc.* 1949, p. 141; *Proc.* 1950, p. 17; *Proc.* 1951, pp. 22–23, 178.
54. *Proc.* 1952, pp. 67, 69; *Proc.* 1953, p. 124; *Proc.* 1959, p. 153. The Association's figures for wildlife funding were sometimes incongruent taken year by year, probably because of varying reporting methods, but the overall picture showed substantial, increasing revenues.
55. *Proc.* 1957, pp. 178–83.
56. *Proc.* 1958, pp. 170, 175–78; *Proc.* 1959, p. 155.
57. *Proc.* 1959, pp. 155–57.
58. Ibid., pp. 166, 170–81.
59. *Proc.* 1947, pp. 63, 140; *Proc.* 1948, pp. 104, 162; *Proc.* 1949, pp. 136–37.
60. *Proc.* 1956, pp. 73–75.
61. U.S., Congress, House, Committee on Merchant Marine and Fisheries, *Duck Stamp and Wildlife Restoration Bills*, Hearings Before the Subcommittee on Fisheries and Wildlife Conservation, 84th Cong., 1st sess., 1955, pp. 114–17; *Proc.* 1958, pp. 144–45, 157.
62. *Proc.* 1949, p. 142; *Proc.* 1950, pp. 157–58; *Proc.* 1953, pp. 159–60.
63. *Proc.* 1957, p. 31.
64. Congressman Clair Engle became a senator in 1958. His bill, H.R. 5538, became PL 85–337. *Proc.* 1957, pp. 162–63.
65. *Proc.* 1958, pp. 173–74; *Proc.* 1959, pp. 57–61, 74–75.
66. Robert L. F. Sikes was a Democratic congressman from Florida. His bill, H.R. 2565, became Public Law 85–337. *Proc.* 1960, p. 133; U.S., Congress, House, Committee on Merchant Marine and Fisheries, *Conservation Programs on Military and Other Federal Lands*, H. Rept. 93–753, 93d Cong., 2d sess., 1974, pp. 2–6; U.S., Congress, Senate, Committee on Environment and Public Works, *Reauthorization of the Sikes Act*, Hearings Before the Subcommittee on Environmental Pollution, Serial No. 97–H44, 97th Cong., 2d sess., 1982, pp. 3–5; Bean, *Evolution of Wildlife Law*, p. 176.
67. *Proc.* 1946, pp. 164–65; Hawkins et al., *Flyways*, p. 376.
68. Hawkins et al., *Flyways*, pp. 2, 376–77; see also Albert M. Day, *North American Waterfowl* (New York: Stackpole and Heck, 1949), pp. 58–68, 71–76.
69. *Proc.* 1951, pp. 163, 170–73, 179; *Proc.* 1952, pp. 120, 152; *Proc.* 1953, pp. 83–87; *Proc.* 1954, pp. 124–32; Hawkins et al., *Flyways*, pp. 382–83. The Association's Committee on Waterfowl Needs gave detailed, thoughtful reports on the work to be done in the flyways separately and throughout the continent, especially in the late 1950s. See, for example, *Proc.* 1957, pp. 84–88; *Proc.* 1958, pp. 157–62.

70. *Proc.* 1952, p. 147.
71. Carlos M. Fetterolf, Jr., "Why a Great Lakes Fishery Commission and Why a Sea Lamprey International Symposium," *Proceedings, Sea Lamprey International Symposium* (Marquette: Northern Michigan University, 1979), pp. 1588–92; see also *Proc.* 1953, pp. 141–44.
72. Clark Walsh, "The Good Old Days: A Review of Game and Fish Administration in Oregon, Part I," *Bulletin of the Oregon State Game Commission* 14 (December 1959):4; *Proc.* 1948, p. 140.
73. Walter B. Barrows's study on the English sparrow and its relation to agriculture was Bulletin no. 1 of what became the U.S. Bureau of Biological Survey in the Agriculture Department. *Proc.* 1948, p. 139.
74. *Proc.* 1949, pp. 42–48; *Proc.* 1951, pp. 24–26.
75. *Proc.* 1956, pp. 107–8.
76. John Gottschalk to author, July 24, 1986; Jack Berryman, telephone interview, August 3, 1986. For a negative view of animal introductions, see George Laycock, *The Alien Animals* (Garden City, N.Y.: Natural History Press for the Museum of Natural History, 1966).
77. *Proc.* 1950, p. 25; *Proc.* 1951, pp. 40–41, 98–99; *Proc.* 1953, p. 32; *Proc.* 1959, p. 10.
78. *Proc.* 1959, pp. 10–11, 217.
79. *Proc.* 1951, pp. 93–94.
80. Ibid., pp. 85–93, 95–106. See also *Proc.* 1952, pp. 96–102. For an optimistic federal view of postwar conservation progress, see U.S., Department of the Interior, *Years of Progress, 1945–1952* (Washington, D.C.: Government Printing Office, 1953), pp. 130–40.
81. *Proc.* 1947, p. 21; *Proc.* 1948, p. 97. This session lasted from January 1947 until August 1948.
82. Stephen Raushenbush, "Conservation in 1952," in *From Conservation to Ecology: The Development of Environmental Concern*, ed. Carroll W. Pursell (New York: Thomas Y. Crowell Co., 1973), pp. 58–61.

4. The Environmental Decade

1. Richard A. Cooley and Geoffrey Wandesforde-Smith, eds., *Congress and the Environment* (Seattle: University of Washington Press, 1970), pp. xiii–xvi; C. R. Gutermuth, interview, April 3, 1986; see also Stewart Udall, *The Quiet Crisis* (New York: Holt, Rinehart & Winston, 1963).
2. Rachel Carson, *Silent Spring* (Boston: Houghton Mifflin, 1962), pp. 64–68, 85; International Association of Game, Fish and Conservation Commissioners, *Public Land Policy Impact on Fish and Wildlife*, December 1971, pp. 29–31.
3. *Annual Report of the Secretary of Interior*, 1950, p. 285; *Proc.* 1953, pp. 90–93.
4. *Proc.* 1958, pp. 126–36; see reports of Pesticide Committee, or Research Committee, which absorbed it, in *Proceedings* of subsequent years.

5. *Proc.* 1962, pp. 88–92.
6. Nelson was a Democrat from Wisconsin. *Proc.* 1966, pp. 189–90; *Proc.* 1968, p. 122. For review articles on pesticides from the points of view of a chemical company and a state conservation agency, see *Proc.* 1970, pp. 60–69.
7. *Proc.* 1929, pp. 111–19; *Proc.* 1948, p. 263. This bill, S. 418, became Public Law 845.
8. Barry Commoner, *The Closing Circle: Nature, Man, and Technology* (New York: Alfred A. Knopf, 1971), p. 96 and chap. 6, passim.
9. *Proc.* 1963, pp. 78–82; *Proc.* 1969, p. 48; *Proc.* 1970, pp. 70–80.
10. *Proc.* 1954, pp. 115–20.
11. *Proc.* 1963, p. 80; *Proc.* 1956, p. 86. John Blatnik was a Democratic congressman from Minnesota. His bill became PL 660, 70 Stat. 498; *Proc.* 1957, pp. 89, 188–90.
12. PL 89–234, 79 Stat. 903. S. 2947 became PL 89–753, 80 Stat. 1246.
13. *Proc.* 1958, pp. 146–47; *Proc.* 1959, pp. 101–6; *Proc.* 1963, pp. 45, 54, 62, 109.
14. H.R. 3846 became PL 88–578, 78 Stat. 898; Michael J. Bean, *The Evolution of National Wildlife Law*, rev. ed. (New York: Praeger Publishers, 1983), pp. 230–31; *Proc.* 1964, pp. 28–30, 68, 71.
15. S. 1229 became PL 89–72, 79 Stat. 213. *Proc.* 1966, p. 192; *Proc.* 1967, p. 157; Keith W. Muckleston, "Water Projects and Recreation Benefits," in *Congress and the Environment*, Richard A. Cooley and Geoffrey Wandesforde-Smith, eds. (Seattle: University of Washington Press, 1970), pp. 121–24.
16. Muckleston, "Water Projects and Recreation Benefits," pp. 124–28; Stanley A. Cain, "Coordination of Fish and Wildlife Values with Water Resources Development Goals," in *Proceedings of the Second Annual American Water Resources Conference*, Kenneth Bowden, ed. (Chicago: University of Chicago Press, 1966), pp. 215–16; Durward L. Allen, "These Fifty Years: The Conservation Record of North American Wildlife and Natural Resources Conferences," *Transactions, 50th North American Wildlife and Natural Resources Conference*, 1985, p. 38; *Proc.* 1963, pp. 112–13; *Proc.* 1965, p. 99; *Proc.* 1966, p. 190.
17. *Proc.* 1956, pp. 191–95.
18. Ibid., pp. 196–200.
19. *Proc.* 1961, pp. 24–27.
20. *Proc.* 1966, pp. 154–58.
21. Ibid., pp. 74–78.
22. "Hunters and Conservationists Share Goals," *National Wildlife* 9 (October-November 1971):18–19; A. Starker Leopold, "The Essence of Hunting," *National Wildlife* 10 (October-November 1972):38–40.
23. *Proc.* 1972, pp. 110–12.
24. *Proc.* 1963, pp. 47–49.
25. *Proc.* 1962, p. 150.
26. *Proc.* 1963, pp. 35–41.
27. Ibid., pp. 46–47.

28. *Proc.* 1964, pp. 48–54.
29. Ibid.
30. 71 I.D. 469 (1964); Bean, *National Wildlife Law*, pp. 22–23; *Proc.* 1965, pp. 101–3.
31. *Proc.* 1965, pp. 19–29.
32. Ibid., pp. 29–31, 148; *Proc.* 1966, p. 192.
33. *Proc.* 1966, pp. 170–78.
34. The Endangered Species Act started out as H.R. 9424, S. 2217; *Proc.* 1966, pp. 122–23, 170–81. The provisions of the Administration bill (H.R. 4758, 93d Cong.) required no more than "best efforts" of federal agencies cooperating to avoid jeopardy to endangered species or their critical habitat. See history of endangered species legislation in chapter 5 of this book.
35. *Proc.* 1966, pp. 154, 170–82. The identical bills (S. 2951 and S. 3212) passed the Senate but not the House; Paul Lenzini correspondence, October 30, 1986.
36. *Proc.* 1968, pp. 103–4; Paul Lenzini, "Summary of Association Participation in Litigation" (hereafter "Litigation Summary"), Memorandum to Government Members, International Association of Fish and Wildlife Agencies, September 1984.
37. New Mexico State Game Commission v. Udall, 410 F.2d 1197 (10th Cir. 1969), cert. denied, 396 U.S. 96.1 (1969), cited in Lenzini, "Litigation Summary," p. 5.
38. *Proc.* 1970, p. 217.
39. Harry R. Woodward, personal letter, June 20, 1985, IAFWA files. See also *SUMAC-GAF*, President Woodward's informal newsletter to his Association colleagues, 1969–70, IAFWA files, for the progress of these legislative and regulatory efforts. Unfortunately, Nixon fired both Hickel and Glasgow within two months, in November 1970.
40. Chester Phelps, press release accompanying letter, September 26, 1985; Lenzini correspondence, October 30, 1986.
41. *Proc.* 1964, p. 34. See also *Proc.* 1966, pp. 159–68, for the Committee's first report to the International, an in-depth study of several aspects of public land law, presented by various committee members. International Association of Game, Fish and Conservation Commissioners, *Public Land Policy Impact on Fish and Wildlife: A Response to the Public Land Law Review Commission's Report "One Third of the Nation's Land,"* December 1971.
42. IAGFCC, *Public Land Policy Impact*, pp. vi, 1–2; see also Public Land Law Review Commission, "One Third of the Nation's Land: A Report to the President and to the Congress" (Washington, D.C.: Government Printing Office, 1970).
43. IAGFCC, *Public Land Policy Impact*, pp. 2–5.
44. Ibid., pp. 7–46.
45. See, especially, Regulation 60 of the PLLRC report, p. 158; IAGFCC, *Public Land Policy Impact*, pp. 49–52.
46. *Proc.* 1960, pp. 77–79; *Proc.* 1962, pp. 43–44.
47. *Proc.* 1960, pp. 81–87; *Proc.* 1962, pp. 43, 48; *Proc.* 1967, p. 33.

48. *Proc.* 1967, pp. 94–97, 100; *Proc.* 1968, pp. 138–43; *Proc.* 1969, pp. 85–89; *Proc.* 1970, pp. 129–30.
49. *Proc.* 1972, pp. 184–86.
50. *Proc.* 1958, p. 171; *Proc.* 1966, pp. 123, 168; Lenzini, "Litigation Summary," p. 1; Lenzini correspondence, October 30, 1986.
51. *Proc.* 1964, pp. 62–63, 108–9; *Proc.* 1966, p. 124; *Proc.* 1967, p. 153; see legislative and legal reports, resolutions of other years for similar statements.
52. *Proc.* 1966, pp. 46–47; *Proc.* 1967, pp. 139–41; *Proc.* 1968, pp. 37–39, 125; *Proc.* 1969, pp. 118–22; *Proc.* 1973, pp. 269–71; *Proc.* 1977, pp. 234–35.
53. *Proc.* 1961, pp. 109–13; *Proc.* 1962, pp. 49–50; *Proc.* 1966, pp. 44–46; see also Professional Improvement Committee reports of other years.
54. *Proc.* 1960, pp. 137–45, 189–92; *Proc.* 1962, pp. 135–39; *Proc.* 1969, pp. 172–76.
55. *Proc.* 1970, pp. 120–28; *Proc.* 1971, pp. 97–106; *Proc.* 1972, pp. 177–84; *Proc.* 1973, pp. 206–14.
56. *SUMAC-GAF*, passim, IAFWA files. President Walter Shannon apparently also issued an irregular informational newsletter, but no copies have surfaced. See reference in *Proc.* 1968, p. 11.
57. *Proc.* 1967, pp. 150, 186; *Proc.* 1968, p. 67.
58. *Proc.* 1970, pp. 137–39.
59. Ibid.
60. Ibid., pp. 139–44, 199–203; *Proc.* 1960, p. 76; *Proc.* 1966, p. 53.
61. *Proc.* 1970, pp. 13–17.
62. *Proc.* 1970, pp. 231–33. The next year the Association exchanged Gordon's owl for one made of Steuben glass, the material of all subsequent awards. *Proc.* 1971, p. 241.

5. The Washington Presence

1. *Proc.* 1971, pp. 16, 94; *Proc.* 1972, pp. 19, 114; *Proc.* 1973, pp. 6, 173.
2. Chester Phelps, interview, August 5, 1985. Phelps incorrectly remembered the timing of Durand's hiring, placing it after Neugebauer's death. The IAGFCC report *Public Land Policy Impact on Fish and Wildlife* clarifies the sequence of events.
3. *Proc.* 1973, pp. 162–63.
4. *Proc.* 1972, pp. 16, 19–21.
5. Ibid., pp. 15–19.
6. Ibid., pp. 19–21; *Proc.* 1973, p. 163.
7. Chester Phelps, interview, August 5, 1985.
8. *Proc.* 1973, pp. 6–8.
9. *Proc.* 1972, p. 151. See IAGFCC *Newsletter*, November 1973, and subsequent issues. The *Newsletter* appeared somewhat irregularly at first, now at least bimonthly. The logo, a stylized fish and deer against an aquatic and mountain background within the circle of a mounted globe, continues to be used. The initials IAGFCC on the globe's base have, of course, become IAFWA.

10. *Proc.* 1973, pp. 6–8; *Proc.* 1974, pp. 22–25.
11. *Proc.* 1974, pp. 153–54.
12. Ibid., pp. 266–70; *Proc.* 1975, pp. 168–70.
13. Harry Woodward, *SUMAC-GAF*, June 1970, p. 1.
14. Chester Phelps, *SUMAC-GAF*, June 1971, pp. 2–3; "NBC Polar Bear TV Sequence in Error, Commissioners Say," Wildlife Management Institute News Release, February 26, 1971, Washington, D.C., Chester Phelps papers; Phelps, *SUMAC-GAF*, September 1971, pp. 3–4.
15. *Proc.* 1975, p. 188.
16. Cleveland Amory, *Man Kind? Our Incredible War on Wildlife* (New York: Harper & Row, 1974); IAGFCC *Newsletter*, March 1974, p. 6.
17. *Proc.* 1971, pp. 107–9.
18. *Proc.* 1972, pp. 39–45.
19. *Proc.* 1973, pp. 149–51.
20. *Proc.* 1975, pp. 149–57.
21. IAGFCC *Newsletter*, December 1975, pp. 4–5.
22. *Proc.* 1982, pp. 77–81.
23. Fund for Animals, Inc. v. Florida Game and Fresh Water Fish Commission, 550 F. Supp. 1206 (S.D. Fla. 1982); Lenzini, "Litigation Summary," p. 34.
24. *Proc.* 1982, pp. 77–81. Only a few months later federal managers lost a similar case involving an overabundance of deer on Smithsonian Institution lands in Virginia, but fortunately, the results were less severe. Berryman, interview, June 5, 1986.
25. Stephen Kellert, "Attitudes and Characteristics of Hunters and Antihunters," *Transactions, 43rd North American Wildlife and Natural Resources Conference*, 1978, pp. 412–23.
26. IAFWA *Newsletter*, July 1979, p. 6; Durward L. Allen, "These Fifty Years: The Conservation Record of North American Wildlife and Natural Resources Conferences," *Transactions, 50th North American Wildlife and Natural Resources Conference*, 1985, pp. 47–48; Michael J. Bean, *The Evolution of National Wildlife Law*, rev. ed. (New York: Praeger Publishers, 1983), pp. 227–30.
27. Correspondence, IAFWA Archives, Box 4, Folder 5.
28. PL 92–522, 86 Stat. 1027. It was widely believed at the time that a Department of Natural Resources, which would consolidate authority over all wildlife resources, would soon be created, but that never happened. U.S., Congress, House, *Marine Mammal Protection Act Amendment*, H. Rept. 97–228, 97th Cong., 1st sess., 1981, p. 11; Bean, *National Wildlife Law*, pp. 282–84; Jack Berryman, interview, June 5, 1986.
29. John Gottschalk, "The Federal-State Partnership in Wildlife Conservation," manuscript chapter for *Wildlife in America*, Howard Brokaw, ed., Council on Environmental Quality, pp. 10–13, IAFWA Archives, Box 4, Folder 5; *Proc.* 1975, pp. 81–82.
30. *Proc.* 1975, pp. 59–66, 81–82; see *Proc.* 1974, p. 291, and *Proc.* 1979, pp. 116–17.

31. The astute Alaska natives sued the federal, not the state, government in order to do so in Washington, D.C., where judges were likely to be more sympathetic than in Alaska. U.S., Congress, House, Rept. 97–228, 1981, pp. 12–13, 20; Bean, *National Wildlife Law*, pp. 302–6; Berryman interview, June 5, 1986; Paul Lenzini, telephone interview, June 10, 1986.
32. The 1966 Endangered Species Preservation Act became PL 89–669, 80 Stat. 926; the 1969 Endangered Species Conservation Act, PL 91–135, 83 Stat. 275; the 1973 Endangered Species Act, PL 93–205, 87 Stat. 884; Gottschalk, "Federal-State Partnership" manuscript, pp. 13–14.
33. U.S., Congress, Senate, Committee on the Environment and Public Works, *Legislative History of the Endangered Species Act of 1973 as Amended in 1976, 1977, 1978, 1979, and 1980*, 97th Cong., 2d. sess., 1982, pp. 1–7, 146–47.
34. Lenzini, telephone interview, June 10, 1986. Interior Department officials also took credit for the strong Section 7 of the 1973 Endangered Species Act. For Interior's point of view on the overall Endangered Species story, see Nathanial P. Reed and Dennis Drabelle, *The United States Fish and Wildlife Service* (Boulder, Colo.: Westview Press, 1984), pp. 87–101. Bean, *National Wildlife Law*, p. 355.
35. Rudy R. Lachenmeier, "The Endangered Species Act of 1973: Preservation or Pandemonium?" *Environmental Law* (Journal of the Lewis and Clark Law School, Northwestern School of Law) 5 (Fall 1974), p. 80, in IAFWA Archives, Box 19, Folder 3; Bean, *National Wildlife Law*, p. 355.
36. The Endangered Species ("God") Committee was composed of the Secretaries of Interior, Agriculture, and the Army; the Administrators of the Environmental Protection Agency, and the National Oceanic and Atmospheric Administration; the Chairman of the Council of Economic Advisors; and a presidentially appointed representative from any affected state. Bean, *National Wildlife Law*, pp. 370–72; U.S., Congress, House, Committee on Merchant Marine and Fisheries, *Oversight Report on the Administration of the Endangered Species Act and the Convention on International Trade in Endangered Species of Wild Fauna and Flora*, by John B. Breaux, Chairman, Subcommittee on Fisheries and Wildlife Conservation and the Environment, Serial No. 96–D, 96th Cong., 2d sess., 1980, pp. 3–4; Thomas L. Kimball to NWF Affiliate Presidents, Executives, Representatives, "Public Works Appropriations/Endangered Species," August 17, 1979, in IAFWA Archives, Box 19, Folder 1.
37. IAGFCC *Newsletter*, January 1974, pp. 1–4; Lachenmeier, "The Endangered Species Act of 1973: Preservation or Pandemonium?" pp. 50–53.
38. *Legislative History of the Endangered Species Act*, 1982, pp. 1–7; *Proc.* 1974, pp. 72–78.
39. Robert L. Herbst, Commissioner, Minnesota Department of Natural Resources, to Lynn Greenwalt, Special Assistant to the Director, U.S. Fish and Wildlife Service, September 30, 1974, in IAFWA Archives, Box 19, Folder 3; *Proc.* 1974, pp. 78–85.
40. Oberstar is a Democrat from northeastern Minnesota. John Gottschalk to

Hon. Robert L. Leggett, Chairman, Subcommittee on Fisheries and Wildlife Conservation and the Environment, U.S. House of Representatives, August 3, 1976, in IAFWA Archives, Box 19, Folder 2.
41. *Proc.* 1975, pp. 45–58.
42. *Oversight Report on the Administration of the Endangered Species Act and CITES*, 1980, pp. 17–19; *Legislative History of the Endangered Species Act*, 1982, pp. 142–43; *Proc.* 1973, pp. 78–84; John Gottschalk, correspondence, September 15, 1986.
43. By 1980 sixty countries had either ratified or acceded to the CITES agreement. *Proc.* 1973, pp. 80–81; *Proc.* 1980, p. 22.
44. *Proc.* 1980, pp. 22–23.
45. *Proc.* 1977, pp. 145–56; IAFWA *Newsletter*, September 1977, p. 3.
46. IAFWA *Newsletter*, June 1978, p. 4.
47. *Proc.* 1978, p. 77.
48. *Proc.* 1980, pp. 22–27.
49. *Oversight Report on the Administration of the ESA and CITES*, 1980, pp. 2, 19–25.
50. John Gottschalk to All U.S. Governmental Members, IAFWA, September 28, 1979, and October 4, 1979, in IAFWA Archives, Box 19, Folder 1.
51. Robert Jantzen to Udall, Rhodes, Stump, and Rudd, October 11, 1979, and Joseph N. Alexander to Hon. Bruce Vento, October 5, 1979, in IAFWA Archives, Box 19, Folder 1.
52. PL 96–159, 93 Stat. 1228; IAFWA *Newsletter*, November 1979 and February 1980, p. 3.
53. Wesley Hayden, Statement of International Association of Fish and Wildlife Agencies to Senate Subcommittee on Environmental Pollution Concerning Possible Changes in the Endangered Species Act, December 8, 1981, in IAFWA Archives, Box 19, Folder 4; see also Box 9, Folder 4. PL 97–304; 96 Stat. 1421.
54. Defenders of Wildlife, Inc. v. Endangered Species Scientific Authority et al., No. 79–3060, U.S. District Court for the District of Columbia (December 12, 1979), rev'd 659 F.2d 168 (D.C. Cir.), cert. denied, 454 U.S. 963 (1981) (Bobcat I), in Lenzini, "Litigation Summary," p. 32; IAFWA *Newsletter*, November 1979 and February 1980, pp. 1–2; IAFWA *Newsletter*, March 7, 1981, p. 3; IAFWA *Newsletter*, May 1981, p. 3.
55. Defenders of Wildlife, Inc. v. Endangered Species Scientific Authority et al., No. 79–3060, U.S. District Court for the District of Columbia (December 1982) aff'd, 725 F.2d 726 (D.C. Cir. 1984) (Bobcat II), in Lenzini, "Litigation Summary," p. 33; *Proc.* 1983, p. 35; Berryman interview, June 5, 1986.
56. IAFWA *Newsletter*, February 1978, p. 2.
57. IAFWA *Newsletter*, February 1979, p. 2; IAFWA *Newsletter*, July 1979, p. 1; *Proc.* 1979, pp. 79–80.
58. IAFWA *Newsletter*, July 1979, p. 1.
59. IAFWA *Newsletter*, October 1980, p. 2; Berryman interview, June 5, 1986.

60. Humane Society of the United States et al. v. Morton et al., no. 73–1566, U.S. Court of Appeals for the D.C. Circuit (July 8, 1974), in Lenzini, "Litigation Summary," 1984, p. 7; *Proc.* 1972, p. 118; *Proc.* 1974, p. 213.
61. Baldwin v. Montana Fish and Game Commission et al., 436 U.S. 371 (1978), and Terk v. Gordon et al., 436 U.S. 850 (1978), cited in Lenzini, "Litigation Summary," 1984, pp. 21–22; Lenzini, correspondence, October 30, 1986.
62. State of Alaska et al. v. Cecil D. Andrus et al., 591 F.2d 537 (9th Cir. 1979) and Defenders of Wildlife et al. v. Cecil D. Andrus et al., no. 77–1611, U.S. Court of Appeals for the D.C. Circuit (March 16, 1979), in Lenzini, "Litigation Summary," 1984, pp. 17–18; Defenders of Wildlife v. Andrus, 627 F.2d 1238 (D.C. Cir. 1980), in Lenzini, correspondence, October 30, 1986; *Proc.* 1980, pp. 10, 89; IAFWA *Newsletter*, July 1979, p. 2; Bean, *National Wildlife Law*, pp. 155–60, 196.
63. Kleppe v. State of New Mexico, 426 U.S. 529 (1976), in Lenzini, "Litigation Summary," 1984, p. 6; *Proc.* 1975, p. 78; IAFWA *Newsletter*, April 1975, p. 2; IAFWA *Newsletter*, August 1976, p. 3; Bean, *National Wildlife Law*, p. 24.
64. Committee for Humane Legislation Inc. et al. v. Cecil D. Andrus et al., no. 78–0430, U.S. District Court for the District of Columbia (June 20, 1979) in Lenzini, "Litigation Summary," 1984, p. 16; Berryman interview, June 5, 1986; *Proc.* 1979, p. 43.
65. IAFWA *Newsletter*, June 1978, p. 1; *Proc.* 1978, p. 47; IAFWA *Newsletter*, July 1979, p. 4; IAFWA *Newsletter*, April 1980, p. 1; Berryman, correspondence, September 11, 1986.
66. IAFWA *Newsletter*, April 1976, p. 1; *Proc.* 1975, p. 169; IAFWA *Newsletter*, April 1980, p. 1; IAFWA *Constitution and Bylaws*, March 1978, July 1980.
67. IAFWA *Newsletter*, February 1979, p. 1; *Proc.* 1979, pp. 41–43; IAFWA *Newsletter*, April 1980, p. 1; IAFWA *Newsletter*, March 1981, p. 1; Berryman correspondence, September 1986.

6. The Agenda Reviewed, a Future Agenda

1. CBS crews for the television program "60 Minutes" taped Watt's presentation, but when the resulting segment was aired, Association members did not recognize what they had witnessed. The program stressed only the protectionist viewpoint. No state conservation director was interviewed. Nor was any part of Watt's Association-arranged press conference used. *Proc.* 1981, pp. 5–13; Jack Berryman, telephone interview, July 8, 1986.
2. *Proc.* 1981, pp. 5–13; Berryman interview, July 8, 1986.
3. Berryman interview, July 8, 1986; *Proc.* 1981, pp. 34–61, 69–71, 76–81; IAFWA *Newsletter*, March 1982, p. 1; *Proc.* 1982, pp. 45, 52–55, 203.
4. June Hall, "Sagebrush Rebellion: Takeover of the Western Lands," position paper for the National Wildlife Federation, Public Lands Resources Defense Division, March 20, 1980; Mike Aderhold, "The Sagebrush Rebellion: Who

Owns the West?" *Montana Outdoors*, November/December 1980, pp. 11–13; League for the Advancement of States' Equal Rights, "Welcome to the West; Property: U.S. Govt.," public relations brochure. All in IAFWA Archives, Box 25, Folder 7.

5. Hall, "Takeover of the Western Lands"; Joseph C. Greeley, Director Nevada Fish and Game Commission, to Jack Berryman, November 17, 1980; Aderhold, "Who Owns the West?" All in IAFWA Archives, Box 25, Folder 7.

6. Greeley to Berryman, November 17, 1980; Douglas Day, Director, Utah Division of Wildlife Resources, to Joseph Greeley, Chair, Land Resources Committee, IAFWA, November 26, 1980, in IAFWA Archives, Boxes 25–26.

7. "Statement of Jack H. Berryman, Executive Vice President, International Association of Fish and Wildlife Agencies, at the National Conference on States' Rights, the Sagebrush Rebellion and Federal Land Policy," November 20, 1980, Salt Lake City, Utah, in IAFWA Archives, Box 26, Folder 2.

8. Ibid.

9. IAFWA *Newsletter*, March 1981, p. 3; IAFWA *Newsletter*, May 1981, p. 2; *Proc.* 1982, pp. 189–90.

10. Department of Interior, "Fifty Years; Restoring America's Wildlife, 1937–1987: The Pittman-Robertson Federal Aid in Wildlife Restoration Act" (hereafter cited as "Fifty Years"), promotional folder with various informational materials, 1986; *Proc.* 1982, p. 185.

11. Rep. Pat Williams, Montana, to John Gottschalk, September 19, 1979; Paul Lenzini to All State Directors, Memorandum of June 26, 1979, on Pittman-Robertson Litigation, the case of Committee for Humane Legislation, Inc. et al. v. Cecil D. Andrus. Both in IAFWA Archives, Box 25, Folder 2.

12. Department of Interior, "Fifty Years."

13. The Randolph-Long bill was S. 1631. IAFWA Archives, Boxes 16–17.

14. Malcolm Wallop is a Republican senator from Wyoming, John B. Breaux a Democratic representative from Louisiana. IAFWA Archives, Boxes 16–17; Jack Berryman, "The International Association: Its Importance to the Fish and Wildlife Resource Worker," address to the 39th Conference of the Southeast Association of Fish and Wildlife Agencies, Lexington, Kentucky, October 28, 1985, pp. 2–3.

15. A. S. Hawkins, R. C. Hanson, H. K. Nelson, and H. M. Reeves, eds., *Flyways: Pioneering Waterfowl Management in North America* (Washington: U.S. Fish and Wildlife Service, 1984), pp. 418–22; Nathaniel P. Reed and Dennis Drabelle, *The United States Fish and Wildlife Service* (Boulder, Colo.: Westview Press, 1984), pp. 50–52.

16. *Proc.* 1980, pp. 140–42; *Proc.* 1981, pp. 131–32; *Proc.* 1982, pp. 133–34; *Proc.* 1983, pp. 119–23.

17. *Proc.* 1982, p. 176; *Proc.* 1975, pp. 192–93; IAFWA *Newsletter*, June 1976, p. 7.

18. IAFWA Archives, Box 3, Folder 3.

19. *Proc.* 1974, pp. 272–75.
20. *Proc.* 1976, pp. 141–43; *Proc.* 1977, pp. 192–93; IAFWA Archives, Box 3, Folder 3; IAFWA *Newsletter*, May 1977, p. 1; *Proc.* 1979, pp. 68–69; *Proc.* 1980, p. 133; *Proc.* 1982, pp. 111, 122–25; *Proc.* 1983, pp. 103–5.
21. IAFWA Archives, Box 3, Folder 3; *Proc.* 1977, pp. 192–93; *Proc.* 1978, pp. 64–65. AWARE still exists and receives donations from time to time.
22. Jack Berryman to Cookingham, Brantly, and Myers, "Association Plans for the Future," August 29, 1985; Statement of Ad Hoc Committee on Association Affairs, March 23, 1986, IAFWA Files.
23. See, for example, Martin Seneca, "Indian Hunting and Fishing Rights," *Proc.* 1975, pp. 71–77; Department of Interior Office of the Special Assistant to the Secretary, Pacific Northwest Region, "Background Information on Indian Fishing Rights in the Pacific Northwest," revised January 1976, pp. 1–3.
24. *Proc.* 1975, p. 74.
25. *Proc.* 1974, pp. 170–90, 288; IAGFCC *Newsletter*, November 1979 and February 1980, p. 4. See also Interior Department, "Background Information on Indian Fishing Rights."
26. Richard Starnes, "New Indian Ripoff," *Outdoor Life*, October 1979, pp. 15–17; Lenzini, "Litigation Summary," 1984, pp. 27–31; IAFWA *Newsletter*, May 1981, p. 4; Berryman interview, June 5, 1986.
27. "Lead-Poisoned Wildfowl," *Forest and Stream*, February 10, 1894, p. 1.
28. Wetmore later became Secretary of the Smithsonian Institution. Alexander Wetmore, "Lead Poisoning in Waterfowl," U.S. Department of Agriculture, Bulletin no. 793, July 31, 1919, pp. 1–13.
29. Frank C. Bellrose, "Effects of Ingested Lead Shot upon Waterfowl Populations," *Transactions, 16th North American Wildlife and Natural Resources Conference*, 1951, pp. 125–33; Frank C. Bellrose, "Lead Poisoning: A Tragic Waste," in Hawkins et al., *Flyways*, pp. 471–73.
30. Bellrose, "Lead Poisoning," in Hawkins et al., *Flyways*, pp. 471–73.
31. *Proc.* 1970, p. 219; Hawkins et al., *Flyways*, pp. 473–74.
32. IAGFCC *Newsletter*, September 1974, p. 4, citing an article by Jim Auckley in *Missouri Conservation*, July 1974; Reed and Drabelle, *Fish and Wildlife Service*, pp. 53–54.
33. *Proc.* 1973, pp. 91–95; *Proc.* 1974, p. 282.
34. *Proc.* 1974, p. 290; IAGFCC *Newsletter*, December 1974, p. 2.
35. *Proc.* 1974, pp. 281–84, 290.
36. Hawkins et al., *Flyways*, pp. 476–77; Reed and Drabelle, *Fish and Wildlife Service*, pp. 53–54; IAGFCC *Newsletter*, August 1976, p. 3; *Proc.* 1978, p. 123.
37. Steve Grooms, "The Steel Shot Controversy," *Fins and Feathers*, Minnesota Department of Natural Resources, December 1980, pp. 26ff. Reprint in IAFWA Archives, Box 27, Folder 5.
38. *Proc.* 1983, pp. 7–20; Ted L. Clark, "Waterfowl Management Plans: Views of the International Association of Fish and Wildlife Agencies," *Transactions*,

48th North American Wildlife and Natural Resources Conference, 1983, pp. 289–91.

39. Jay D. Hair, National Wildlife Federation, to Hon. William P. Horn, Assistant Secretary for Fish, Wildlife and Parks, Department of the Interior, April 10, 1986, in IAFWA files; Lenzini, correspondence, October 30, 1986.

40. Statement of the International Association of Fish and Wildlife Agencies on Non-Toxic Shot, March 23, 1986, in IAFWA files.

41. Department of Interior News Release, "Assistant Secretary Horn Announces Planned Phase Out of Lead Shot for Waterfowl Hunting: Nontoxic Shot Zones for 1986–87 Waterfowl Season Set," June 25, 1986; Jay D. Hair, Executive Vice-President, National Wildlife Federation, to Interested Parties, "Steel Shot Lawsuit," July 2, 1986; see also Paul Lenzini, Memorandum to IAFWA Government Members, "1986 Steel Shot Litigation," July 2, 1986; Durward L. Allen, "These Fifty Years: The Conservation Record of the North American Wildlife and Natural Resources Conferences," *Transactions, 50th North American Wildlife and Natural Resources Conference*, 1985, p. 31.

42. U.S. Department of Agriculture, "Policy on Fish and Wildlife," Secretary's Memorandum 9500–3, July 20, 1982; U.S. Department of Interior, "Department of Interior Fish and Wildlife Policy: State-Federal Relationships," March 18, 1983.

43. Draft, Resource Policies of the IAFWA, October 14, 1983, in IAFWA files. See Appendix G.

44. IAFWA Archives, Box 1, Folder 8.

45. North American Waterfowl Management Plan: press releases, summaries, memoranda of Jack Berryman, May 1986, in IAFWA current files.

46. See, for example, Stephen R. Kellert and Miriam O. Westervelt, "Historical Trends in American Animal Use and Perception," *Transactions, 47th North American Wildlife and Natural Resources Conference*, 1982, pp. 649–64.

47. See Robert H. Connery, *Governmental Problems in Wild Life Conservation* (New York: Columbia University Press, 1935), pp. 177–202; Clifton J. Whitehead, "State Fish and Wildlife Agency Responses to Funding Challenges," *Transactions, 48th North American Wildlife and Natural Resources Conference*, 1983, pp. 139–45; *Proc.* 1983, pp. 190–94.

Sources

The primary resources for the writing of this book have been the published *Proceedings* of the Association's annual conventions. The only surviving records of the pre–World War I years, however, are journalists' reports of the conventions that appeared in *Forest and Stream* and *The American Field*, two contemporary weekly sportsmen's newspapers. These brief columns were copied in total for their historical interest as a Supplement to the 1980 *Proceedings*. Printed *Proceedings* for the years 1912 and 1917 were later found and included with the bound *Proceedings* for 1965–70.

The *Proceedings*, verbatim transcripts of convention action, have the strength of immediacy and completeness, the weakness (for later researchers) of the conversation of intimates who assume the reader, or listener, is already familiar with the topic under discussion. Context is often absent, as is follow-up to complete the account of a settled issue. Still, the scientific and political challenges emerge from the pages; diverse interacting personalities enliven them.

The Regional Associations (Northeastern, Southeastern, Midwestern, and Western) have also published *Proceedings*, which have been consulted on occasion but are not uniformly accessible. They have tended to emphasize the more technical aspects of game management, although regional political concerns have generated considerable attention. Individual state fish and wildlife agencies have also provided materials that shed light on both local and broader problems; some have answered specific questions.

Since November 1973 the IAGFCC *Newsletter* (after January 1977 the IAFWA *Newsletter*) has provided timely news to members, especially legislative updates, which have been particularly useful for revealing wildlife managers' priorities and interpretations of current issues. Earlier, some individual Association Presidents issued their own informally produced newsletters, such as the *SUMAC-GAF* of Harry Woodward and Chester Phelps.

After the International Association established its Washington office in 1972, it began accumulating correspondence and operational files. These have been recently organized, properly stored, and indexed to form a functional archives for researching action on concerns of the past fifteen years. In particular, memoranda, legislative testimony, legal opinions, and position papers from various sources have proved their worth.

Paul Lenzini, the Association's Legal Counsel, has guided the telling of its legal history, providing references, summaries, and interpretations of both specific rulings and the International's reasoning. Bean's *Evolution of National Wildlife Law*, the only compilation on the subject, has been helpful, but its biases for federal authority and against management meant using it with caution.

From the earliest period the Association has maintained close, though not evenly cordial, relations with the federal government, so various types of official documents have been essential. Specific titles are listed below, but certain series can be referred to in general, such as the *Annual Reports* of the Interior and Agriculture Departments (which include those of the Bureau of Biological Survey, Bureau of Fisheries, Forest Service, and Fish and Wildlife Service), technical bulletins of federal agencies, departmental histories of varying intent and value, and congressional documents such as hearings, reports, and the statutes at large. The *Congressional Record* provided the flavor of debate on several contested issues. Specialized publications such as the *Pittman-Robertson Quarterly* and *Dingell-Johnson Quarterly* gave overviews and synopses of the federal aid for wildlife restoration programs. A nongovernmental publication that reported on legislative events was the National Wildlife Federation's *Conservation News*, which began after World War II under Carl Shoemaker's editorial leadership.

Other conservation organizations have worked closely with the International Association over the years, and their publications illuminate both their working relationships and their mutual interests. The *Bulletin of The American Game Protective Association*, for example, augmented sparce records for the early decades, while the *Transactions of the North American Wildlife and Natural Resources Conference* and others have been useful supplements for many years up to the present, highlighting the work of many resource managers active in multiple forums. Protectionists, too, both organizations and individuals, have widely published. A sampling of their literature has provided a necessary look at another point of view.

The popular press, especially in its outdoors periodicals, has helped to reveal the interests and perceptions of anglers, hunters, and other wildlife enthusiasts and outdoors recreationists. Time constraints prevented a thorough search of this abundant material, but referenced articles proved useful.

Secondary literature on the wildlife conservation movement in general, and specific aspects of it, has been plentiful since the first late nineteenth-century flowering of interest in the subject. These contributions vary widely in quality and scope, but taken sequentially they show the evolution of conservationists' topical and methodological emphases.

Finally, past and current leaders of the International Association of Fish and Wildlife Agencies have given their recollections and viewpoints of its history through taped and informal oral history interviews, in person and by letter and telephone. Their knowledge and insight have illuminated the story at every point.

Sources

Specific references to the general sources cited above are found in the notes. The following works merit individual mention:

Aderhold, Mike. "The Sagebrush Rebellion: Who Owns the West?" *Montana Outdoors*, November-December 1980, pp. 11–13, 36–37.

Allen, Durward L. *Our Wildlife Legacy*, rev. ed. New York: Funk and Wagnalls, 1962.

———. "These Fifty Years: The Conservation Record of North American Wildlife and Natural Resources Conferences." *Transactions, 50th North American Wildlife and Natural Resources Conference*, 1985, booklet edition.

The American Field (a weekly sportsmen's newspaper). Chicago, 1902–16.

American Game Association. "American Game Policy." *Transactions of the Seventeenth American Game Conference*, 1930, pp. 281–89.

Amory, Cleveland. *Man Kind? Our Incredible War on Wildlife.* New York: Harper & Row, 1974.

Amsler, Guy. Arkansas Game and Fish Commission, retired, Little Rock. Interview with John C. Sunderland, June 27, 1985.

Barker, Elliott. New Mexico Department of Game and Fish, retired, Santa Fe. Interview with Jesse Williams, October 21, 1983.

Bates, J. Leonard. "Fulfilling American Democracy: The Conservation Movement, 1907 to 1921." *Mississippi Valley Historical Review* 44 (June 1957): 29–57.

Bean, Michael J. *The Evolution of National Wildlife Law*, rev. ed. New York: Praeger Publishers, 1983.

Bellrose, Frank C. "Effects of Ingested Lead Shot upon Waterfowl Populations." *Transactions, 16th North American Wildlife and Natural Resources Conference*, 1951, pp. 125–35.

———. "Lead Poisoning: A Tragic Waste." In *Flyways: Pioneering Waterfowl Management in North America*, edited by A. S. Hawkins et al. Washington, D.C.: U.S. Department of Interior, Fish and Wildlife Service, 1984.

Berryman, Jack. International Association of Fish and Wildlife Agencies, Washington, D.C. Interview, June 4, 1986.

———. "Report of the Executive Vice President." Association Convention. Sun Valley, Idaho, September 11, 1985.

———. "The International Association: Its Importance to the Fish and Wildlife Resource Worker." Address to the 39th Conference of the Southeast Association of Fish and Wildlife Agencies. Lexington, Kentucky, October 28, 1985.

———. "The Sagebrush Rebellion and Federal Land Policy." Statement to the National Conference on States' Rights. Salt Lake City, November 20, 1980. IAFWA Archives, Box 26, Folder 2.

Cain, Stanley A. "Coordination of Fish and Wildlife Values with Water Resources Development Goals." *Proceedings, Second Annual American Water Resources Conference*, edited by Kenneth Bowden. Chicago: University of Chicago Press, 1966.

Cameron, Jenks. *The Bureau of Biological Survey: Its History, Activities and*

Organization. Service Monograph of the U.S. Govt., no. 54. Baltimore: Johns Hopkins Press, 1929.

Carson, Rachel. *Silent Spring*. Boston: Houghton Mifflin, 1962.

Commoner, Barry. *The Closing Circle: Nature, Man, and Technology*. New York: Alfred A. Knopf, 1971.

Connery, Robert H. *Governmental Problems in Wild Life Conservation*. New York: Columbia University Press, 1935.

Cooley, Richard A., and Wandesforde-Smith, Geoffrey, eds. *Congress and the Environment*. Seattle: University of Washington Press, 1970.

Coyle, David Cushman. *Conservation: An American Story of Conflict and Accomplishment*. New Brunswick, N.J.: Rutgers University Press, 1957.

Cross, Whitney R. "Ideas in Politics: The Conservation Policies of the Two Roosevelts." *Journal of the History of Ideas* 14 (June 1953):421–38.

Darling, J. N.; Gabrielson, I. N.; and Bode, I. T. *Proposed Dams on Missouri River Watershed*. Washington, D.C.: National Wildlife Federation, 1945.

Day, Albert M. *North American Waterfowl*. New York: Stackpole and Heck, 1949.

De Sorno, Maitland. *John Bird Burnham—Klondiker, Adirondacker and Eminent Conservationist*. Saranac Lake, N.Y.: Adirondack Yesteryears, Inc., 1978.

Durisch, Lawrence L., and Macon, Hershal. *Upon its Own Resources: Conservation and State Administration*. N.p.: Universities of Alabama, Georgia, South Carolina, and Tennessee, 1951.

Fetterolf, Carlos M., Jr. "Why a Great Lakes Fishery Commission and Why a Sea Lamprey International Symposium." *Proceedings, Sea Lamprey International Symposium*. Marquette: Northern Michigan University, 1979, pp. 1588–92.

Flader, Susan L. *Thinking Like a Mountain: Aldo Leopold and the Evolution of an Ecological Attitude Toward Deer, Wolves, and Forests*. Columbia: University of Missouri Press, 1974.

Forest and Stream: A Weekly Journal of the Rod and Gun. New York, 1894–1916.

Gabrielson, Ira N. "Concepts in Conservation of Land, Water, and Wildlife." *Smithsonian Report for 1948*, Publ. no. 3965. Washington, D.C.: Government Printing Office, 1949.

———. *Wildlife Conservation*. New York: Macmillan Co., 1959.

———. *Wildlife Management*. New York: Macmillan Co., 1951.

———. *Wildlife Refuges*. New York: Macmillan Co., 1943.

Gordon, Seth. Seth Gordon Papers. University of Wyoming, Laramie.

Gottschalk, John. International Association of Fish and Wildlife Agencies, Washington, D.C. Interviews, August 5 and September 30, 1985.

———. "The Federal-State Partnership in Wildlife Conservation." Manuscript chapter for *Wildlife in America*, by the Council on Environmental Quality, 1978. IAFWA Archives, Box 4, Folder 5.

Sources

Graham, Edward H. *The Land and Wildlife*. New York: Oxford University Press, 1947.

Graham, Frank, Jr. *Man's Dominion: The Story of Conservation in America*. New York: M. Evans & Co., 1971.

———. *Since Silent Spring*. Boston: Houghton Mifflin, 1970.

Graham, Otis, and Wander, Meghan R., eds. *Franklin D. Roosevelt, His Life and Times: An Encyclopedic View*. Boston: G. K. Hall & Co., 1985.

Grinnell, Dr. George Bird. "The Game Is Not for Us Alone." *Bulletin of The American Game Protective Association* 8 (April 1919):15.

Grinnell, George B., and Sheldon, Charles, eds. *Hunting and Conservation: The Book of the Boone and Crockett Club*. New Haven: Yale University Press, 1925; reprint ed. by Arno and the New York Times, 1970.

Grooms, Steve. "The Steel Shot Controversy." *Fins and Feathers*, Minnesota Department of Natural Resources, December 1980, pp. 26ff.

Gutermuth, C. R. Wildlife Management Institute, retired, Arlington, Virginia. Interview, April 3, 1986.

Hall, June. "Sagebrush Rebellion: Takeover of the Western Lands." Position paper for the National Wildlife Federation, Public Lands Resources Defense Division, March 20, 1980. IAFWA Archives, Box 25, Folder 7.

Hawes, Harry B. *Fish and Game: Now or Never*. New York: D. Appleton Century Co., 1935.

Hawkins, A. S.; Hanson, R. C.; Nelson, H. K.; and Reeves, H. M., eds. *Flyways: Pioneering Waterfowl Management in North America*. Washington, D.C.: U.S. Department of Interior, Fish and Wildlife Service, 1984.

Hayden, Wesley. Statement of International Association of Fish and Wildlife Agencies to Senate Subcommittee on Environmental Pollution Concerning Possible Changes in the Endangered Species Act, December 8, 1981. IAFWA Archives, Box 19, Folder 4.

Highsmith, Richard M.; Jensen, J. G.; and Rudd, R. *Conservation in the United States*. Chicago: Rand McNally & Co., 1969.

Hoover, Herbert. "United States Food Administration Memorandum on the Use of Game as Food." *Bulletin of The American Game Protective Association* 7 (April 1918):26.

Hornaday, William T. "Does the Supply of Game Justify any Relaxation in the Laws that Regulate its Taking?" *Bulletin of The American Game Protective Association* 7 (April 1918):24.

———. *Our Vanishing Wild Life: Its Extermination and Preservation*. New York: Charles Scribner's Sons, 1913.

———. *Thirty Years War for Wild Life: Gains and Losses in the Thankless Task*. New York: Charles Scribner's Sons, 1931.

———. *Wild Life Conservation in Theory and Practice*. New Haven: Yale University Press, 1914.

"Hunters, Conservationists Share Goals." *National Wildlife* 9 (October-November 1971):18–19.

International Association of Game, Fish and Conservation Commissioners. *Public Land Policy Impact on Fish and Wildlife: A Response to the Public Land Law Review Commission's Report, "One Third of the Nation's Land."* n.p., 1971.

Kellert, Stephen. "Attitudes and Characteristics of Hunters and Antihunters." *Transactions, 43rd North American Wildlife and Natural Resources Conference*, March 1978, pp. 412–33.

———. "Perceptions of Animals in American Society." *Transactions, 41st North American Wildlife and Natural Resources Conference*, 1976, pp. 533–46.

Kellert, Stephen, and Westervelt, Miriam O. "Historical Trends in American Animal Use and Perception." *Transactions, 47th North American Wildlife and Natural Resources Conference*, 1982, pp. 649–64.

Kibbe, A. S. "A Western View of the Game Refuge Bill" and Sheldon, Major H. P. "The Game Refuge Bill—An Eastern View." *Bulletin of The American Game Protective Association* 14 (January 1925):5–10.

Lachenmeier, Rudy R. "The Endangered Species Act of 1973: Preservation or Pandemonium?" *Environmental Law* (Journal of the Lewis and Clark Law School, Northwestern School of Law) 5 (Fall 1974):29–84.

Laycock, George. *The Alien Animals*. Garden City, N.Y.: Natural History Press for the American Museum of Natural History, 1966.

LeDuc, Thomas. "The Historiography of Conservation." *Forest History* 9 (October 1965):23–28.

Lendt, David L. *Ding: The Life of Jay Norwood Darling*. Ames: Iowa University Press, 1979.

Lenzini, Paul A. "Summary of Association Participation in Litigation." Memorandum to Government Members, International Association of Fish and Wildlife Agencies, September 1984.

Leopold, Aldo. "Ten New Developments in Game Management." *American Game* 14 (July 1925):7–8, 20.

———. *Game Management*. New York: Charles Scribner's Sons, 1933.

———. "The State of the Profession." *Journal of Wildlife Management* 4 (July 1940):343–46.

Leopold, A. Starker. "The Essence of Hunting." *National Wildlife* 10 (October-November 1972):38–40.

Linduska, Joseph P., ed. *Waterfowl Tomorrow*. Washington, D.C.: Government Printing Office, Department of Interior, 1964.

Matthiessen, Peter. *Wildlife in America*. New York: Viking Press, 1959.

Montana Outdoors 11 (1979). Special issue on hunting.

Muckleston, Keith W. "Water Projects and Recreation Benefits." In *Congress and the Environment*, edited by Richard A. Cooley and Geoffrey Wandesforde-Smith. Seattle: University of Washington Press, 1970.

Nash, Roderick, ed. *The American Environment: Readings in the History of Conservation*. Reading, Mass.: Addison-Wesley, 1968.

National Association of Audubon Societies. *Federal Power and Duck Bag Limits: Facts.* Foreword by T. Gilbert Pearson. New York: National Association of Audubon Societies, 1926.

Nixon, Edgar B., ed. *Franklin D. Roosevelt and Conservation, 1911-1945.* 2 vols. Hyde Park, N.Y.: Franklin D. Roosevelt Library, National Archives and Records Service, 1957.

North American Wildlife Conference. *Proceedings, Wildlife Restoration and Conservation.* Conference called by President Franklin D. Roosevelt. Washington, D.C.: Government Printing Office, 1936.

Palmer, T. S. "Lest We Forget." *Bulletin of The American Game Protective Association* 14 (January 1925):11–12.

Phelps, Chester. International Association of Fish and Wildlife Agencies, Washington, D.C. Interview, August 5, 1985.

Phillips, John C., and Lincoln, Frederick C. *American Waterfowl: Their Present Situation and the Outlook for their Future.* Boston: Houghton Mifflin, 1930.

Pinchot, Gifford. *Breaking New Ground.* New York: Harcourt, Brace & Co., 1947.

———. *The Fight for Conservation.* Introduction by Gerald D. Nash. Seattle: University of Washington Press, 1967.

Public Land Law Review Commission. *One Third of the Nation's Land: A Report to the President and to the Congress.* Washington, D.C.: Government Printing Office, 1970.

Raushenbush, Stephen. "Conservation in 1952." In *From Conservation to Ecology: The Development of Environmental Concern*, edited by Carroll W. Pursell. New York: Thomas Y. Crowell Co., 1973.

Reed, Nathanial P., and Drabelle, Dennis. *The United States Fish and Wildlife Service.* Boulder, Colo.: Westview Press, 1984.

Regenstein, Lewis. *The Politics of Extinction: The Shocking Story of the World's Endangered Wildlife.* New York: Macmillan, 1975.

Rutherford, Robert M. *Ten Years of Pittman-Robertson Wildlife Restoration.* Washington, D.C.: Wildlife Management Institute, 1949.

Scheffer, Victor. *A Voice for Wildlife.* New York: Charles Scribner's Sons, 1974.

Shoemaker, Carl. "Flash—Dingell-Johnson Bill Vetoed—Flash." *Conservation News* 14 (October 15, 1949):1.

Smith, Frank E. *The Politics of Conservation.* New York: Pantheon Books, 1966.

Starnes, Richard. "New Indian Ripoff." *Outdoor Life* (October 1979):15–17.

Stroud, Richard H., ed. *National Leaders of American Conservation.* Washington, D.C.: Smithsonian Institution Press, for the Natural Resources Council of America, 1985.

"Success Crowns the Canadian Treaty Campaign" and "Complete Text of the Treaty with Canada." *Bulletin of The American Game Protective Association* 5 (October 1, 1916):1–3.

Swain, Donald C. *Federal Conservation Policy, 1921–1933*. Berkeley: University of California Press, 1963.

Swift, Lloyd. U.S. Forest Service, retired, Falls Church, Virginia. Interview, March 6, 1986.

Trefethen, James B. *Crusade for Wildlife: Highlights in Conservation Progress*. Harrisburg, Pa.: Stackpole Co. and New York: Boone & Crockett Club, 1961.

Udall, Stewart L. *The Quiet Crisis*. New York: Holt, Rinehart and Winston, 1963.

U.S. Congress. House. *Aid to States in Wildlife Restoration Projects*. H. Rept. 1572, 75th Cong., 1st sess., 1937.

U.S. Congress. House. *Marine Mammal Protection Act Amendment*. H. Rept. 97–228, 97th Cong., 1st sess., 1981.

U.S. Congress. House. *Protection of Migratory and Insectivorous Birds of the United States*. H. Rept. 680, 62nd Cong., 2d sess., 1912.

U.S. Congress. House. *Providing That the United States Shall Aid the States in Fish Restoration and Management Projects*. H. Rept. 2327, 81st Cong., 2d sess., 1950.

U.S. Congress. House. Committee on Merchant Marine and Fisheries. *Conservation Programs on Military and Other Federal Lands*. H. Rept. 93–753, 93rd Cong., 2d sess., 1974.

U.S. Congress. House. Committee on Merchant Marine and Fisheries. *Duck Feeding and Duck Stamp Legislation*. Hearings Before the Subcommittee on Fisheries and Wildlife Conservation, 85th Cong., 1st sess., 1957.

U.S. Congress. House. Committee on Merchant Marine and Fisheries. *Duck Stamp and Wildlife Restoration Bills*. Hearings Before the Subcommittee on Fisheries and Wildlife Conservation, 84th Cong., 1st sess., 1955.

U.S. Congress. House. Committee on Merchant Marine and Fisheries. *Oversight Report on the Administration of the Endangered Species Act and the Convention on International Trade in Endangered Species of Wild Fauna and Flora*, by John B. Breaux, Chairman, Subcommittee on Fisheries and Wildlife Conservation and the Environment. Serial no. 96–D, 96th Cong., 2d sess., 1980.

U.S. Congress. House. Select Committee on Conservation of Wildlife Resources. *Conservation of Wildlife*. H. Rept. 3112, 76th Cong., 3d sess., 1941.

U.S. Congress. Senate. *Aid to States in Fish Restoration and Management Projects*. S. Rept. 2029, 81st Cong., 2d sess., 1950.

U.S. Congress. Senate. *Policies, Standards, and Procedures in the Formulation, Evaluation, and Review of Plans for Use and Development of Water and Related Land Resources*. S. Doc. 97, 87th Cong., 2d sess., 1962.

U.S. Congress. Senate. *To Protect Migratory Game and Insectivorous Birds of the United States*. S. Rept. 675, 62nd Cong., 2d sess., 1912.

U.S. Congress. Senate. *United States Aid to States in Wildlife Restoration Projects*. S. Rept. 868, 75th Cong., 1st. sess., 1937.

Sources

U.S. Congress. Senate. Committee on the Environment and Public Works. *Legislative History of the Endangered Species Act of 1973 as Amended in 1976, 1977, 1978, 1979, and 1980*. 97th Cong., 2d sess., 1982.

U.S. Congress. Senate. Committee on the Environment and Public Works. *Reauthorization of the Sikes Act*. Hearings Before the Subcommittee on Environmental Pollution, Serial no. 97–H44, 97th Cong., 2d sess., 1982.

U.S. Department of Agriculture. *Policy on Fish and Wildlife*. Secretary's Memorandum 9500–3, July 20, 1982.

U.S. Department of Agriculture. *The Wildlife Restoration Program under the Pittman-Robertson Act of 1937*, by Albert M. Day. Misc. Publ. no. 350, 1939.

U.S. Department of Agriculture, Bureau of Biological Survey. *Chronology and Index of the More Important Events in American Game Protection, 1776–1917*, by T. S. Palmer. Bulletin no. 41. Washington, D.C.: Government Printing Office, 1912.

U.S. Department of Agriculture, Bureau of Biological Survey. *Digest of Game Laws for 1901*, by T. S. Palmer and H. W. Olds. Bulletin no. 16. Washington, D.C.: Government Printing Office, 1901.

U.S. Department of Agriculture, Bureau of Biological Survey. *Game as a National Resource*, by T. S. Palmer. Bulletin no. 1049. Washington, D.C.: Government Printing Office, 1922.

U.S. Department of Agriculture, Bureau of Biological Survey. *Hunting Licenses: Their History, Objects and Limitations*, by T. S. Palmer. Bulletin no. 19. Washington, D.C.: Government Printing Office, 1904.

U.S. Department of Agriculture, Bureau of Biological Survey. *Laws Regulating the Transportation of Game*, by T. S. Palmer. Bulletin no. 14. Washington, D.C.: Government Printing Office, 1900.

U.S. Department of Agriculture, Bureau of Biological Survey. *Lead Poisoning in Waterfowl*, by Alexander Wetmore. Bulletin no. 793. Washington, D.C.: Government Printing Office, 1919.

U.S. Department of Agriculture, Bureau of Biological Survey. *Migratory-Bird Treaty-Act Regulations and Text of Federal Laws Relating to Game and Birds*. Service and Regulatory Announcements—B.S. 75, 1931.

U.S. Department of Interior. *Department of Interior Fish and Wildlife Policy: State-Federal Relationships*, March 18, 1983.

U.S. Department of Interior. "Fifty Years; Restoring America's Wildlife, 1937–1987: The Pittman-Robertson Federal Aid in Wildlife Restoration Act." Public Information Folder, 1986.

U.S. Department of Interior. *Years of Progress, 1945–1952*. Washington, D.C.: Government Printing Office, 1953.

U.S. Department of Interior, Office of the Special Assistant to the Secretary, Pacific Northwest Region. "Background Information on Indian Fishing Rights in the Pacific Northwest," rev. ed., January 1976. IAFWA Archives, Box 4, Folder 3.

Sources

Walsh, Clark. "The Good Old Days: A Review of Game and Fish Administration in Oregon, Parts I and II." *Bulletin of the Oregon State Game Commission*, December 1959 and January 1960.

Index

Acklen, J. H., 23
Agriculture. *See* Land use, agricultural
Alaska game laws, 26–27, 128–29, 173
Aldrich, A. D., 87, 95
Alexander, Joseph, 137
Alexander, M. L., 26, 28
Allen, Durward, 91, 164
Alligators, 132, 133
American Association for Conservation Information, 155
American Field, 17, 18, 19
American Fisheries Society, 67, 87, 170
American Fishing Tackle Manufacturing Association, 4
American Forestry Association, 99, 170, 173
American Fur Resources Institute, 4
American Game Protective Association, 21–22, 27, 37, 49, 172
American League of Anglers, *Dingell-Johnson Expansion Bill Newsletter,* 153
American Wildlife Institute, 45, 46, 48, 49, 175, 177, 209 n.47. *See also* Wildlife Management Institute
Amory, Cleveland, 124, 126; *Man Kind? Our Incredible War on Wildlife,* 123
Amsler, Guy, 41, 189; *Arkansas Deer,* 60
Anadromous Fish Conservation Act, 179, 198
Andreson, August, 39
Andrus, Cecil, 144
Animal rights, 123, 125–26, 136, 137, 139, 141–44. *See also* Hunting, opposition to
Antelope, 13, 91, 170
Anthony, Daniel R., 34
Antiquities Act, 171
Ants, fire, 91–92
Association for Conservation Information, 4
Atomic energy, effects of, on wildlife, 72, 93
Audubon, John James, 84
Audubon Society, 17, 22, 37, 99, 170, 171, 173
Australia, 140
Avery, Carlos, 28, 34
AWARE (America's Wildlife Association for Resource Education) Foundation, 156, 182

Bache, Richard, 31
Bagley, Lester, 71, 73, 189
Baird, Spencer, 170
Barker, Elliott, 46–48, 53, 56, 58, 59, 70, 189
Bass, 59, 173
Bears, 43; grizzly, 133; polar, 122, 128
Beavers, 132
Beck, Thomas, 45, 174
Bell, Daniel W., 51
Bellrose, Frank, 160
Berne Criteria, 135

Index

Berryman, Jack, 148, 150–51, 157, 159, 165; as IAFWA official, 145, 164, 182; on legislation, 128, 144
Besadny, C. D., xi
Bible-Price-Young Act, 75, 178
Big game. *See* Wildlife, big game
Biggs, John A., 80, 93
Birds, 32–40, 83–87, 90–91, 108–10, 175, 178; game, 12, 24, 31–32, 88, 169; watchers of, 98–99. *See also* Wildlife, migratory birds
Bison, 32, 41, 129, 170
Bitely, Ralph, 161–62
Blackbirds, 15
Blatnik Federal Water Pollution Control Act, 93–94
Boating Industry Association, 153
Bobcats, 8, 135–39, 154, 182
Bode, I. T., 64–65, 66, 69, 74, 93
Boldt, George H., 158
"Bonn Convention," 139–41, 182
Boone and Crockett Club, 14, 15, 170
"Bottle bill," 196
Bowers, Glenn L., xi, 165, 190
Brantly, Robert, 125, 126, 164
Breaux, John B., 136–37
Brooks, James, 128
Brown, William Y., 135
Buck, Frank, 62
Buffalo, 13, 90
Bulletin of the American Game Protective Association, 35–36
Bump, Gardiner, 87
Burnham, John B., 21–22, 23, 36
Burros, 143, 180

Callison, Charles, 93
Cameron, Jenks, 43
Camp Fire Club, 15, 171
Canada, 88, 136, 137, 172, 198; accords with, 23–24, 38, 58–59, 85, 108–10, 140, 166, 175, 176, 183; in IAFWA, 4, 20, 28, 58–59, 66–67, 114, 173, 182
Canadian Wildlife Service, 4, 120
Caribou, 40, 140, 142
Carp, 86, 88
Carson, Rachel, *Silent Spring,* 90–92
Chalk, John, 54–55, 56
Chapman, Duff and Lenzini (law firm), 119. *See also* IAFWA, and litigation
Chapman, Oscar, 111
Chickens, prairie, 12, 16, 88, 170
Cisco, 93
CITES, 8, 133–41, 146, 154, 182, 199
Civilian Conservation Corps, 44, 46, 166, 174
Civil Works Administration, 46
Clapp, Earle H., 56
Clark, Arthur, 54
Clark, Joel B., 57
Clark, Ted, 164
Clarke-McNary Act, 173
Clean Water Restoration Act, 94, 179
Coalitions, 8, 155
Coerr, Wymberley, 133, 134
Commercial Fisheries Research and Development Act, 198
Conservation movement, 14, 30, 43, 88–116, 171, 172, 173; ecology, 63, 90, 99, 115, 122–27, 197; and energy sources, 72, 196; federal role in, 33, 48, 68–71, 75, 81–83, 147; history of, xi, xii, xiii, 3, 13–17, 88, 169; on international level, 3, 48, 58, 60, 75, 83–85, 133–41; and legislation, 90, 149; in national parks and forests, 14, 41–43, 100–102, 142, 169, 171, 172, 173, 201; and natural resources, 3, 5, 14–15, 44, 154, 174, 194, 201; and private interests, 75, 83, 88; and public works, 44–48, 90, 166–67, 174, 200; and recreation, 94–101, 107, 178, 179, 195, 196, 197, 198; regional role in, 3, 75; reserves, 7; states' role in, 3, 75, 88, 95–96, 136–39; and water projects, 68–71, 93, 94–96, 100, 177, 201; and wildlife conservation, 14, 15, 19, 51, 61, 95. *See also* IAFWA; Pollution; Wildlife; Wildlife management
Convention on International Trade in Endangered Species of Wild Fauna and Flora (CITES), 8, 133–41, 146, 154, 182, 199
Cookingham, Russell, 164
Coolidge, Calvin, 33, 39
Cooperative Wildlife Research Unit Program, 49, 53, 60, 62–63, 92, 112, 167, 174, 175
Coordination acts (water projects), 45, 69, 70, 93, 174, 177
Coots, 23

Index

Cottam, Clarence, 70–71, 86–87, 88, 91–92
Cougars, 41, 43
Cox, Nelson, 102
Coyotes, 41, 43
Crane, Harold, 101
Cranes, sandhill, 88
Crossley, S-D Surveys, Inc., 96, 178. *See also* National Survey of Fishing and Hunting
Crowe, Douglas, 137–38

Damage by wildlife. *See* Wildlife, damages of
Darling, Jay N., 45–49, 50, 64, 71, 87–88, 174
Davis, Herbert, 63
Day, Albert M., 51–53, 69, 78, 84, 85–86, 190
Deer, 12, 16, 40, 54–56, 120–21, 125–26, 141, 169, 173, 219 n.24. *See also* Mule deer
Denmead, Talbott, 61, 66
Denver Conservation Library, 111–12, 179
Dilg, Will H., 36
Dingell, John, 76
Dingell-Johnson Act, 76–78, 92, 111–12, 148, 152–53, 179, 182–83, 214 n.52; implementation of, 102; as model legislation, 94, 167, 198; passage of, 76–78, 177. *See also* Wallop-Breaux Act
Doig, Herbert, 162
Doves, 5
Dowdell, R. L., 161
Drought. *See* Land use, drought
Ducks, 12, 20, 32–40, 80–81, 85, 88, 148, 159–64; baldpate, 160; black, 170; canvas-back, 160; mallard, 31; redhead, 160; ring-necked, 160; scaup, 160; wood, 170
Duck Stamp Act. *See* Migratory Bird Hunting Stamp Act
Durand, Forrest V., 118

Eagles, bald, 164, 169
Earth Day, 115, 180
Ecology, 43, 63, 90, 126–27, 197–98. *See also* Conservation movement, ecology
Educational programs, 6, 60, 83, 145, 196
Egrets, 91, 124
Eisenhower, Dwight D., 82
Elk, 32, 40, 41, 75, 129, 170
Endangered species: international agreements (*see* CITES; Bonn Convention); legislation, 8, 104–5, 130–34, 136–38, 140, 180, 181, 182, 199, 217 n.34, 220 n.36; litigation, 138–39; Management Authority, 134, 136–38; Scientific Authority, 135–39
Energy policy, 196
Engle, Clair, 82
Engle Act, 82, 178
Ernest Thompson Seton Award, 193
Erosion, 7, 175
Eskimos, 128–29, 181, 220 n.31
Evans, Thomas, 109
Everglades deer hunt, 125–26
Exotics, 85–87, 197, 215 n.76

Farm Bill, 7
Feast, Cleland N., 66, 69, 189
Federal-aid funding, xiv, 40, 48–53, 76–80, 140–41, 147–48, 151–53, 172, 176, 177, 198; withholding of surplus, 74–75. *See also* names of individual federal legislative acts
Federal Aid in Wildlife Restoration Act. *See* Pittman-Robertson Act
Federal Emergency Relief Act, 174
Federal Land Policy and Management Act, 142, 149, 181
Federal legislation. *See* names of individual acts
Federal-state relations. *See* State-federal relations
Federal Water Pollution Control Act, 93, 178
Federal Water Project Recreation Act, 95, 179
Federal Water Quality Control Act, 94, 179
Fielding, F. R., 73
Firearms industry, 33, 65, 159–64; and wildlife conservation, 21, 49, 79, 124, 172
Fish, 45–46, 59–60, 76–78, 93, 96, 130–31, 157–59, 179, 194, 198
Fish and Wildlife Coordination Act (Non-game Act), 127, 178

Index

Fishing, 9, 76–78, 96–101, 124, 152–53, 194, 195, 196; bag limits, 12, 30; excessive, 16, 76; in Great Lakes, 18; as industry, 96–101; licenses, 10, 77, 98, 159; restrictions on, 26, 167, 171, 173, 174–75, 178; rights, 157–59, 166, 181, 195. *See also* names of individual fish
Fishing tackle industry, 79, 177
Fish restoration. *See* Dingell-Johnson Act
Flooding. *See* Land use, flooding
Florida Everglades Deer Hunt, 125–26
Flyways, 39, 83–85, 154, 160–63, 177, 178, 208 n.26, 214 n.69
Forest and Stream, 10, 11, 18, 21, 159
Forester, Frank. *See* Herbert, Henry William
Forest Reserve Act, 170
Fred Bear Sports Club, 156
Friends of Animals, 155
Frogs, 91
Frye, Earle, 115
Fullerton, Sam, 11–12, 188
Furbearers Conference, Worldwide, 154, 182
Fur Seal Convention, 5

Gabrielson, Ira, 48, 58, 62, 64, 65, 71, 91, 111, 190
Game farming, 19, 25, 31
"Game hogs," 15–16, 167
Game laws, 16, 19, 20, 40; bag limits (*see* Hunting, bag limits); closed season, 16, 40, 169, 170; market hunting, 20, 23, 25, 170; spring shooting, abolition of, 11, 18, 20, 170
Game managers, xiii, xiv, 7, 52–53, 57, 169; and conservation, 15, 16, 44; education of, 49, 61–62, 167, 174, 175, 209 n.47; on federal level, 34, 36, 38, 142; jurisdiction of, 23, 52, 55, 80, 85, 158–59; organization of, 10, 17, 63–64; professionalism of, 4, 57, 61, 62–64, 113, 152, 167; on state level, 10, 16, 63–64, 74, 81, 107, 125–27, 149–51
Game Refuge-Public Shooting Grounds Bill (New-Anthony), 30, 34–38
Game refuges. *See* Refuges, game
Garfield, Charles D., 26
Geer v. Connecticut, 12, 42, 171
Geese, 20, 32, 88, 163
Glasgow, Leslie, 106, 122
Goats, mountain, 170
Gordon, Ladd, 106
Gordon, Seth, 30, 46, 54–55, 60, 64, 103–4, 189; as conservationist, 37, 39, 41–42, 92–93, 208 n.31; as IAFWA official, 56, 65–68; Seth Gordon Award, 116, 180, 192, 218 n.62
Gottschalk, John, xi, 98, 109, 114, 125, 127–28, 131–32, 137, 153, 190; as IAFWA official, 120–21, 133, 145, 181, 182
Grazing. *See* Land use, grazing
Great Britain, 23–24
Great Lakes, 18, 77, 85, 93, 109, 132, 177, 178
Great Lakes Fishery Commission, 85, 109, 178
Green, R. G., 161
Greenley, Joseph, 150
Greenwalt, Lynn, 132
Grinnell, George Bird, 15, 21, 23, 159–60, 170, 171
Grooms, Steve, 163
Grouse, 91, 169
Groves, Frank, 101–3
Gun control, 20, 111, 141, 152, 155, 197
Gutermuth, C. R., 66, 68, 190

Habitat, 6–7, 30, 32, 38, 83, 107, 133, 154–55, 196, 201
Halleck, Charles, *Forest and Stream,* 15, 170
Harding, Warren G., 33
Harkin, J. B., 58
Harris, Peyton Randolph, 55, 56
Harrison, Benjamin, 31, 170
Hatch, Orrin, 149
Hatcheries, fish, 31, 198
Hawes, Harry B., 175
Hawes Act, 59, 173
Hayden, Wesley, 137–38, 140, 145–46, 190
Heath hens, 169
Herbert, Henry William ("Frank Forester"), 15
Herbst, Robert, 132
Herter, Christian A., Jr., 133

Index

Hewitt, C. Gordon, 23
Hickel, Walter J., 106, 115
Higgins, Elmer, 72
History Associates Incorporated, xi
Hodel, Don, 152, 166
Hoffmaster, Peter J., 65, 69, 70
Holland, Ray P., 35, 57, 67, 189
Homestead Act, 170
Hoover, Herbert, 27, 33, 44, 174
Hornaday, William T., 23, 26–27, 33–39, 43
Horses, wild, 143, 180
Houston, David F., 23
Huey, William, 134–36
Humane Society of the United States, 141
Hunt v. United States, 42, 173
Hunting, 34, 62, 71, 96–101, 122–25, 165, 169, 194, 195, 196; bag limits, 12, 20, 30, 33–34, 39, 45, 53, 170; as game conservation, 14–15, 62, 152, 181, 197; as industry, 96–101; licenses, 7, 10–11, 16, 18, 34–35, 39–40, 53–57, 98, 124, 141–42, 170, 171, 182; in national parks, 100–101; opposition to, 99, 117, 122–27, 141–44, 146, 152, 163, 167; for profit, 11, 12, 16, 20, 23, 25–27, 39, 90–91, 133, 182; prohibitions on, 11, 169, 170, 171, 172, 174, 175; for recreation, 13, 21, 23, 25, 32, 96–99, 124; restrictions on, 12, 16, 19, 20–21, 24, 30, 48, 81–85, 157–64, 174–75; rights, 157–59, 166, 195; sports clubs, 33–34; for subsistence, 26, 128; waterfowl, 11, 32–40. *See also* names of individual animals

IAFWA. *See* International Association of Fish and Wildlife Agencies
Indians. *See* Native Americans
International affairs, 8, 23–25, 108–10, 166, 178, 197, 198
International Association of Fish and Wildlife Agencies (IAFWA), 37, 45, 49; *American Outdoors,* 155, 181; beginning, xi, 3, 10–29, 30, 57, 166, 171, 172; bylaws, 28, 66–68, 114–15, 145, 172; committees, 5, 29, 66, 110, 113; conservationists' role in, 9, 10, 64; *Earth One,* 156, 182; executive committee, 4–5, 65–66, 67, 144–45, 156–57; federal role in, 4, 7–8, 64–65, 120; finances, 6, 28, 87, 119, 121, 144; function of, 3–4, 8, 18, 87, 145, 160, 166–68; headquarters (*see* Washington office); honorary life members, 18, 67, 188–91; and legislation, 26, 28–29, 34–40, 60, 81, 104–6, 107, 110–11, 130–31, 138–40, 182; and litigation, 7, 53–56, 104, 106, 110–11, 119–21, 138–39, 141–44, 164, 178, 180, 195; and media, 122–24, 126, 155–57, 182, 222 n.1; member numbers, 28, 57, 87, 114, 211 n.81; members, types of, 4, 20, 67; membership dues, 28–29, 66–67, 114, 118, 121, 144, 173, 177, 180, 181, 182; name of, 11, 28, 58, 68, 145, 172–73, 181, 203; *Newsletter,* 120, 123, 131, 135, 158, 162, 181, 218 n.9; *North American Furbearers: A Contemporary Reference,* 154; organization of, 4–7, 18, 28–29, 66–68, 113–16, 118–21, 144–46, 156–57, 180, 181; *Proceedings,* xi, 20, 47, 67, 85, 120, 121, 154; provinces' role in, 4, 67, 68, 114; *Public Land Policy Impact on Fish and Wildlife,* 107, 150; Resource Policies of, 165, 194–201; State Associate program, 6, 182; states' role in, 4, 8, 10–13, 68, 114; *SUMAC-GAF,* 113–14; *Transactions,* 67. *See also* Conservation movement; Game managers; Regional Associations of Fish and Wildlife Agencies; Wildlife; Wildlife management
International Association of Game, Fish and Conservation Commissioners. *See* IAFWA
International Convention Advisory Commission, 137–38
International Convention for the Conservation of Migratory Species of Wild Animals (Bonn Convention), 139–41, 182
International Union for the Conservation of Nature, 145
Izaak Walton League, 36, 37, 92, 99, 173

Jantzen, Robert, 137, 190
Janzen, Daniel, 97
Japan, 140

Index

Johnson, Edwin C., 76
Johnson, Lyndon B., 90
Joslyn, Charles, 18, 189

Kaibab deer crisis, 41–43, 60, 173
Kasmire, Robert D., 122
Kellert, Stephen, 126
Kennedy, John F., 90, 111, 167, 179
Kimball, Thomas, 56, 78, 98–99, 107, 121, 131, 133, 190

Lacey, John F., 23
Lacey Act, 12–13, 21, 43, 86, 171
Lachenmeier, Rudy, 130–31
Lampreys, sea, 85, 177, 178
Land and Water Conservation Fund, 94–95, 99, 179
Land grant colleges, 63, 167, 175, 209 n.47
Landon, Alf, 48
Land use, 7, 62, 63, 68–71, 99–100, 194, 197, 201; agricultural, 5, 7, 32, 50, 88, 107, 170, 195; drought, 32, 38, 39, 50, 98, 121, 175; erosion, 7, 175; federal, 72–73, 81–83, 94–95, 101–8, 149–51, 176, 178, 179, 181, 200–201; federal role in, 38, 104, 130–31, 148–51, 154, 177, 181, 196; flooding, 44, 59, 68, 70, 125; grazing, 5, 41, 46–47, 58, 83, 150–51, 175, 196; military, 82–83; private, 60, 83, 99–100, 151, 154; public, 47, 83, 106, 149–51, 169, 175, 196; reclamation, 32, 38, 46, 196, 201; recreational, 97, 99, 101; reservations, 157, 159, 181; state, 149–51; states' role in, 196. *See also* Wetlands
Larks, 169
Lau, Glen, 156
Lawrence, W. Mason, 114, 190
Lawyer, George, 34
Lead and Zinc Institute, 162
Lead poisoning. *See* Nontoxic shot
League for the Advancement of States' Equal Rights, 149
League of American Sportsmen, 15, 17, 171
LeCompte, E. Lee, 37, 52, 58
Legislation. *See* names of individual acts
Legislative Service Bureau, 66
Lenzini, Paul, 111, 119, 126, 143, 180
Leonard, Justin, 124
Leopards, 133
Leopold, A. Starker, 99
Leopold, Aldo, 30–31, 45, 49, 63, 174; *Game Management,* 43–44
Lewis, Harrison, 66, 189
Licenses. *See* Fishing, licenses; Hunting, licenses
Lincoln, Frederic C., 84
Lions, mountain, 149
Litigation. *See* IAFWA and litigation; U.S. Supreme Court
Livestock, 47, 83, 86, 91, 132, 143
Lloyd, Hoyes, 48, 58, 189
Lobbies, 27, 115; counter to IAFWA, 136; for IAFWA, 6, 28, 69, 93, 118, 121, 137, 153, 157
Long, Russell, 153
Lydecker, R. P., 171
Lynx, 135

MacMullan, Ralph, 119
Madsen, David H., 36, 38
Magnuson, Warren G., 104
Management. *See* Wildlife management
Manning, Laura, 157
Marine Mammal Protection Act, 127–29, 140, 180
Market hunters. *See* Game laws, market hunting; hunting for profit
Marsh drainage, 30, 32, 38
Matson, JoAnna, 119–20
McGee, WJ., 14, 30, 62
McGowan, Carl, 142
McLean, George P., 22, 23
McMillan, Thomas, 166
McNary, Charles, 39
Mercier, Honore, 58
Mexico, 59, 136, 172, 198; accords with, 28, 39, 48, 57, 59, 108–9, 140, 166, 175, 176; in IAFWA, 4, 20, 87, 114, 145, 182, 198
Micronesia, 4
Migratory Bird Act (Weeks-McLean), 21–24, 60, 172
Migratory Bird Conservation Act (Norbeck-Andreson), 38–39, 52, 173
Migratory Bird Hunting Stamp Act (Duck Stamp), 39–40, 45, 60, 62, 80–81, 154, 174, 177, 178, 179

Index

Migratory Bird Treaty, 23–25, 28, 32–33, 35, 39, 49, 58–59, 85, 108, 166
Migratory Bird Treaty Act, 24, 172, 175
Miles, Lee, 40
Missouri v. Holland, 24, 173
Mondell, Frank W., 22, 23
Moose, 40, 96, 132
Morgan, Ben, 66
Morton, Rogers, 141
Mule deer, 32, 40–43, 91
Multiple use, 107–8, 127, 196

National Association of Game and Fish Wardens and Commissioners (predecessor), 11, 18
National Committee on Wild Life Legislation, 37, 38, 173
National Environmental Policy Act, 117, 142, 144, 151, 180, 200
National Forest Refuge Act, 174
National forests: established, 41, 170, 172, 173, 174, 176; hunting in, 14, 42, 53, 55, 83, 100, 101–2, 172, 175
National Hunting and Fishing Day, 124, 180
National Marine Fisheries Service, 4
National parks: established, 169, 170, 172, 174; hunting in, 14, 16, 100, 101–2, 105, 171
National Rifle Association, 155, 162
National Shooting Sports Foundation, 124
National Survey of Fishing and Hunting, 96–99, 178
National Waterfowl Council, 84–85, 178
National Wilderness Preservation System, 179
National Wildlife, 99
National Wildlife Federation, 99, 121, 161–64, 176; *Conservation News,* 76
National Wildlife Refuge System, 32
Native Americans, 5, 157–59, 166, 175, 181, 195
Nelson, Edward W., 24–25, 27, 33, 39
Neugebauer, Russell J., 119–20, 180, 181
New, Harry S., 34
New-Anthony Bill, 30, 34–38
New Deal, 44–48, 59, 174
New Mexico State Game Commission v. Udall, 105–6, 180
New York Association for the Protection of Game, 15
New York Sportsmen's Club, 169
Nixon, Richard M., 106, 123, 180, 217 n.39
Nongame, 99, 127, 178
Nontoxic shot, 159–64, 171, 183, 195
Norbeck, Peter, 38
Norbeck-Andreson Act, 38–39, 52, 173
North American Waterfowl Management Plan, 166, 183
North American Wildlife Conference, 48, 175
Nowlin, D. C., 11, 188

Oberstar, James, 132
Olds, Hayden, 100
Olds, Nicholas, 101–3, 105, 110
Osborne, Livingston, 88
Otters: river, 135; sea, 156, 172
Outdoor Recreation Resources Review Commission, 94
Overgrazing, 41–43, 46, 53, 55

Palmer, T. S., 15, 17, 18–20, 172, 188; *Chronology and Index of American Game Protection,* 19; *Game as a National Resource,* 40
Partridges, 31; chukar, 87; Hungarian, 86
Patton, Clyde, 83
Patton, R. D., 97
Pearson, T. Gilbert, 11, 16, 17, 22–23, 26, 34, 37, 42, 188
Peck (commissioner to IAFWA), 57
Pelicans, 26
Pesticides, 90–92, 199
Pheasants, 31; Chinese, 85
Phelps, Chester F., xi, 106, 114, 118, 120–21, 122, 190
Phelps, John, 106, 190
Phillips, John M., 34
Pick, Lewis A., 70
Pigeons, 13
Pinchot, Gifford, 14–15, 62, 166; *Breaking New Ground,* 14, 172
Pisgah National Forest, 54–57, 58, 60, 62, 176
Pitcher, John G., 18
Pittman, Key, 50, 62

Index

Pittman-Robertson Act, 63–64, 86, 92, 111–12, 143–44, 148, 151–52, 168, 177, 179, 210 nn.58, 69, 211 n.70; enforcement of, 102, 167, 178, 182; implementation of, 49–53, 59, 73–75; as model legislation, 60, 62, 76–78, 93, 94, 147, 198; passage of, 49–53, 176
Plover, golden, 88
Pollution, 8, 85, 154, 198; acid rain, 5, 8; nuclear, 72, 93; pesticides, 90–94, 199; petrochemical, 93; thermal, 93; toxic shot, 157, 159–64, 166, 171, 182, 183, 195; water, 8, 32, 45, 47, 59, 61, 71, 91–94, 174, 177–79
Ponder, Amos, 19
Poole, Daniel, 149, 191
Predators. *See* Vermin; Wildlife management, predator control
Price, Overton, 14
Professionalism, 5, 29, 49, 57, 60, 62–64, 88, 112, 120, 155–57, 167; lack of early, 16–17, 25
Project WILD, 6
Public Land Law Review Commission, 106, 115, 118, 179, 180; *One Third of the Nation's Land,* 107; *Public Land Policy Impact on Fish and Wildlife,* 107
Public lands, 106–8, 143, 149–51, 196, 200; war surplus, 72–73, 177; military, 81–83, 178
Public shooting grounds, 30, 34–38, 141, 197
Public works policy, 200, 201

Quail, 169
Quarles, E. A., 31
Quinn, I. T., 46, 57, 189

Rabbits, 91
Raccoons, 127
Randolph, Jennings, 153
Raushenbush, Stephen, 89
Reagan, Ronald, 147
Recreation, 15
Recreation policies, 94–96, 98–99, 173, 178, 179, 196, 197
Redington, Paul G., 39, 42
Reed, Nathaniel P., 161
Refuges, game, 19, 31–39, 41–43, 44–45; established, 171, 172, 173, 174, 175; hunting in, 191
Regional Associations of Fish and Wildlife Agencies, 5, 57–58, 145; Midwestern, 5; Northeastern, 5; Southeastern, 5, 165; Western, 5, 36–37, 58, 110, 145, 165, 173
Regulation G–20–A, 53–57, 58, 103, 174, 176
Regulation W–2, 56, 103, 176
Republic of China (Taiwan), 4
Resource Policies, IAFWA, 194–201
Richey, Charles, 144
Roads and wildlife, 108, 201
Robertson A. Willis, 50, 69
Robertson, Gordon, 146
Robins, 169
Robinson, Joseph T., 174
Roosevelt, Franklin D., 44–48, 49, 51, 58, 76, 166, 174, 175, 176
Roosevelt, Theodore, 3, 14–16, 25–26, 31, 41, 166, 170, 171, 172
Root, Elihu, 22, 23
Roster, Tom, 164
Rouault, Theodore, Jr., 25
Ruhl, Harry R., 74, 78, 81
Rutherford, Robert, 74

Sagebrush Rebellion, 149–51, 166
Salmon, 59, 96, 159, 176
Scholastic Magazine, 123
Scott, William F., 10, 13, 17, 18, 65, 171, 188
Scott, Walter, 119
Seals, 128; fur, 172, 176
Seth Gordon Award, 116, 180, 192, 218 n.62. *See also* Gordon, Seth
Seton, Ernest Thompson, 193
Shannon, Walter, 105
Shantz, Homer L., 53–55, 62
Sharp, John, 11, 17
Shawhan (commissioner to IAFWA), 54
Sheep: bighorn, 149; mountain, 170
Sheldon, Charles, 27
Shields, George Oliver, 15, 18, 171
Shiras, George, III, 21, 23, 171
Shoemaker, Carl, 45–46, 49–51, 75, 76, 78, 81, 93, 189
Shrimp, brine, 77

Index

Sierra Club, 99
Sikes Act Extension, 181
Sikes Military Reservation Act, 83, 178
Sloan, William G., 70
Smith, Anthony Wayne, 100
Smith, Frank E., 33
Smithsonian Institution, 135, 219 n.24
Snail darter, 131
Snipes, 170
Soil Conservation Act, 175
Solicitor's Opinion, 102–5
Soviet Union, 140
Sparrows, English, 43, 86
Spring-Rice, Cecil, 24
State Associate Program, 6
State-federal relations, 7, 18, 19, 21, 22, 53–57, 100, 101–6, 127–33, 140–41, 148–51, 165, 168, 194
State sovereignty: and migratory species, 8, 21, 24, 139–40; relinquishment of, 13, 54–56; over resident wildlife, 7, 12, 42, 100, 102, 105, 108, 142–43, 162, 165
Steel shot. *See* Nontoxic shot
Steen, Melvin, 81, 115
Stevens Amendment, 163, 182
Stras (commissioner to IAFWA), 54
Stuart, Russell, 110
Sturgeon, 93
Sulzer Bill, 27
Sulzer, Charles, 26
Surplus lands, disposal of, 72–73
Swans, trumpeter, 88

Taft, William Howard, 22, 23
Taft-Barkley Act, 93, 177, 178
Taylor Grazing Act, 46–47, 58, 175
Tennessee Valley Authority, 4, 131, 174
Terk v. Ruch, 7
Towell, William E., 79, 93, 104, 115
Train, Russell, 133
Trapping, 125, 137, 154
Trefethen, James, 12, 21, 27, 49
Trout, 12, 85, 96; brown, 86
Truman, Harry S., 76, 111
Turkeys, 169

United Nations, 133–34
U.S. Army Corps of Engineers, 65, 68, 69, 96, 169
U.S. Atomic Energy Commission, 83
U.S. Bureau of Biological Survey, 18, 42, 43, 64, 84, 176; beginning of, 19–20, 86, 170; and legislation, 12, 23, 27, 28, 33, 47, 50, 52
U.S. Bureau of Fisheries, 59, 64, 76, 176
U.S. Bureau of Indian Affairs, 169, 175
U.S. Bureau of Land Management, 4, 83, 142, 149, 177, 201
U.S. Bureau of Outdoor Recreation, 94
U.S. Bureau of Reclamation, 69, 70
U.S. Bureau of Sport Fisheries and Wildlife, 111, 112, 161
U.S. Bureau of the Budget, 78
U.S. Census Bureau, 97
U.S. Department of Agriculture, 14, 19, 50, 52, 56, 64, 107, 165
U.S. Department of Commerce, 64
U.S. Department of Defense, 82
U.S. Department of Interior, 64, 73, 103, 147–48, 161, 164, 165, 170
U.S. Environmental Protection Agency, 117, 180
U.S. Federal Bureau of Investigation, 64
U.S. Federal Communications Commission, 123
U.S. Federal Emergency Relief Administration, 46
U.S. Fish and Wildlife Service, 68, 75, 78, 96–97, 110, 128, 144, 161–64; beginning of, 52, 64, 170, 176; and IAFWA, 4, 7, 65, 74, 80, 84, 86, 102–3, 114; and legislation, 52, 69–70, 73, 77, 136–38, 154, 200
U.S. Fisheries Commission, 170
U.S. Food Administration, 27
U.S. Forest Service, 4, 42, 53–57, 100, 103, 125, 149, 171, 201
U.S. Internal Revenue Service, 115
U.S. National Aeronautics and Space Administration, 83
U.S. National Park Service, 100, 105, 172
U.S. Office of Management and Budget, 148
U.S. Public Works Administration, 45
U.S. Supreme Court, 23, 24, 54–56, 106, 138, 143, 176; specific cases of, 12, 42, 131, 141, 159, 171, 173, 181, 182
U.S. Treasury Department, 52, 78, 94

Index

U.S. War Assets Administration, 72, 73
U.S. War Department, 68
U.S. Water Pollution Control Administration, 94
Udall, Stewart, 90, 91, 92, 104–5, 167

Vermin, 41, 43–44, 72
Vietnam War, 111
Voigt, Les, 119, 191
Volstead Act, 39

Wallace, Henry A., 51
Wallace, John H., 34, 63
Wallop-Breaux Act, 9, 153, 168, 182–83. *See also* Dingell-Johnson Act
Walruses, 128–29
Washington office: establishment of, 114–15; proposed, 66, 87, 115, 177; significance of, 6, 118; staffing of, 118–21, 145–46, 157
Water Bank Program, 154
Waterfowl, 45, 52, 72, 75, 84–85, 108–10, 154, 159–64, 166, 178, 183, 208 n.26; hunting of, 11, 48, 80–81, 98, 170, 171; international management of, 108–10, 166, 183; refuges, 32–40, 50, 62, 64, 95–96, 102, 173
Watergate, 117, 123
Water policies, 68–71, 95–96, 174, 177, 201
Water pollution. *See* Pollution, water
Water-Pollution Control Act (Taft-Barkley Act), 93, 177, 178
Watt, James, 147–48, 151, 222 n.1
Weather modification, 195
Weeks, John W., 21–22
Weeks Act, 172
Weeks-McLean Act, 21–24, 60, 172
Western Lands Distribution and Regional Equalization Act, 149
West Germany, 139–40, 182
Wetlands, 30, 32–33, 38, 71, 88, 148, 160, 175; IAFWA policy on, 5, 8, 107, 196, 201; and legislation, 7, 34, 39, 81, 154, 179
Wetlands Loan Act, 154, 179
Wetmore, Alexander, 160
Whales, blue, 124
Wherry, Kenneth, 72
Wherry-Burke Act, 72–73, 82, 177
White, James (Canadian Department of Conservation), 23
White, James B. (IAFWA public land law expert), 107
Whitefish, 18
Wildcats, 41
Wilderness, 179, 201
Wilderness Society, 99
Wild Free-Roaming Horses and Burros Act, 143
Wildlife, 13, 69, 101–6, 108, 122–23; big game, 13–14, 32, 40–43, 60, 98, 142; damage of, 42, 53, 100, 105, 132, 199–200; depletion of, thru hunting, 12, 13–14, 71–73, 129, 175; disease, 5; exotic, 85–87, 197; as factor in economic growth, 13, 44, 52, 61–89, 128, 166–67, 174; as food, 25–26, 32, 40, 85, 128, 140, 181, 198; furbearers, 124, 133, 154, 172, 176, 182; mammals, 127–29, 180; migratory birds, 5, 15, 20–25, 34, 38, 39–40, 45, 47, 50, 83–85, 108–10, 162, 171, 208 n.26 (*see also* Convention on International Trade in Endangered Species; Endangered species; Migratory Bird Act; Migratory Bird Hunting Stamp Act; Migratory Bird Treaty); migratory fish, 60, 77, 176; nongame, 127, 169; overpopulation, 41–43, 55, 56, 62, 85, 100, 109, 129; predators of, 41–43. *See also* Fishing; Hunting; names of individual animals
Wildlife in America, 127
Wildlife management, xiii–xiv, 3–4, 9, 30–31, 52, 56, 63, 123–24, 194–95, 199–200; animal refuges, 19, 28, 31–44, 44–45, 104–5, 141, 171, 172, 175; animal restoration, 48, 52, 61–62, 151–52, 175, 176, 177, 199 (*see also* Pittman-Robertson Act); bird sanctuaries, 31–32, 38, 39–40, 171; conservation, 14–15, 19, 44–45, 51, 61–62, 122, 145, 156, 165; conservationists' role in, xiv, 4, 21, 30–31, 33, 40–41, 43, 155; constitutionality of, 22, 23, 24, 36, 179; definition of, 4, 166–67; educational programs in, 6, 48, 60, 83, 122–25, 145, 155–57, 196; endangered species,

Index

14, 83, 124, 129–39, 146, 157, 195, 199, 201 (*see also* Endangered species); and environment, 31, 152, 154–55, 166, 180, 195; federal role in (from beginning to 1932), 12–13, 15, 18–24, 26, 34, 36, 42, 169, 171, 172, 173; federal role in (1933–1959), 44–48, 49–57, 174–75, 176, 177; federal role in (1960 to present), xiii, 101–6, 108, 127–33, 139, 142–43, 148, 151, 162–63, 165, 168, 180, 194; fisheries, 5, 31, 76, 83–85, 154, 157, 177, 178, 198; fish restoration, 8, 59, 62, 122, 147, 179, 199 (*see also* Dingell-Johnson Act; Wallop-Breaux Act); game production, 7, 25, 31; habitat preservation, 139, 148, 181, 196, 199; habitat restoration, 6, 75, 78, 83, 108–9, 183; international accords, xiii, 23–24, 166, 172, 175, 176, 177, 181, 182, 183; on international level, 178, 197, 198; laws, 12–13, 33, 45, 57, 61, 88 (*see also* names of individual acts); opposition to, 98, 115, 123–27, 152, 155–57, 163, 167, 222 n.1; predator control, 41–43, 132, 142, 172, 178, 198; states' role in (from beginning to 1932), 13, 15, 18–24, 36, 42, 170, 171, 173; states' role in (1933–1959), 48, 50–53, 53–57, 58, 74, 175, 176, 177; states' role in (1960 to present), xiii, xiv, 8, 100–106, 108, 127–33, 141–43, 148, 162–63, 165, 168, 179, 180, 181, 182, 194, 195. *See also* Conservation movement; Fishing; Hunting; IAFWA; Wildlife

Wildlife Management Institute, 68, 149, 209 n.47. *See also* American Wildlife Institute
Wildlife Reference Service, 111–12
Wildlife restoration. *See* Pittman-Robertson Act
Wildlife Society, 63, 99, 176
Willard, E. V., 54
Williams, Pat, 152
Wilson, Chester, 78
Wilson, G., 160
Wilson, Woodrow, 24
Winn, Roberta, 112
Wolper Productions, 122
Wolves, 41, 43, 142; timber, 132
Woodcocks, 170
Woodstream Corporation, 4
Woodward, Harry, 106, 107, 113–15, 119, 122
World War I: immediate effects of, 25–27, 32, 68; prior period, 24, 41; resumption of wildlife management after, 36
World War II: immediate effects of, 61, 64–75, 82, 89, 167, 177; prior period, 41, 44, 53, 57, 63, 93; resumption of wildlife management after, 76, 83, 87
Worms, 91

Yancey, Richard, 139
Yellowstone Park: first meeting, 10–12; ban on hunting in, 16, 19

Zaunbrecher, Dusty, 145
Zinser, Juan, 48, 59